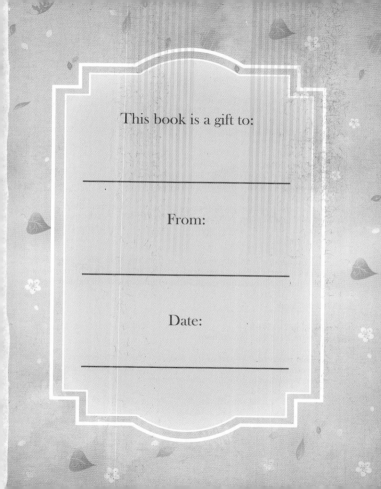

This book is a gift to:

_____

From:

_____

Date:

_____

One-Minute Devotions® for Moms

© 2010 Christian Art Publishers, RSA
      Christian Art Gifts Inc., IL, USA

Designed by Christian Art Gifts

First edition 2010
Second edition 2016

Images used under license from Shutterstock.com

Printed in China

ISBN 978-1-4321-1541-8
ISBN 978-1-4321-2926-2 (SA edition)

18 19 20 21 22 23 24 25 26 27 – 14 13 12 11 10 9 8 7 6 5

ONE-MINUTE DEVOTIONS®

for
MOMS

CAROLYN
LARSEN

christian
art gifts®

*The thoughts in this book cover every
stage of motherhood, from anticipating your
child's arrival to watching your adult children
parent their own little ones. Motherhood is a
full-time, life-time commitment that holds our
children deep in our hearts. Moms need God's help,
strength, guidance, patience and love every single
step of the way. My prayer is that these devotions
will encourage you to make God an active partner
in the motherhood experience. Lean on Him,
love Him and trust Him because He loves
your children even more than you do!*

Carolyn Larsen

January

A New Trust

Unfailing love surrounds those who trust the LORD.
Psalm 32:10 NLT

I was certain I would be way too cool and calm to check … but when it came down to it, calmness flew out the window. Even before the exhaustion of thirty hours of labor and delivery had passed, I peeled the blanket away from my newborn daughter and carefully counted every finger and toe, and made sure everything was there and in the right place.

It was – and that made me smile. I should have known I could trust God. After all, He knit her together in my womb. Before I ever laid eyes on her, everything that will ever cross her path was written down in God's Book. I know that my husband and I are not alone as we raise our precious child. God is with us every step of the way. His guidance, wisdom and discernment are available to us; we just need to go to Him daily, even hourly, to draw on His power.

Dear God, I'm going to need a lot of help over the next years. I know that as my baby grows up I need to trust You. Because she was Your child first – she's only on loan to me. Amen.

Scared Silly

In everything, by prayer and petition, with thanksgiving, present
your requests to God. And the peace of God, which transcends
all understanding, will guard your hearts. Philippians 4:6-7

"Going out"? She's "going out" with a boy? What does that mean? She's only twelve so actual dating is waaaay down the line, right? OK, I have noticed recently that my opinions have become less and less important to my daughter, and her friends' opinions have become more and more important. That scares me silly.

Have we instilled values and morals in her heart? Does she respect herself enough to stand firm in the face of temptation and peer pressure? I am hanging on to that first time I held her in my arms and gave her to God. I know He loves her even more than I do (that's amazing). So I must stay on my knees – lifting her up to Him. I must ask for His protection, His discernment and His guidance to always be in the forefront of her mind.

As she gets older the temptations will get stronger and the consequences bigger. What can I do? Pray. Pray. Pray. Love. Love. Love. I can do that.

Dear God, the idea that my little girl is noticing boys now is scary. Guide her, protect her and keep her close to You. Help me always to model Your love and care in my words and actions. I love her so much. I know You do too. Amen.

When Did Life Get So Crazy?

*It is good to praise the LORD and make music to Your name,
O Most High, to proclaim Your love in the morning
and Your faithfulness at night. Psalm 92:1-2*

The phone is ringing, the spaghetti has boiled dry, the dog just threw up, my two-year-old is drawing on the kitchen wall with a permanent marker, my six-year-old is flushing chocolate chip cookies down the toilet and I don't even know where my eight-year-old is ... probably trying to tie up the cat. Sigh.

I had no real idea what lay ahead ten years ago when I walked down the church aisle to my handsome Prince Charming. I thought I was ready for marriage and children. But it's a whole lot more work than I ever imagined.

The truth of the matter, however, is that when one of my children hugs me and gives me a sloppy kiss, or draws a picture especially for me, then every burned pot, missed phone call, decorated wall and flushed cookie is worth it. I love being their mom. And I must remember that life is a journey ... enjoy it.

Dear God, thank You for letting me have the experience of being a mom. I pray that I never take the responsibility lightly. God, help me as I teach my children about You, by the way I live my life. God, help me to show You to them. Amen.

Temper Tantrums

The fruit of the Spirit is love, joy, peace, patience, kindness, goodness, faithfulness, gentleness and self-control. Galatians 5:22-23

Oh my, that's my son lying on the floor, kicking and screaming ... right here in the grocery store. Everyone is looking at us and it is all because I won't buy him a bag of cookies. Sigh.

Sometimes I'd like to get inside the mind of my two-year-old just to see what he's thinking. I've got a couple of choices here – I can walk away and pretend he isn't mine. I can pick him up and leave the store. I can buy the silly cookies. Or, I can just stand here beside him until he's done. It seems like this should be an easier choice. Why can't he just trust my judgment? Why? Why? Why?

Hmmm ... I wonder if God ever feels this way about me? Why do I have my own temper tantrums? Why don't I trust Him? Just as He is so patient with me, I need to be patient with my son. It's really hard sometimes, but I want to be a good mom. I pray for patience to handle his tantrum calmly, just as God handles mine. My Father God is a good example of parenting; patient, calm ... and loving.

Dear Father, please help me to be like You. Give me the patience to handle my son's tantrums calmly. Keep me from reacting in anger. Father, help me to be like You. Amen.

JANUARY 4

Miracle Worker

"God so loved the world that He gave His one and only Son, that whoever believes in Him shall not perish but have eternal life." John 3:16

I barely have the energy to speak. The sheer labor of doing my part to bring this baby into the world has left me exhausted. If I had my way, I would sleep for a week. Although one part of me longs to rest, another part is exploding with excitement! A baby is a miracle, showcasing God's creative power. This miracle happens every day all around the world – but this time, with this miracle, I GOT TO HELP!

This new human being is God's creation, made in His image. He is a little bit of me and a little bit of my husband. Helping to bring my child into the world was an incredible privilege. The pain that wracked my body moments ago is nearly forgotten, replaced with awesome wonder at who God is and how much He loves me! In this instant I understand the sacrifice God made in sending His Son to earth. I already know that I would give my life for my child. Yet God willingly gave His Son, knowing what Jesus would go through here on earth. It must have been hard, but God still did it.

God, I understand Your sacrifice now more than ever before. I'm overwhelmed by Your amazing love. Help me to emulate that as I begin my parenting career. Amen.

Teenage Stress

"Come to Me, all you who are weary and burdened, and I will give you rest. Take My yoke upon you and learn from Me, for I am gentle and humble in heart, and you will find rest for your souls." Matthew 11:28-29

Someone once said something like: The best way to handle the teenage years is to get a barrel, stick your child inside, seal it shut and leave her there until she's twenty-one. I used to think that was funny. Now it actually seems like a pretty good idea.

If I shut her away from the rest of the world I can protect her from peer pressure and worrying about whether or not she's "cool." I know that God is paying attention and that lots of teens make it through these high-pressure years just fine, but peer pressure is so powerful. What girl doesn't want to be popular or at least not be considered weird? I must stay on my knees asking God to protect her and keep her in His Word, searching for guidance and strength.

I will try my best to keep the lines of communication open without adding more pressure on her. I will work to make home a safe place for her. These next few years are crucial and I must trust them to God.

Dear Father, I do trust You with this most precious child. I know You love her, too, so protect her from harm, Father. Strengthen her to face temptation and not give in. Keep her heart clos[e] Yours. Amen.

Thankfulness

*Every good and perfect gift is from above, coming down
from the Father of the heavenly lights, who does
not change like shifting shadows. James 1:17*

Is there anything more precious than watching a baby sleep? Even though I'm worn out from chasing him around all day, standing here looking at my precious child sleep, I am overwhelmed with love for him.

I am so thankful for the energy that kept him running and playing today; even for the fearlessness that makes him take chances. I am thankful that he hasn't gotten seriously hurt. He will recover from the few bumps and bruises he has. I'm thankful for the joy of seeing my familiar world through the eyes of my son who is noticing it for the first time.

I'm amazed once again at God's creativity. I'm thankful for this little guy's curiosity – we are learning new things together. I'm thankful for the joy he finds in the simplest of things. Now, in the dark stillness of his room, I watch my sleeping son and am so thankful for him. He is an amazing, incredible, miraculous, loving gift from God.

Dear Father, You must feel the same way about Your Son. I love my little guy more with each passing day. Now I understand the magnitude of Your gift of Jesus better. What an amazing sacrifice. Thank You. Amen.

Busy, Busy, Busy

These commandments that I give you today are to be upon your hearts. Impress them on your children. Talk about them when you sit, walk, lie down and when you get up. Deuteronomy 6:6-7

Seriously ... could life get any busier? I had no idea how busy the parenting years would be. I feel like an entertainer spinning plates on the tips of sticks, running from plate to plate to keep them spinning so they don't fall. But I can't always catch them before they crash to the floor.

For example, I forgot to take treats to my son's baseball game; my daughter's negligence in practicing piano slipped through the cracks; and I can't remember the last time I had a facial. I never realized all the elements of being a mom: housekeeper, cook, laundress, chauffeur, nurse, counselor, bedtime story reader ... the list is endless.

However, what concerns me is the one thing I don't want to lose in the busyness: being a spiritual guide to my children. I don't want to get so caught up in the busyness that I rush through prayer times with my kids or miss the opportunities to read stories from God's Word. I know the most important thing I can do for them is to teach them about the Father.

Dear Father, help me to prioritize so that praying with my children and reading Your Word to them never gets pushed aside. Amen.

JANUARY 8

A Time to Speak ...
A Time to Be Quiet

There is a time for everything, and a season for every activity under heaven ... a time to be silent and a time to speak. Ecclesiastes 3:1, 7

I have the answer. Why can't my child see that I have the answer to her problem? My years of living on this planet, combined with my vast experience in relationships and my deep faith, have given me great wisdom.

She could truly benefit from listening to me but she doesn't even ask my advice. Sigh ... OK, I have to learn when to keep quiet. Even if I can see the freight train that will knock her down because of her choices or behavior I need to keep my opinion to myself.

Funny, the saying used to be, "Children should be seen and not heard." Now, it's, "Parents should keep their opinions to themselves." Yikes. It's hard! This thing called "tough love" is as tough on the mom as it is on the child. I'm supposed to let her make mistakes and get hurt so that she can hopefully learn from them and become a stronger, person. It's just so hard. I need God's wisdom to know when to speak and when to be quiet ... and the strength to actually keep quiet.

Dear Father, You're really going to have to help me with this, OK? I don't like to see my child hurt, but I guess she has to learn some things for herself. So help me to be quiet and to be there. Amen.

So Tired

The LORD replied, "My Presence will go with you,
and I will give you rest." Exodus 33:14

Will I ever be able to sleep again? I mean for an entire night – uninterrupted? I'm so tired that I could fall asleep standing up. The saying, "I slept like a baby" now seems utterly ridiculous! It doesn't create an image of a restful night but rather two hours of sleep at a time ... if that.

When do babies start sleeping through the night? My brain is so tired that I can't make good decisions, my temper is short, I'm not pleasant to be around and I'm not even enjoying this child because I'M TOO TIRED. This whole parenting thing is so new to me and I'm not even sure I'm doing it right.

When I'm up with my child in the middle of the night I feel so lonely. It would be nice to know that someone else is up too ... oh, right ... God is up. It's a good time to pray, then, isn't it? Just me, God and my precious baby. If I've ever needed God's strength and patience, it is now. My friends promise it will get better – until the teenage years come of course.

Dear Father, I'm so tired. Please, give me rest without sleep. Strengthen my body and keep my mind alert when it needs to be. Help me to lie down and sleep when my baby sleeps ... the laundry can wait. Thanks, Father. Amen.

JANUARY 10

The Best Day Ever!

Let us come before Him with thanksgiving and
extol Him with music and song. Psalm 95:2

Today started out just like any other. I had a much needed cup of coffee and a bagel. My toddler woke up early and padded down the hallway to the kitchen. Then, the usual: spilled orange juice, splashed cereal, minor temper tantrum about getting her face washed, major temper tantrum about watching television. Same old, same old. But then one little blip of time changed everything. I was on the floor picking up blocks when my precious child ran up behind me, wrapped her pudgy little arms around my neck and said, "I love you, Mommy." That one moment changed my whole attitude, in fact, my whole day.

It was such a simple thing but I'm so grateful to God for those little love moments when I am gently reminded of His love – sometimes through something as simple as a hug from my child. Those little hugs are a reminder of the privilege of parenting. Those moments put the mundane to rest. Every moment is special and I am thankful when I'm reminded of that!

Dear Father, love moments make dreary days so wonderful. Thank You for planning those. Thank You for spontaneous hugs and jelly kisses and words of love from my precious child. Amen.

JANUARY 11

Moody Girl

"Be strong and courageous. Do not be terrified; do not be discouraged, for the LORD your God will be with you wherever you go." Joshua 1:9

What happened to my sweet little girl? One day my daughter thought I was the smartest, most wonderful mom ever, but by eight o' clock the next morning I had become uncool, unsmart, unbeautiful and unfunny.

My little girl is suddenly so critical of everything I say, wear and do. Of course, part of the problem is that I keep calling her my little girl although she is in junior high already – definitely NOT a little girl. This is a whole new era of parenting. My little girl … excuse me, my daughter, is becoming independent. She is pulling away from me. She is like a baby bird testing her wings, but wanting to know that her nest is nearby.

The hard part is that my emotions don't go in and out like that. I really need wisdom and discernment to know how to parent now. I don't want to build walls between us, but I don't want to let her go either. I need God's help to be firm enough to still be her mom, but give her enough freedom to test her wings.

Dear Father, OK, I'm trying to walk the fine line between being a mom and not smothering with my mothering. Please help me to know where that line is. Give me the courage I need to be firm. Amen.

JANUARY 12

First Steps

You created my inmost being; You knit me together in my mother's womb.
Psalm 139:13

He walked! My baby boy took a step all by himself today! He's been trying so hard ... pulling up, standing alone, falling down, walking along holding onto the furniture. But today he let go and just walked! He was so pleased with himself! It seems like just yesterday he was a tiny baby. He is changing so quickly. It seems like he is learning new things every day. Now the fun begins. This is the beginning of his growth to independence. He's going to start exploring the whole house, climbing and jumping and ... whew. What's amazing is that my super-intelligent little boy just knew how to walk.

He knew what to do because God planted the intelligence in his mind. God gave his muscles the information they needed to grow and strengthen to hold up his body. It is truly a miracle. I am constantly amazed at God's plan to start every human life as a newborn baby. When you think about it, every single human is a testament to God's power and love!

Dear Father, I don't know how anyone can see a newborn baby and watch him grow and not believe in Your power. Every baby is a miracle – born with everything that tiny body needs to become an adult. Thank You for Your wisdom and Your wonderful plan. Amen.

Knowing God Early

This is how God showed His love among us: He sent His one and only
Son into the world that we might live through Him. 1 John 4:9

I read my Bible each morning and pray often throughout the day. I'm happy when my children see me doing this. As a family we thank God for our food before each meal, we attend church and small groups, and participate in church ministries.

My husband and I try to model our obedience to God by the way we live. We strive to make our Christian walk more than just words so that our children will see that our faith is important to us. I pray with our children and read Bible stories to them. I pray with all my heart that they will come to know God early and give their lives to Him.

I know they will have some tough choices ahead and some pressures that will be difficult to resist as they grow older. The earlier their relationships are established with Jesus, the stronger they will be when the tough times come.

Dear Father, help me show my children the way to You. I know I must be very consistent in my Christian walk. Help me to notice and take advantage of teachable moments to help them understand how much You love them. Help them understand how to obey You and honor You in their lives. Amen.

JANUARY 14

The Beat Goes On

Give thanks to the LORD, for He is good; His love endures forever.
1 Chronicles 16:34

One of the most wonderful things about being a parent is becoming a grandparent! What a blessing! It's amazing that my baby girl is now a mom herself. What a joy it is to hold my tiny new granddaughter in my arms and see the resemblance she has to her mother as a newborn. I see my daughter's eyes and snub little nose. It warms my heart to watch my daughter hold her baby and see the love and amazement in her eyes. I know she will be a wonderful mother. Most importantly, she and her husband will teach their daughter about God's love.

As for me ... I can't wait to babysit! I want to bake cookies with my granddaughter and have tea parties and go shopping. I want to read her stories and take her on vacations. I want her to see a strong woman from an older generation who loves and follows God and shows kindness and compassion to people as I passionately live out God's command to love others.

Dear Father, I'm a grandmother! I don't feel old enough to be one, but this little baby I'm holding means that I am! What an honor this is. Father, show me how to support and encourage my daughter and her husband as they parent this little one. Help me to know where my boundaries are as a loving grandmother. Amen.

Am I Doing This Right?

Above all, love each other deeply, because love covers over a multitude of sins. 1 Peter 4:8

What if I'm doing this all wrong? Sometimes I wish my baby had come with an instruction manual. Why does it seem like some new mothers instinctively know what to do? I don't think I got that automatic maternal gene.

What if I mess my child up? I don't want her to go from kindergarten to counseling. I really want to be a good mom. I love her so much. I need help learning how to be a little less intense and a little more fun. OK, stop and take a deep breath here. My mom did the "parent of a new baby" thing and she did a good job. So, maybe asking for her advice would be good. Plus, some of my friends have babies just a bit older than mine so I could ask them some things too.

My husband and I need to talk through our parenting style so that we start out being consistent with our little one. We're in this together and the bottom line is that we love our baby more than anything. Will we make mistakes? Yes, in fact, we may have already – but love covers a multitude of wrongs.

Dear Father, wow, parenting is a big responsibility! I want to do it right so I need to cry out to You for guidance, wisdom and patience daily. Help me to be a good, consistent, loving mom. Amen.

JANUARY 16

Prayer Commitment

Pray in the Spirit on all occasions with all kinds of prayers and requests. With this in mind, be alert and always keep on praying for all the saints. Ephesians 6:18

I liked it better when my son was six and not sixteen. Life was easier when my husband and I got to decide where he was going and who he was spending time with. It's a bit more difficult with a teenager, especially one with a driver's license. Well, this stage of his life is where "the rubber meets the road." It will keep me on my knees, that's for sure. It's time to pray that the foundations we gave him as a child, will make a difference in our son's choices now.

I know the temptations and pressures on kids these days are incredible, and the opportunities for trying things when he's away from us are certainly available. Will he make mistakes? Of course – we all did. But I'll pray and pray and pray … for his choices in friends, in activities, and for wisdom as he "tests his wings." Maybe I'll get a group of his friends' moms together to pray. There's strength in numbers!

Dear Father, I know You love my son even more than I do. I know he will make some mistakes along the way, but please protect him from serious consequences. Guide his choices, thoughts and actions. Show us how to parent him through these teenage years! Amen.

Quality vs. Quantity

Trust in the LORD with all your heart and lean not on your own understanding; in all your ways acknowledge Him, and He will make your paths straight. Proverbs 3:5-6

I have a job. There isn't much I can do about it because we need my income to keep the household going. But parenting is also a full-time job! Some of my friends make me feel guilty for working and for the fact that I enjoy my job. They don't seem to realize that their pressure just makes it more difficult for me. It's not that I enjoy my work more than I enjoy my children – that's ridiculous. But if I have to work, isn't it OK that I enjoy what I do? Does it mean I'm not a good mom? I don't think so.

I've made a commitment that the time we do spend together will be quality time. We have so much fun together, whether we're snuggled on the couch or walking through a museum. I love my children with all my heart, but I don't have the privilege of being a stay-at-home mom so I make the best of the time we have. Thanks to my husband and to good baby-sitters, I think my kids are doing OK.

Dear God, maybe I care too much about what other people think. It hurts that my friends don't think I'm a good mom. You know how much I love my children. Help me make the most of the time I have with my children. Amen.

Discipline Pain

No discipline seems pleasant at the time, but painful. Later on, however, it produces a harvest of righteousness and peace for those who have been trained by it. Hebrews 12:11

When I was a child my mom would say, "This hurts me more than it does you," just as she was about to discipline me. I didn't believe her. But now that I'm the parent doing the disciplining I understand that comment. Disciplining my children is not something I look forward to. I don't enjoy it when they feel punished and I don't enjoy the tears and attitude that follows discipline. It makes me sad when privileges they enjoy are taken away from them. I can honestly say that disciplining my children hurts me more than it does them.

However, as the adult in this situation, I know that discipline is important even though it's difficult. I must stay focused on the reason behind discipline. It is important to teach my children the difference between right and wrong because it will make them more pleasant to be around. Discipline helps my children become responsible, wise adults. Whew. It's hard, but it is also a great responsibility.

Dear Father, please give me wisdom in disciplining my children. Help me to never react in anger but to always act in love. Amen.

Miracle Smile

Let everything that has breath praise the LORD.
Psalm 150:6

Something just happened that wiped away every ounce of exhaustion from my body. My mind is suddenly lifted from its tired fog and is racing with energy. What happened? My baby SMILED! I had no idea how much joy would flood my heart when he looked into my eyes, showed recognition and purposefully, intentionally smiled ... at me! That simple act made every sleepless night, every load of laundry, every pound gained, every lost lunch with friends, everything ... absolutely worth it.

His genuine smile – the first one that can't be chalked up to gas bubbles – has warmed my heart. Almost daily now I will see him changing and growing as his personality develops. What a privilege to be the mother of this little guy! I'm so thankful to God that He knew how much it would help, mixed in with the work and tiredness, these spontaneous moments of joy. And all it took was one little smile! A miracle smile!

Dear Father, thank You for the gift of my son's miracle smile. I love him so much. Thank You for the encouragement that it gives to keep me going. Help me, Father, to enjoy every evidence of my son's growth and maturing. Help me celebrate these moments! Amen.

JANUARY 20

Am I Cheating Him?

"I know the plans I have for you," declares the LORD,
"plans to prosper you and not to harm you,
plans to give you hope and a future."
Jeremiah 29:11

I'm a little nervous, no, I'm a lot nervous. I just found out that we're going to have our second child early next year. This is a bit of a surprise; actually, a big surprise. Of course I'm happy, but, well … honestly, in some ways I'm not so sure how I feel about it. Our first baby will only be eighteen months old when his brother or sister is born. He's still a baby too. Will he be cheated out of the "mommy time" he needs because of this new baby?

I'm afraid that I'll miss some wonderful times with my little guy because of the new baby. I guess I'm scared that I can't do it all. I believe that God's plan is perfect and that both of these children are providential, but what if I don't have the energy or patience to deal with an active, curious eighteen-month-old and a newborn at the same time?

Dear Father, thank You for this new baby. I believe children are a gift from You. Please give me the energy to give both of my children the attention they deserve. Don't let me miss anything in their lives. And give me the wisdom to ask for help from family and friends when I need it. Amen.

Good Reports

*Therefore, as God's chosen people, holy and dearly loved,
clothe yourselves with compassion, kindness, humility,
gentleness and patience.* Colossians 3:12

My son's first grade teacher called today. I'll be honest, when I heard her voice on the phone, my first thought was, "What has he done now?" He has always been an active little boy and he doesn't always think before he acts. Thankfully though, he wasn't in trouble this time. I was glad to give her ten minutes as she shared how my rough-and-tumble son was kind, considerate and helpful to a little boy in his class who is confined to a wheelchair.

What do you know … my son has a sensitive side! He took the time to talk to the boy on the playground instead of playing soccer with his buddies. He sat by the little boy at lunchtime. In other words, he was a friend to this little boy.

What a heartwarming phone call that was! Parents always wonder how their children behave when they aren't around. It is comforting to learn that my children are kind, compassionate and considerate of others – especially to those with special needs.

Dear Father, I've tried to teach my children to love others by modeling that to them. Thank You that they have picked up on that. Thank You for each time my children reach out to someone else. Amen.

JANUARY 22

The Future

*May the Lord direct your hearts into God's love and
Christ's perseverance. 2 Thessalonians 3:5*

I am simply overwhelmed with love for my little girl. Standing here in the darkness and watching her sleep, my mind is racing with all the dreams I have for her. I want her to have every opportunity to explore any interests she has. I want her to know she's loved. But as I think about her future, one thing keeps popping into my mind – her future spouse. With half of all marriages ending in divorce these days I want to protect her from that pain. So ... I pray.

I pray for the young man who will someday be a part of her life to experience a loving family, to be taught early to walk with God. I pray that this child will grow to be a compassionate man who will love God first and my precious daughter second. I pray for her to grow into a woman who will be kind and sensitive, who will be a support and encouragement to her husband. I pray that they will serve God side by side.

Dear Father, I pray for my daughter and for the man who will one day be her husband. Please guide and direct each of them as they grow up. Protect them from the temptations and dangers of this life. I pray that they will each come to know You early and that their lives will be blessed in service to You. Amen.

Group Effort

*Two people are better off than one, for they can help each other
succeed. If one person falls, the other can reach out and help.
But someone who falls alone is in real trouble.* Ecclesiastes 4:9-10 NLT

I am so thankful for the people around me who have an influence on my child. The old saying, "It takes a village to raise a child" is really true. I'm very aware of the nursery workers and Sunday school teachers who love and care for my child. I'm thankful every time the pastor takes the time to stoop down and talk to her face to face. I'm grateful for my friends who have become beloved aunties to her — especially since her actual aunties are so far away.

I want to hug my dear neighbor who is often my daughter's stand-in grandma. She bakes cookies with her and plays in the backyard with her. She even goes to Grandparent Day at pre-school when our own parents can't make it. There are times when I simply don't know the right way to handle the situation, but there is always someone I can call for advice. All of these people are making a difference in my child's life. They make her feel loved and give her confidence. They model God's love and care.

Dear Father, I don't know how we'd do this parenting thing without our friends and church family. Parenting is a 24/7 job and I'm so grateful for these dear friends who help share the load. Thank You for bringing them into our lives. Amen.

JANUARY 24

Saying Goodbye

Where, O death, is your victory? Where, O death, is your sting?
The sting of death is sin, and the power of sin is the law. But thanks
be to God! He gives us the victory through our Lord Jesus Christ.
1 Corinthians 15:55-57

How do I tell my eight-year-old son that his beloved grandpa has died? I've dreaded this day ever since we were told how sick my father was. My son and my father were so much alike; my little guy shadowed Dad every chance he got. Dad taught my son how to do so many things and I know they often talked as they worked.

I see Dad's influence in so much of my son. How will my little guy take the news that he no longer has his grandpa in his life? It will break his heart. I wish I could protect him from this ... but I can't. Somehow, even through my own pain, I now have to show my son the reality of the hope of eternity and that we will one day be together with Dad again. I've got to help him understand that Dad is now with Jesus and that's a good thing. Sigh ... I'm going to need a lot of wisdom for this conversation!

Dear Father, this must be one of the most difficult things a mom has to do. Help me to convey the hope of heaven in a way that an eight-year-old will understand. Thank You for Dad's influence on my son. I pray that he will always remember it. Amen.

Disappointment

Each man has his own gift from God; one has this gift, another has that.
1 Corinthians 7:7

This is breaking my heart. My daughter has tried out and auditioned for everything her school offers, from the Show Choir to the Glee Club to the Volleyball team ... and made none of them. My aching mother's heart wonders why this school that encourages students to participate keeps choosing the same kids for everything. It seems that to foster school spirit each student should be allowed two extracurriculars. Then more students could join in. Sigh.

Well, the problem at hand is how to pick up my daughter's broken spirit since her name has not appeared on the "made-the-team" list. She is so smart and so talented that I truly do not understand why she is continually passed over. I just know that I don't want to her lose hope in herself. I want her to see that God has made her exactly the way He wants her to be. I want her to believe in her gifts and talents. I want her to see that junior high doesn't last forever and one day she will be able to do the things she loves to do. I want her to believe in herself.

Dear Father, this is going to be hard because my daughter's going to say that I have to say these things since I'm her mother. Of course I do love her and I see the best in her, but I know that You have a plan for her too. Show me how to encourage her and give her hope. Amen.

Trust

If you need wisdom, ask our generous God, and He will give it to you.
He will not rebuke you for asking. James 1:5 NLT

I carried this baby inside me for nine months. I felt her gentle movements, her powerful kicks and I laughed at her hiccups. I talked to her and sang to her and spent a lot of time imagining how she would look. I persevered through twenty hours of labor and did my part to push her into this world. She is my daughter; my child. But now, I think these people ... these supposedly wise medical people ... are going to let my husband and me walk out of here WITH THIS CHILD! What makes them think we have any clue what to do with this helpless little baby? What if we do something wrong? What if I don't know what she needs? Do they really trust me with this child?

OK, I'm scared, I'll admit it. I'm scared. It's an overwhelming responsibility to be trusted with this child's well-being; with her very life! I'm going to need God's help.

Dear Father, HELP! Thank You for trusting us enough to give us this precious, little girl. Please give us the wisdom to know how to raise her. Surround us with knowledgeable friends and family who will give good, sound advice. Father, keep us both completely dependent on You. We can't do this without You. Amen.

Potty Training

Love is patient, love is kind. It does not envy,
it does not boast, it is not proud. 1 Corinthians 13:4

I'm spending a lot of time these days focused on my child's body fluids. It's not a lot of fun. These days I feel tied to the house by my two-year-old's bladder. I know it's important and we will celebrate when she has mastered this grown-up function of "going on the big girl's potty."

I've read the books, studied the websites, talked with my experienced friends and ... she is still having accidents. Sigh. Oh, she's into the whole potty thing, in fact, we have to visit the restroom of every store, library, church or friend's house we go to. She seems to have some weird fascination with restrooms.

I love it when she goes and we can celebrate! We cheer and sing and applaud! But I don't love it when she gets too busy to go and then I get impatient with the mess. I have to remember that this is a learning process for her. I know I must be patient and encouraging and motivating. That's funny ... exactly the things I want God to be to me!

Dear Father, I'm somewhat stunned that we're at the potty training stage already. In some ways it seems like my daughter was just born. Please help me to be patient with this process. And help me to enjoy the journey of this stage of her life. Amen.

JANUARY 28

Mother of the Bride

*The wisdom that comes from heaven is first of all pure;
then peace-loving, considerate, submissive, full of mercy
and good fruit, impartial and sincere. James 3:17*

I can't believe it – my baby is getting married. We've been planning, shopping (and even arguing a bit) for a year now. Who knew that a wedding could be so much work? My daughter has impeccable taste and I love the young man she is marrying. He's good to her and considerate to my husband and me. He loves my daughter and he loves God. I couldn't ask for anything more. But I shudder when I think about the wedding planning ... Usually my daughter and I agree on things, but we have disagreed on everything from flowers to frosting colors. Trust me, there are a lot of things to disagree on!

Having my daughter disagree with my opinions has been difficult. I have to remind myself daily that she is an adult and that this is her wedding. My baby is getting married. I don't want to be a problem, I want to be part of the celebration. I love her so much and this is a send-off to her new life. I want us all to enjoy it.

Dear Father, I need Your help to back off and not push to have my way in my daughter's wedding plans. But the process of letting go isn't easy. The truth is ... I'm going to miss her a lot, so I want this wedding to happen with us on good terms. Help me, Father, please. Amen.

Yesterday, Today and Tomorrow

Do not exasperate your children; instead, bring them up in the training and instruction of the Lord. Ephesians 6:4

Some days my children drive me crazy. I love them with all my heart, but some days it feels like they are ganging up on me so they can push me over the edge.

On days like these I know it's more important than ever to be consistent in my responses and even my punishments. I need to be consistent with my rules of what is acceptable behavior and what is not. It's hard, though, because they throw little tantrums and push me to the limits of my patience. Some days I'm so frustrated that I react in anger to their misbehavior. There isn't any consistency in that. Some days I don't have the energy to deal with disciplining them and then they try to get away with all kinds of things. Days like these make me realize just how full time parenting is. I'm tired ... but I want to do a good job. That means setting rules that always remain the same. How will they learn what is acceptable and what isn't if the boundaries keep moving?

Dear Father, this is hard, but I know it's so important. Help my husband and me to set rules that are fair. Then give me the energy and strength to consistently enforce them and explain them. Please help me with the process. Amen.

JANUARY 30

Teaching about God

"Love the Lord your God with all your heart and with all your soul and with all your mind and with all your strength. The second is this: Love your neighbor as yourself. There is no commandment greater than these." Mark 12:30-31

I've come to realize that words alone aren't going to do it. If I want to teach my children about God it won't work to just read them stories or quote Scripture verses or even take them to church every Sunday. The best way to show them what a life lived for God looks like is to live that life in front of them. Whew! Of course I want them to see me reading my Bible and praying, and I want to pray with them. That's important. But more than anything, I want them to see a life that is filled with love for others.

I can't quote Scripture verses about love and then turn around and make negative comments about someone. I have to be careful about criticizing, complaining about and belittling others. I must live generously; giving of my time, energy, creativity and money to help others. I've got a constant audience watching me. The best way to teach my children how a God-follower lives is to show them.

Dear Father, Jesus said that the two greatest commandments are to love God and to love others. I want that to show in my life so that my children pick it up. Help me to be an example to my children – at home and in public. Amen.

February

The Attitude of Success

Encourage one another and build each other up, just as in fact you are doing. 1 Thessalonians 5:11

My daughter won the state gymnastics championship! I'm so proud of her and she's so proud of herself! She has worked so hard and sacrificed so much to get to this point. I want to tell the world how proud I am of her!

Winning feels so good and does so much for the self-esteem. But then the Mom-i-tude kicks in: on the one hand I'm celebrating with her, but on the other hand I want her to understand that winning is not everything. There is the very real danger of becoming so obsessed with winning that people get pushed aside or pushed down in the vicious climb to success.

There is a healthy attitude toward success that is balanced by motivation to work hard and expect the best from herself without being so obsessed with winning that she hurts others in her quest. Sometimes someone else will be the winner instead of her and I want her to be able to celebrate with them.

Dear Father, there is such a fine line between doing our best and being able to cheer when someone else wins. Help me to communicate this to my daughter. Help her develop a healthy attitude toward success; one that keeps love for others in the forefront. Amen.

Copycat

Be imitators of God, therefore, as dearly loved children and live a life of love, just as Christ loved us and gave Himself up for us as a fragrant offering and sacrifice to God. Ephesians 5:1

This is scary. Over the last week or so I've noticed my child trying to do things that he has seen my husband or I do. We laugh so hard when he tries to put a cell phone on his belt "just like Daddy," or insists on putting things in the dishwasher (even if they aren't dirty) because that's what I do.

Yes, it's cute, but when you stop and really think about it, it is also scary. It means he is watching us. He's paying attention to what we do and how we do it. He notices how we spend our time and interact with others. Wow, that means we have to be careful.

It's a sobering thought to know that we're role models for our son. The first time he copies something we do in anger – like slam a door or throw something across a room – and we want to punish him, we have to stop and realize that he is just copying something he has seen us do. It's a good reminder to make our walk of faith match our talk of faith.

Dear Father, it's so easy to tell my son how to behave. It's much harder to actually model good behavior. Father, I want to be a good role model of Your love and consideration for him. Help me to be a mom who is worthy of my son's copycat behavior. Amen.

Writing in the Dust

Be joyful always, pray continually; give thanks in all circumstances,
for this is God's will for you in Christ Jesus. 1 Thessalonians 5:16-18

I can't remember the last time I dusted my furniture. It's not so bad – as long as no one moves anything. But, with three kids in the house, things get moved. Yesterday my ten-year-old thought it would be funny to write a message on one of the end tables: "PLEASE DUST ME." He thought it was funny. I did not.

I'm really not such a bad housekeeper, I actually enjoy cleaning; but who has the time? For the time being I've traded "Domestic Engineer" for "Soccer Mom." Yeah, by the time I drive one kid to soccer practice three days a week, another one to choir rehearsals and the third one to gymnastics; then attend all their games, plus church activities and the multitude of other things that they are each involved in ... I don't often have time to clean.

Now, I could feel guilty about not keeping a spotless house ... but I'm not going to. Right now I think the "job" God has put in front of me is to be available to my kids; to encourage them and invest in them. I can do that!

Dear Father, OK, sometimes I get tired of being a taxi, sports fan, music aficionado and so on. Help me to remember that my children are young for only a short time. Investing in them is a privilege, so help me to enjoy this time to the fullest! Amen.

A Toddler's Frustration

Sensible people control their temper; they earn respect by overlooking wrongs. Proverbs 19:11 NLT

I don't understand this. My son is only fifteen months old. I've never spanked him or struck him in any way. So why, when he gets frustrated, is he now hitting whoever is around him? Where did he learn that? Is this an example of the inherent sinful nature of mankind? Sigh. More importantly, how do I handle this? It doesn't make sense to spank him. I need the patience, wisdom and control of a saint to do this parenting thing.

I love my little guy and want him to be a child who others want to be around, a child who other moms want their children to play with. He has to learn to control his frustrations or handle them in a way that is acceptable. Wow, I wonder how often God feels that way about me ... My frustrations may come out in other ways, but they definitely come out. Maybe patience and control is a lesson my son and I need to learn together.

Dear Father, help me to be a model for my son of correct ways to handle frustrations. Show me how to teach him now, even at this young age, to have control over his actions and reactions. Whew ... I really need Your patience, wisdom and control to do this right. Thanks for Your help. Amen.

Broken Heart

Be kind and compassionate to one another, forgiving each other, just as in Christ God forgave you. Ephesians 4:32

I remember the pain of a teenage girl's anguish when her special guy no longer wants to be her special guy. It hurts. I can hear my daughter sobbing in her bedroom. I know her heart is breaking and my heart aches for her. I want to see her laughing again and racing out the door to meet her friends at the mall. I even want to hear her incessant chatter (that I got so tired of before) about her special guy. I just want to stop her pain. But ... I can't.

Everyone goes through the pain of a broken heart ... usually several times before the "real" one comes along. Of course, I know that she will heal and that one day this lost love won't matter at all. But she doesn't realize that right now so I must be compassionate with her. I don't want to be overbearing and push her to feel better. I know I must be patient with her pain and, if I'm allowed, show her healthy ways to deal with it. I must empathize with her, love her, cry with her, pray with her and wait with her for this to pass.

Dear Father, it hurts me to see my child hurt so much. Give me wisdom to know what to say. Help me to be compassionate and caring. Give me words of encouragement and hope. Amen.

Peacemaker

*Do not repay anyone evil for evil. Be careful to do what is right
in the eyes of everybody. If it is possible, as far as it depends
on you, live at peace with everyone. Romans 12:17-18*

Why am I so often in the middle? Is it really part of a mom's job description to be the mediator between brother and sister, sister and sister and (most frustrating) between Dad and each of them? It's tiring to have this responsibility and yet it seems to come with the territory. Being part of a family is wonderful when everyone is getting along. But when they aren't it is up to me to be the "bridge" of communication, to help them hear each other and help them understand the emotions behind each other's actions.

I can see the domino effect of one person's unkind words, which causes the next person's selfish behavior and the next one's impatience ... so I intercede before it starts, because peace means harmony in our family. It's a lot of work and takes a lot of emotional energy ... but it's what a mom does.

Dear Father, sometimes I get tired of being the peacemaker ... but I can't seem to stop. I love my family and I want them to love each other. I know they do, but when there is conflict I want to make it stop. Father, help me to let go of my control issues – to bring peace when I can but also to let them learn how to solve their own problems. Amen.

Make It Stop!

The LORD is my strength and my song; He has become my salvation.
Exodus 15:2

Five weeks. It has been five weeks since my baby was born. She has cried 24/7 for five weeks. Seriously, her sleep times have been no more than forty-five-minute segments. Then she's awake again ... crying. I can't figure out how to make her stop. She's not hungry, her diaper is not wet — I hold her, I put her down, but no matter what I do, she keeps on crying. After five weeks of this, I'm exhausted, frustrated and my patience is very, very thin. I feel like a failure as a mother and I've only been one for five weeks! What's wrong with her? What's wrong with me? How do I make it stop?

OK, deep breath. I'm going to put her down in her crib and walk away for ten minutes. I will spend those ten minutes talking to God; asking for help, strength and patience. I'd like Him to just make the crying stop. Maybe He will, but even if He doesn't, I know it will end eventually. My goal right now is to be a godly mother who has the patience to show unconditional love to this little one.

Dear Father, I can't do this without Your help. I'm tired. My patience is gone. I'm frustrated. Please give me the patience and strength to treat her with love and compassion. Help me ... no, help us get through this. Amen.

Baby Bird Time

The LORD gives wisdom, and from His mouth come knowledge and understanding. Proverbs 2:6

Many of my friends are bemoaning this stage of parenting. There's no doubt that the pre-teen and early teen years do have their challenges, but I'm secretly kind of enjoying it. My child's desire for freedom from Mom and Dad is the normal beginning stage of independence. After all, we are trying to raise her to be an independent adult. It's kind of fun to watch her fly out from the nest and test her wings. She probably doesn't even realize that she keeps looking back to make sure the "nest" is still there.

She tries her wings and then comes back. I know that as she gets older she will fly farther away each time, but I believe that as long as I keep the lines of communication open, she will always come home. I'm thankful for the privilege of being her guide during this time. I'm going to need a lot of wisdom and discernment from God to know when to pull her back to the nest, when to let her fly and when to let her crash. And then be there to pick up the pieces and hug and console her.

Dear Father, that wisdom and discernment can only come from You. Letting go is hard because the dangers seem so massive. My child needs to know how to make good choices. Show me now, with my child craving independence, how to be a strong guide. Amen.

The Learning Curve

Let us consider how we may spur one another on toward love and good deeds. Hebrews 10:24

"Mommy, can I wash the dishes?" "Can I clean the bathroom sink?" "Can I make my own bed?" My sweet little girl is yearning to do "grown-up" things and is eager to help me with the housework. I love it and I'm going to enjoy it while it lasts! I'm glad she wants to learn these things and I certainly appreciate the help, but, here's the rub ... I have to let go of my perfectionism and accept the way she does these chores. If I was washing the dishes, the dishes would be rinsed better, the sink would be cleaner and the water drops would be wiped away. If I was making the bed, the bedspread would be smoother and it would hang evenly along the side. But if I go back and re-do her work, what is that teaching her? That her efforts aren't good enough.

Yes, I can teach her the best way to do things, but I want to be patient enough to accept her best efforts; knowing that they will improve with practice and maturity. God accepts me in the same way. He allows me a learning curve. He knows when I try my best. It's a good idea for me to do the same for my daughter.

Dear Father, thank You for accepting my best efforts and allowing me time to learn. Please help me to do the same for my daughter. Help me to have the patience to praise her efforts. Amen.

Born into My Heart

God decided in advance to adopt us into His own family by bringing us to Himself through Jesus Christ. This is what He wanted to do, and it gave Him great pleasure. So we praise God for the glorious grace He has poured out on us who belong to His dear Son. Ephesians 1:5-6 NLT

I love my son. It's true that I didn't carry his forming body inside me. It's true that I didn't bring him into this world. It's true that his DNA does not match my husband's or mine. Yes, he is the biological child of another man and woman. But none of that matters because this little boy, my son, has been born into my heart.

From the moment he was placed in my arms and my eyes caressed his little body, my heart claimed him as my own. Yes, he is adopted into our family but he is born into my heart. Friends and family members who don't understand sometimes comment about how I feel about this adopted boy in relation to my real child. They just don't get it. The physical ability to birth a child does not make you a parent — that comes from the heart. This boy makes our family a family. I love and cherish him.

Dear Father, when this little guy joined our family I gained a new understanding of how You feel about me. I was adopted into Your family when I claimed Christ as Savior — but in Your eyes (heart) we are related by blood ... Christ's blood. Thank You for the privilege of being this boy's mother. Amen.

Thunder and Lightning

*When I am afraid, I will trust in You. In God, whose word I praise,
in God I trust; I will not be afraid. What can mortal man do to me?*
Psalm 56:3-4

Bolts of lightning and crashes of thunder slice the stillness of the dark night. The house literally shakes with the power of this storm. It takes only a few seconds before all the children have raced to our bedroom, pillows and blankets in hand. I guess it just feels better to be together when you're afraid. We spread their makeshift beds on the floor and they all snuggle close together, with me in the middle. I remind them that God is watching over us and that He controls the wind, thunder and lightning. One by one my kids fall asleep as the storm moves on its way.

I could climb back into my bed now, but I don't. It's nice to be here together, snuggled against their fear. I cherish these times to comfort them, knowing that all too soon they won't need me to do so anymore. I silently pray over each of them, for their faith and trust in God to carry them through frightening times. I pray for His love to be their strength throughout their lives.

Dear Father, thank You for these times when I can comfort my children and remind them of Your love and care. I pray that they will always turn to You with their fears and find their strength in You. Amen.

Broken Dreams

Dear friends, let us love one another, for love comes from God.
Everyone who loves has been born of God and knows God. 1 John 4:7

This is not going to be easy. How do I tell my children that Daddy is moving out because he doesn't want to live with us any more? No, that isn't right – he doesn't want to be married to me any more but he still loves them very much.

Divorce is hard ... on everyone. As angry as I am at my husband right now, I know that this experience is hard on him too. I'm hurting so much, but I must be careful not to be spiteful and say mean things about him to the children. I want them to know that he's not leaving them.

This is not how I expected our lives to turn out – I thought we'd grow old together and the kids would come home to visit and bring the grandchildren. Instead, we've got to work together to make time for the children to see each of us. We've got to put the children first. Yes, it will be harder to find time for the kids to spend with their father, but if my husband and I can remain amicable and cooperative, that will only be easier for the children. I must do that ... for them.

Dear Father, I need You more than ever right now. My heart is hurting so much. But I want to think of my children first. Take away the anger toward my husband. Fill it with love and understanding so that this difficult experience can be as easy as possible for my children. Amen.

Happy Tears

"Go and make disciples of all nations, baptizing them in the name of the Father and of the Son and of the Holy Spirit. And surely I am with you always, to the very end of the age." Matthew 28:19-20

From the day my baby entered this world we have tried to teach her to be independent, to make wise decisions, to be mature and to honor God in her life. There have been ups and downs in that journey. But now she is all grown up and believes that God is directing her to travel halfway around the world to share the gospel with the people there. This is exactly what I prayed for and I am so grateful to God. But now ... I have to let her go. Whew, that's more difficult than I thought it would be.

What a weird emotional place to be in – I'm glad that my daughter is willing to obey God and I'm so very proud of her, but I'm also going to miss her and worry about her. Even though I'm crying today as her plane pulls away – they are tears of joy. I'm going to miss her every moment of every day, but I'm also going to be praying for her and asking God to use her and bless her ministry. So, my tears are happy tears.

Dear Father, thank You for how far my daughter has grown in her life with You. Bless her now as she goes across the world to serve You. Protect her and bless her ministry! Amen.

A Miracle Heart

You yourselves have been taught by God to love each other.
1 Thessalonians 4:9

It amazes me that when my first child was born, I immediately loved her with all my heart – all of it! In fact I was relatively certain that I probably had no more love to give. My heart was completely full. Then my second child was born and, amazingly, I loved him with all my heart too. But I still loved my first child with all my heart, too. How does that work? Now my third baby has just been born and ... I LOVE HER WITH ALL MY HEART!

As the birth of my second child approached, I remember worrying that I wouldn't be able to love him as much as I loved my firstborn, and I didn't want to have the struggle of having a favorite child! I'm completely amazed at the capacity for love that God has placed within the human heart. He really knew what He was doing!

Instead of our hearts being forced to make choices as to who to love most, our capacity to love grows and grows. Our hearts envelop all the precious ones in our lives. In fact, it seems that the more we love, the more we are able to love. What a loving arrangement from a loving God!

Dear Father, thank You so much for Your incomparable love. I truly believe Your love is unending. Thank You for sharing that capacity to love with us. Thanks for Your plan! Amen.

Worry Expert

Cast all your anxiety on Him because He cares for you.
1 Peter 5:7

Why does it scare me silly to watch my son play football? He loves playing and he is good at it, but when I see him hurling his little body at the other players and them hurling their bodies at him, my heart leaps into my throat. I worry that he will get hurt, but he doesn't worry about that at all. I'm actually fighting the urge to put my son in a glass box to keep him safe. Then there will be no chance of him getting hurt, or even dirty! That wouldn't be much fun for him, would it?

Oh my, I must somehow learn to worry less. I guess I even need to be OK with him getting a little hurt once in a while. I know that in everyday life he will sometimes be in pleasant situations, I also know that he might get hurt once in a while and that he will have to learn to make choices and decisions for himself. That's a good thing. He must learn how to choose between good and bad. I need God's help to learn to worry less and let my son live life to the full.

Dear Father, OK, I just said it. I worry too much and that makes me want to stop my son from participating in normal activities. Father, help me to trust You with him. Help me to be willing to let him experience normal activities without me hovering over him. Amen.

Happy Birthday!

Clap your hands, all you nations; shout to God with cries of joy.
Psalm 47:1

What a fun day! It is my little girl's fifth birthday. Wow, where did the time go? This year she understands that it is her birthday and her excitement simply cannot be contained. It's been fun to plan her parties – one with streamers, games, cake and ice cream for her little friends. I love watching them play together and seeing how much my daughter's friends care about her. Then there's the family party with grandparents and special adult friends. What a celebration of love. It's such a blessing to share this event with others who love my daughter and join in thanking God for her presence in our lives.

This day makes me think back over the last five years and how she has grown each year. I'm aware of the things she has learned to do and of how her likes and dislikes have changed. I see how the influence of friends colors her preferences. I know that with every passing year her independence will be more evident. She's growing up so quickly and I want to enjoy every moment. I'm taking photos with my camera ... and with my heart!

Dear Father, thank You so much for my daughter's birthday. Thank You so much for her presence in my life and the privilege of being her mother. Remind me, often, to enjoy every day. Amen.

Celebration!

The LORD is near to all who call on Him,
to all who call on Him in truth. Psalm 145:18

My son prayed tonight ... he prayed! We did our usual nightly routine – we read a story from his little Bible story-book and talked about it a bit, then I suggested it was time to talk to Jesus. "I want to talk to Him myself, Mommy!" he said. For the first time ever my son talked to Jesus about the things on his heart. What a joy to hear him pray for Grandma to feel better and to thank God for fishing trips with Grandpa. I learned that he is worried about a friend who is feeling sad. He prayed for Daddy's job and for the Bible study I teach. What a blessing to hear my son thank God for his family and friends.

It was so precious to hear his simple appreciation of God's gift of Jesus. I learned a lot tonight about what my son has absorbed. I'm so thankful that we have been diligent in praying often with him. Even though there were times when he didn't pay attention or even complained that he had to take time for prayer ... we were establishing that prayer is important. Praise God!

Dear Father, thank You for the privilege of being able to talk with You at any time. I'm thankful that my son understands that You care about the things that concern us. Thank You for the blessing of hearing my son's little voice talk with You! Amen.

FEBRUARY 17

The Longest Day

We also rejoice in our sufferings, because we know that suffering produces perseverance; perseverance, character; and character, hope.
Romans 5:3-4

The kids are in bed ... finally. What happened today? From the moment their little feet hit the floor (way too early this morning), we were engaged in a difficult power struggle. They were just so grouchy today. My efforts to distract them with activities that normally interest them did not work. They disobeyed pretty much every established rule in our household and were basically unhappy all day.

These kinds of days are so tiring and make me question my parenting ability. Did I start the day with an attitude or action that kicked off this behavior from them? If so, it was unintentional, but now that the children are in bed I'm reviewing my words and actions to see how I reacted and responded. On days like this I need God's help more than ever to be loving and consistent with my kids. Oh my, this is not easy and I know I can't do it on my own. On a day like today I'm reminded to stay close to God and to begin each day with a prayer for His help.

Dear Father, this has not been a fun day of parenting. I need Your help to be loving, patient and consistent with my children. Fill me with Your love and strength. Help me to measure my words and even the tone of my voice as I speak with them. Amen.

A Puppy?

Listen to a father's instruction; pay attention and gain understanding.
Proverbs 4:1

My kids want a puppy. They are presenting a well-organized and very persistent onslaught of requests. It feels like every time I turn around I'm hearing the "dog plea." Is it a good idea? I don't know. There are several things to consider. There would be added pressure on our budget to feed and care for a dog. There is also the time element to consider; I simply do not have time to take care of one more creature. My kid's promises to do all the work is so convincing but I know they really have no idea of how constant the care of a pet can be.

My children could learn some great lessons of responsibility by caring for a pet. They could also experience the true love and companionship that a dog offers. For this to work, I've got to be disciplined and insistent about them fulfilling their promises to take care of this puppy. I've got to put up with the puppy's training stage and with the children's complaints about doing their jobs. I know this is going to be a good learning experience for both my children and me ... so let's go get a puppy.

Dear Father, this could be a great learning experience for my children, but I'm going to need lots of strength and patience to make this work. Father, help me keep the big picture in mind. Amen.

Giving Back

"Your love for one another will prove to the world that
you are My disciples." John 13:35 NLT

I'm looking forward to today; my children and I are visiting a senior citizens' home. We're going to help serve cake and ice cream for a birthday party and take part in a little program. My children are singing with a few other children from church. I know my little ones are a bit nervous about this, but I also know that they will do great. They are so loving and compassionate.

I know the residents of the home will love having them there and I think my children will understand the joy of spending time with them. I hope that we can build some relationships that will take us back to the home, even apart from the church group's visits.

I believe it is important for my children to experience the joy of giving to others. We are so blessed to be in a loving family and to know that we have each other. Some of the dear people in the home do not have family close by and it takes so little for us to stop in for a chat. I'm grateful for the chance to share this time with my children.

Dear Father, I pray that this will be a great experience for my children. I pray that it will give them a chance to see how they, as children, can serve others. I pray that it will reinforce the opportunity to love others. Bless them with joy and love. Amen.

Is There a Better Way?

You will keep in perfect peace all who trust in You, all whose thoughts are fixed on You! Isaiah 26:3 NLT

I seriously wonder if I'm doing this mother thing right. Today I totally lost it over something really silly. My kids must think I'm a "psycho mom." Some days I'm so incredibly patient, loving and kind. Occasionally I have these bursts of creativity and think of amazing things for them to do. Then, for hardly any reason at all, I have one of these days when my children can do nothing right. I become impatient about everything and today I even shouted at them! I'm so disappointed in myself. What am I teaching them by this crazy, erratic behavior?

I love my children very much and I love being a mom. I take the responsibility of teaching my kids how to behave and how to treat others seriously. But my own crazy actions don't match the things I teach them. I really need God's help to stop this craziness. Maybe I need a little alone time to refuel. I definitely need sleep, exercise and nutritious meals too ... all of which take time! I'd better start with prayer.

Dear Father, I need help! I want to be a good mom. I don't want my kids to think of me as a "psycho mom." I want them to know that I love them, no matter what. Father, show me how to refuel and relax so I can react less and love more. Amen.

The Highest Calling

"Let the little children come to Me, and do not hinder them, for the kingdom of God belongs to such as these." Luke 18:16

When I was a little girl I had such big dreams of what I wanted to be when I grew up ... a doctor, a writer, a nurse, a cowgirl (OK, that one didn't last long). Even when I went to college I was preparing for a career. Now, I'm pretty much in the house 24/7, picking up macaroni from the floor, changing diapers, wiping drippy noses, reading the same children's book over and over, doing laundry and ... well, mom stuff.

I used to feel bad about not being out in the business world, I used to feel like I wasn't making a difference with the life I've been given. But I don't struggle with that anymore. I've learned that motherhood is truly my highest calling. When I see my little one learn something new, when I see her generosity and love toward someone, and when I hear her simple, heartfelt prayers, I KNOW this is my calling. What a privilege to care for, love, teach and train this young life to be a Christ-following person in this world. For now, I thank God for this privilege and I constantly seek His help in being the best mom I can be.

Dear Father, some days the job of motherhood is just so ... constant. But Father, please help me to never take it lightly. Thank You for this wonderful job! Amen.

Listening and Learning

*Everyone should be quick to listen, slow to speak
and slow to become angry.* James 1:19

My mother is driving me crazy! Her constant advice and suggestions about parenting sound like flat-out criticism. I'm at the end of my patience with her. Just because something worked for her does not mean it will work with my children. Times have changed, customs have changed, medicine has changed, technology has changed. Can't she see all of that? I know she cares and that she thinks she is helping, but . . .

OK. I am going to calm down and think this through. My mom loves me and she loves my kids. I know that when she sees me struggling she just wants to help. Now that I think about it, I turned out OK so Mom did do something right. The Bible says that older women should teach younger women; so perhaps I need to relax a little and see what I can learn from my mom. I can filter what she says through the twenty-five or thirty years since she had a toddler of her own and make it work today. I know she just loves me and my kids and wants the best for all of us.

Dear Father, help me to relax a little and not consider my mom's advice a threat. I know she loves us and just wants to help, so please let me listen to her with a heart that wants to learn. Amen.

On the Run

"Be still, and know that I am God; I will be exalted among the nations, I will be exalted in the earth." Psalm 46:10

First I pick up my daughter at junior high, then my younger daughter and son. Next, we head to gymnastics to drop off my older daughter. Then I take my son to baseball and my little one to piano. Fifteen minutes to run to the grocery store then back to pick up my pianist and go to the ball field to wait for my son's practice to end. Then run home and make a quick dinner and get the kids started on their homework.

After my husband gets home, we gobble down dinner before I run back out to pick up the gymnast and hurry home so she can do homework. After this … let's face it, I'm toast. But I still need to do laundry, clean up the kitchen and do some work on a project for church. Sometimes I just want to run away from it all and be still. I'd be a better mom, wife and person if I could just get some space in my life. I seriously don't have time to read my Bible and pray … except at stoplights. Something has to change and I'm the only one who can change it, but I can't do it without God's help.

Dear Father, I need to simplify my life. I barely have time to breathe these days. God, help me to prioritize my life. I want to enjoy these days of being with my children and be the best mom I can be. Amen.

Cruel Words

We know how much God loves us, and we have put our trust in His love. God is love, and all who live in love live in God, and God lives in them. 1 John 4:16 NLT

Kids can be so mean. Why does it make one girl feel good to say cruel and hurtful things to someone else? My heart breaks every day that my daughter comes home with tears in her eyes. I don't know how anyone could want to hurt her. Some days I wonder what I could change to make them stop – buy her different clothes, suggest a different hairstyle – but deep in my heart I know that won't stop them. They are doing what they do just because ... not for any specific reason.

The thing is, all people are created by the same loving God and all are created in His image. So, is one person better than another? It is especially hard to understand how a Christian can do this. Christians are supposed to love, aren't they? How do I help my daughter through this? How do I help her keep her self-esteem and remember that God loves her very much? How do I advise her to respond to this treatment? I don't want her to respond in the same way back – no matter how much she is hurting.

Dear Father, please help me. My daughter is hurting so much and I just want to make the hurt go away. I don't know how to do that, but I know You do. Help her to remember that You love her. Amen.

Climbing the Walls

The joy of the LORD is your strength. Nehemiah 8:10

My daughter makes me laugh so hard. She is never still. At eight years old she walks around the house ... on her hands! We have to watch TV between her legs! She does cartwheels and flips all around the room. I can't recall the last time she entered a room by simply walking into it. She literally climbs the walls by putting a foot and a hand on each side of a doorframe and scooting up to the very top! It sure shocks houseguests when they see her hanging near the ceiling!

What a precious gift this energetic little girl is. Her zest for life shows in so many ways. She attacks life and brings laughter and joy to pretty much everyone. I'm so thankful for her joy and for the energy she brings to our family.

I pray that her joy will be reflected in my own attitudes and actions. It teaches me to let go of little things and celebrate life more often. I pray that I never do anything to dull her spirit. I pray that throughout her life her interactions with other people will only increase her joy and will never put that light out.

Dear Father, I think the world needs more people like my daughter; more people who live life with joy. Thank You for her Father, keep her joy shining even as she grows up and faces some harsh realities in life. Amen.

FEBRUARY 26

A Learning Curve

We urge you, warn those who are idle, encourage the timid,
help the weak, be patient with everyone. 1 Thessalonians 5:14

So many of my toddler's firsts seem to sneak up on me. One day she stayed exactly where I put her on the floor, and the next day she rolled over, then crawled, pulled herself up, stood, and then walked. Wow, those firsts rolled in so fast! Her first words happened the same way; at first unintelligible babbling, then slowly words became understandable. It is so much fun to see her grow up. However, the "first" we're working on now is not going so easily ... potty training. Some days she is so into it, and other days I might as well be talking to a brick wall.

I need a lot of patience to get through this and do it right. If I lose my temper then this won't be a fun time for her, either. Other things have come so easily to her that I want this to come easily too ... by my standards. I suppose that the learning curve for this could be steeper than other things. I need to remember that she used to fall when she was learning to walk. So, when she has accidents, it is just like falling down.

Dear Father, please help me to be patient enough not to frustrate my daughter. I know this is a learning process for her, so help me to be patient to allow for her learning curve. Amen.

Stranger Danger

The fear of the LORD is the beginning of wisdom; all who follow His precepts have good understanding. To Him belongs eternal praise.
Psalm 111:10

Every parent wants her child to be safe. I'm not unique in that desire. I try to do all the right things by teaching her not to play around fire and not to stick things in outlets ... all the basics. But one kind of teaching is so hard: I want my daughter to be friendly and kind to all people she meets, but I also want her to be safe. It's a sad statement on our world that we have to teach children about the danger of strangers.

I pray for the wisdom to teach her to be safe but also not destroy her childlike trust in humanity. Whew, that's a fine line to walk; one that I can't possibly walk without God's wisdom and help. I don't want to terrify her but I don't want to be lax, either. It's such a contradiction to tell her not to talk to strangers but then encourage her to say hello to people we meet in the grocery store. I'm thankful for the wisdom and advice of parents with older children on how to handle this.

Dear Father, help me to be smart about this lesson. Show me how to teach my daughter to be safe, but not ruin her opinions of people. I don't want her to be afraid, I want her to be friendly and respectful, but also be safe. Show me how to do this. Amen.

Simple Joy

Come, let us sing for joy to the LORD; let us shout aloud to the Rock of our salvation. Let us come before Him with thanksgiving and extol Him with music and song. Psalm 95:1-2

Joy! Joy! Joy! My heart swelled with joy over the simplest of things today. My grandson spent the day with me. He is eighteen months old and full of energy, curiosity, demands, tears, giggles ... he wears me out. The joy moment came when we settled down for lunch. He was buckled safely into his little chair and watched quietly while I put his plate and cup on the tray.

Then I sat down and looked at him to suggest that we thank God for our food. He already had his little head bowed and his hands folded. He quietly "prayed" for a few minutes, said a firm "amen" and looked at me with a sweet grin. He prayed! I couldn't understand what he said, but I know God did!

My joy comes from the knowledge that his mommy and daddy are consistently teaching him to thank God and that he understands that. What joy!

Dear Father, thank You that my little grandson understands already to thank You for what You give. I pray that he will come to know You early in his life and have the joy of serving You. Thank You for parents who openly live their faith in front of him. Amen.

March

What Happened?

Who hopes for what he already has? But if we hope for what we do not yet have, we wait for it patiently. Romans 8:24-25

OK, no one told me about this and I don't think it's fair. I made it through nine months of pregnancy, struggling to keep my weight gain at a reasonable level. Then I delivered a healthy, beautiful baby and I fully expected to walk out of the hospital at my pre-pregnancy figure. Why is my mom laughing so hard? Probably because my body still looks six months pregnant.

My mom says this is the first of many little "surprises" that will accompany this new experience of motherhood. So I guess my first challenge as a mother is to learn patience and perseverance while I wait for my body to return to its former self (or as close as it will ever be). My mom says that motherhood is going to be one lesson in patience after the other. Since patience isn't one of my strong points, I suppose I'd better begin seeking God's help right now. But God often teaches patience through some pretty intense situations, and as I'm already IN an intense situation as a new mom, it's probably safe to pray for help!

Dear Father, You know I've always taken care of myself and been proud of my fitness. That's what makes this weight gain harder to handle. Help me to learn patience. Amen.

Ouch!

The LORD gives strength to His people;
the LORD blesses His people with peace. Psalm 29:11

Who knew that a fourteen-year-old girl could have such a sharp tongue? I can't imagine that I talked to my mom like that when I was a teenager. Honestly, if I spoke to my mom the way my daughter speaks to me ... I need to call my mom and tell her that I'm really sorry. It hurts a lot when my daughter says such sarcastic, hurtful things to me when all I've ever wanted is to love her and be her friend. I thought I had taught her to be respectful to adults. While she may be to others, she is definitely not to me.

I have to admit, I miss our fun conversations, I miss knowing what's going on in her life, I miss ... her. I think this new attitude is a sign of her struggle toward independence, but I sure miss my little girl.

As much as this hurts, it gives me pause to think of how I sometimes react and respond to my heavenly Father. So, as I thank Him for His constant, unconditional love; even through my rudeness and rebelliousness, I will learn from Him and seek to love my daughter steadily and constantly. I know we'll get through this stage

Dear Father, my daughter's words and tone of voice sometimes hurt. Please give me the strength not to react to her with anger. Help me to love her unconditionally ... as You love me. Amen.

MARCH 2

Frustrating Free Will

*Praise be to the God and Father of our Lord Jesus Christ, who comforts us
in all our troubles, so that we can comfort those in any trouble with
the comfort we ourselves have received from God.* 2 Corinthians 1:3-4

My children are adults, but I'm still their mother. I will always
be their mother. Parenting adults is more difficult than parenting toddlers or even teenagers. Because they are adults
they get to make their own decisions (which are not always
wise ones) and I can't say anything … unless I'm asked, of
course. Now, granted, the fact that I'm not supposed to offer my advice doesn't always keep me from doing so, but I
do know that I should be quiet.

It's just difficult to let my children make mistakes that will
cause them pain when I could help them. I wonder why they
don't choose to benefit from the wisdom I have garnered
through my life experiences and the practice I've had in
parenting. I've made many wrong choices and learned such
hard lessons from those experiences. I guess I must allow
my children to learn in the same way I did … Of course, any
time my children ask for my advice I will gladly share it. Otherwise, I will just be there to support and love them through
whatever happens.

Dear Father, it is hard to see my children in pain. Give me the
wisdom to know when to be quiet and the patience to stay by my
kids to support them when they need me. Amen.

What Is Perfection?

Love is patient, love is kind. It always protects, always trusts,
always hopes, always perseveres. 1 Corinthians 13:4, 7

My baby is here. We waited nine long months for this precious baby to come. It amazes me that I started loving this little girl from the minute I knew she was growing inside me. I've been praying for her, dreaming about her, and imagining what she would look like and what she would become when she grew up. But my precious little girl has been born with some special challenges. The hopes and dreams I had for her will probably never happen.

Of course my heart aches for lost dreams and for the challenges ahead of her, but I believe God is good. So, almost as soon as my heart began aching, God began blessing. I love my precious little girl and will do all I can to help her live a full and happy life. I will enjoy the unconditional love she will give me and count her as an "angel unaware." I will be the best mom I can be to this child. Recognizing that some gifts from God give me the opportunity to grow in my strength, faith and love.

Dear Father, OK, I won't deny that this is hard, but I know I will never be alone in caring for my daughter. You will be with me each step of the way. Show me how to parent her. Show me how to help her and teach her. Father, help me to be the best mom I can to her. Amen.

The World in Which We Live

*But you, dear friends, build yourselves up in your most
holy faith and pray in the Holy Spirit. Jude 1:20*

Sometimes this world scares me. The pressures on teenagers today are so much more oppressive than when I was a teen. The things my son must face in the hallways of his school each day, the language he hears in gym class, the things his friends talk about, the movies he wants to see, the music he wants to listen to, how badly he wants to fit in – it scares me.

I know I can't keep my son in a box to protect him but I sure would like to. We've taught him biblical standards and morals and to respect others; both girls and guys. I believe that my son wants to honor and obey God, but the pressures around him are so strong. I must continue praying for him to be strong, for God's protection, for the friends he chooses and the choices he makes. I must pray for the world we live in and for the influence of Christians, living for Christ, to improve it.

Dear Father, I pray for this world and for the sinking standards of what is acceptable and what isn't. Father, I pray for Christians of all ages to take a stand. I pray that we can be a light in a dark place. Help my son to make good choices even when it isn't the popular thing to do. Amen.

Do You Trust Me?

Commit your way to the LORD; trust in Him and He will do this:
He will make your righteousness shine like the dawn,
the justice of your cause like the noonday sun. Psalm 37:5-6

Ummm, I think there may be a problem ... Seriously, someone should be paying attention over here! These medical people, these experts, are really going to let me take this newborn baby home. They must think that I know what I'm doing. OK, yes, she is my daughter, and my husband and I do love her; but we don't really have a clue what to expect or what lies ahead for us. Scary.

Whew, I realize that my fear may be what's making me so nervous. I don't want to do things wrong. I want to be a good mother, but how will I know what she needs when she cries? How do I protect her and teach her how much God loves her? Wow, I've never felt so unprepared and unskilled.

I'm going to depend on God to empower and strengthen me minute by minute. I'm also going to call on my experienced friends who are already moms and my mother for advice. This is going to be a "learn-on-the-job" experience so I'll need all the help I can get.

Dear Father, help! Help me to be wise and loving. Help me to be firm but kind. Help me, Father, to be the best mom I can possibly be to this precious child. Amen.

MARCH 6

Playtime

*Get wisdom, get understanding; do not forget my words
or swerve from them.* Proverbs 4:5

My seventeen-month-old son seems to think it is appropriate behavior to bounce a ball off the head of his one-week-old brother. It is a soft, rubber ball, but still, I have to keep reminding myself that he is still a baby, too. And that he is not purposely trying to hurt his brother. It only took about an hour of being home from the hospital to realize that for the next few months I can't do anything alone. Not laundry, washing dishes, vacuuming, showering or even going to the bathroom. My children need to be constantly supervised in order for them both to be safe.

I know parenting is a full-time job, but this is a bit overwhelming. I want both of my boys to be safe so I've got to be very attentive. I also need to be patient with my older son. He will learn to be kind and gentle if I teach him that. I pray that someday my boys will be really good buddies and that will happen more easily if I do not make the baby a problem for my older boy. I want to teach them to love, respect and enjoy each other. Wow, I really need God's wisdom, guidance and patience here.

Dear Father, I cannot do this without You. Please give me wisdom to teach my son to be gentle with his younger brother without making him resent the baby. Amen.

Failure: A Learning Curve

We have different gifts, according to the grace given us. Romans 12:6

She struck out again. My daughter just finished playing her fifth softball game of the summer and she has struck out every single time she went to the plate. Every time. This time she hung her head and walked back to the bench, but I could see the tears in her eyes. She didn't even want to lift her head and look at me, let alone at her friends. My heart aches for her. She wanted to be part of a team and have the camaraderie of teammates and the joy of playing together so badly. But some of the girls laugh at her behind her back.

I thank God for the other girls and for her coach who continually tell her that she'll get it next time and encourage her to keep on trying. I know some wonderful lessons can be learned from failure, such as persistence, strength of character and ... I want to help her focus on those positive lessons. I want to teach her that failure is no reason to give up, but only to try harder or to look around for something else. Failure isn't the end, it's just a corner to go around.

Dear Father, help me to be an encourager to my daughter. Help her find the things she is good at and help her believe in herself by focusing on those things. Thank You for her coach and her friends who encourage her. Amen.

Birthday Joys

*May the Lord make your love increase and overflow for each other
and for everyone else, just as ours does for you.* 1 Thessalonians 3:12

Today began with a gentle nudging on my shoulder that woke me from a comfortable sleep. My two little girls stood beside my bed with the silliest, proud-of-themselves grins on their faces. As soon as they saw my eyes open they shouted, "Happy birthday, Mommy!" They jumped onto the bed and we giggled and hugged and sang silly songs for the next half hour. Then they remembered that they had made breakfast for me. Breakfast in bed!

The tray placed before me had orange juice (which splashed around the tray as they carried it to the bedroom), a dried out piece of toast that had been made an hour before, a bowl of cornflakes that had sat in the milk for too long ... yummy, and an orange. The best part was a red flower which my older daughter drew, colored and cut out, and birthday notes from each girl. As I ate the soggy cereal and rock-hard toast, I thought, *This is the best birthday ever!* I will treasure the memory of their efforts. I am so blessed with these precious girls.

Dear Father, thank You for my daughters. Thank You for their love for me, which they so practically expressed today. Father, I pray that their sensitive hearts will continue to express their love; not just for me, but for all the people they come into contact with. Amen.

Hot Dogs in a Cave

Make sure that nobody pays back wrong for wrong, but always try to be kind to each other and to everyone else. 1 Thessalonians 5:15

I want my children to be healthy. I am careful about what they eat, how much sleep they get and how active they are. I take that stuff very seriously. However, my mother-in-law isn't quite so conscientious. She knows my rules and, for the most part, she abides by them, but once in a while, she feels the children need a treat. On those "free days" as she calls them, the children can have hot dogs for lunch, which they eat in a cave (on the floor under the dining room table). No wonder they love visiting Granny.

OK, in my heart, I know that she is just making memories with them. I also know that an occasional hot dog won't kill them, but isn't she undermining my authority when she breaks my rules? I don't want to ruin my relationship with her, and I don't want my children to pick up on my negativity. Even though I'm going to ask her to cut back on the hot dogs (and explain why), I want to encourage more cave lunches and cave chats and cave reading times. She's really a good granny who loves my children and I am so thankful for her!

Dear Father, we're so blessed to have a granny close by who wants to spend time with our children. Help me to explain my feelings to her in love. Help me to focus on the good things she does for us. Amen.

MARCH 10

Middle School Blues

Make every effort to add to your faith goodness; and to goodness,
knowledge; and to knowledge, self-control; and to self-control,
perseverance; and to perseverance, godliness; and to godliness,
brotherly kindness; and to brotherly kindness, love. 2 Peter 1:5-7

I love being a mother. From the time my first daughter was born I have loved each stage of her life. As her siblings came along I used what I had learned during her young life to enjoy them more and more. Now she is ready to start middle school and I'm nervous. My friends who have older children have often shared how difficult these years are. The competition in middle school is tough and girls especially can get snippy and critical.

It can be a very lonely time for a girl who is pushed to the fringe of the group of friends she used to be in the center of. My heart already aches with anxiety for my daughter. I don't want her to be hurt or to hurt others. I pray that the foundations of God's love for her and all people will see her through these years, whether they be good or bad for her. I pray that she will be kind to others and be strong enough to withstand life's storms. Prayer will definitely be our lifeline through these years.

Dear Father, I pray that these middle school years will not be as difficult as I fear. But however they turn out, I pray for my daughter to be a beacon of Your love and care for those in her world. Amen.

Secret Smiles

Enter His gates with thanksgiving and His courts with praise;
give thanks to Him and praise His name. Psalm 100:4

My daughter has been very firm that she will raise her children without my advice. She is doing a great job and I'm very proud of her. I've been careful to guard my words so that I'm not giving unsolicited advice, which is not always easy. So, today when I stopped by to see her and the children, I heard something that made me smile so broadly I had to turn my head away.

When one of my grandchildren threw a little tantrum about something, my daughter handled the situation. What made me smile was that the words she spoke were mine!

Yes, even though she does not want my advice, I heard my words coming from her mouth! I realized that I have taught her about parenting from the time she was a child herself and now, her responses to her children are often the same things I said to her as a child. My secret smile warmed my heart because of the domino effect of parenting ... passed from generation to generation – even when we are unaware of it.

Dear Father, I'm so grateful that the way I raised my daughter has settled in her heart. I must have done something right for it to stick in her mind. Thank You for her heart which seeks to teach her children well. Amen.

An Honest Question

Create in me a pure heart, O God,
and renew a steadfast spirit within me. Psalm 51:10

When I get a chance to sit down with God and ask Him a question face to face, this is what I want to know: Do You know how difficult it is to parent with patience, love and gentleness all day long without ANY SLEEP?

Seriously, when my younger child keeps me up night after night, allowing only a few hours of sleep over four or five days, I'm not very patient! But I don't want my children to think their mom is a raging fool or be frightened of me. I have come to realize that the term "sleeping like a baby" is not really a good thing.

I've always wanted to be a patient, forgiving, longsuffering, FUN mom. But, it's not happening and that is because I'm tired – so tired. Sometimes I wonder if God knows how hard this is. I don't want to just "get through" this time of my children's lives. I want to enjoy it and even create some memories for us to cherish. Yep, I'm going to need God's strength for that to happen.

Dear Father, it is a good thing to be completely dependent on You, I'm not complaining about that. I'm just so tired! Please refresh my spirit and my body with Your strength and love. Just help me, Father. Please, help me to be patient, gentle and loving. Amen.

A New World

In the beginning God created the heavens and the earth. Genesis 1:1

What a joy to see the world through the eyes of my toddler. His complete awe of a bee hovering over a flower or a bird hopping across the lawn reminds me that I am often too preoccupied to notice the miracles of God's creation every day. In fact, I take them for granted. Since my son began noticing things and pointing them out to me I have marveled at an ant that busily crawls across the driveway, and squirrels that seem to play tag in our yard. I've enjoyed his giggles as he blows the fuzz from a dandelion.

We've enjoyed picking up pine cones along the lane and shells at the beach. Yes, we have enjoyed the big things – mountains and oceans – and the small things – flowers and fireflies. The world God created is one amazing, marvelous miracle after another. I probably knew that when I was a toddler but that awe is something we adults lose along the way. I'm so grateful that I get to share these discoveries with my son and teach him that all these wonderful things are here because of our creative God.

Dear Father, thank You for this amazing world. You are so creative! You've made something for every one of us to enjoy. I'm so thankful I get to see this world through the eyes of a toddler. By doing that I can teach him about You and together we can thank You for all You've made. Amen.

Spelling Quiz

*Let us therefore make every effort to do what leads to
peace and to mutual edification.* Romans 14:19

Do you need proof that my life is out of control and just
too busy? Here it is: Tonight my son asked me a simple
question, "Mom, how do you spell Hawaii?" You see, my
husband is all things Math and I am all things English. So, I
began with great deliberation to spell this word for my son.
"H ... a ... w ..." (I had to wait for him to write out each letter so, of course, I was spelling slowly). After a few minutes
I realized that my son, my two daughters and my husband
were laughing hysterically. Why? Had I misspelled the word?
Nope, I had fallen asleep in the middle of spelling it!

Once the laughter died down and I finished spelling the
word, my husband and I had a heart to heart. I realized that
for right now my main career goal is to be the best mom for
my children. I am blessed not to have to work outside our
home right now, but I am also very involved with church and
school activities. It's time to say, "Sorry, not right now," to
a few things and get the rest I need so I can spell a whole
word in one waking moment!

Dear Father, it's hard to say no. I need adult conversation and the
stimulation of using my creativity. But I also need to take care of
myself sometimes. Please guide my choices and give me wisdom
as to what tasks to accept and which not. Amen.

Cloud Pictures

Shout with joy to God, all the earth! Sing the glory of His name;
make His praise glorious! Psalm 66:1

I had the best time with my daughter today. We didn't do anything fancy or expensive. We didn't do shopping or go to a museum or to a music lesson. We didn't go out to eat or even meet up with friends. We didn't just ride around in the car together while she played video games and I talked on my cell phone. This memory was not made while we did something else. We had Mommy–Daughter time. We had a simple picnic in the backyard and then lay back on the blanket and chatted while we watched the clouds float by.

I discovered once again what an amazingly imaginative little girl she is. She saw a puppy in one cloud formation, which slowly morphed into an old woman eating an apple. We giggled and imagined and dreamed together until the clouds slowly drifted away. What a wonderful memory we made on a relaxing afternoon. With our busy lifestyle these opportunities are not possible very often. I was reminded that God provides plenty of entertainment for us, we just need to take time to enjoy it together.

Dear Father, thank You for my daughter. Thank You for the relaxing time together. I'm so grateful for this afternoon and the precious time we had. Amen.

Consistent Living

Fools vent their anger, but the wise quietly hold it back.
Proverbs 29:11 NLT

I wonder what God would consider to be justifiable anger? Jesus' anger at the moneychangers in the temple is always said to be justified because they were profaning His Father's house. Somehow I doubt that my angry outbursts over spilled milk, muddy footprints on the floor or toys left lying around are considered justified.

I don't enjoy losing my temper and screaming at my children ... but I let it happen all too often. Why? Some days I secretly fear that I'm losing my mind. Perhaps I'm too " me-focused," so I evaluate everything that happens by how it affects me. Sometimes I even imagine that my children are plotting together to frustrate me.

Perhaps I'm over-committed so I'm too tired and therefore I react irrationally. I don't know. I just know that I want to stop this. I need God's help to be more controlled, more patient, more accepting and to worry less about spills, mud and toys. I want to model godly behavior for my children, and irrational outbursts definitely do not do that!

Dear Father, my children are little for such a short time. Please help me to enjoy them and not stress over spills, dirt and messes. Help me to react and speak in a way that always honors You. Amen.

Can It Get Worse?

There is a time for everything ... a time to weep and a time to laugh,
a time to mourn and a time to dance. Ecclesiastes 3:1, 4

By the time I get my three kids piled in the car I'm already tired. The baby is in his car seat, screaming loudly, the two older ones are buckled in, but fighting like cat and dog. I buckle myself in the driver's seat and turn to "encourage" my children to stop arguing. As we pull out of the driveway I simultaneously whip around to once again "encourage" silence and hit the button to roll up my window.

As the backseat noise escalates so does my temperature, until finally I jerk my head around to really let them have it ... only to discover that when I rolled my window up, my long hair got caught in it. I nearly rip myself half bald and quickly forget the children's fight. I just wanted to cry. Seriously cry. Until I notice the woman in the car next to me laughing hysterically. As tears run down her face she touches her heart and waves at me. I know ... she's been there. So I take a deep breath, roll down the window to free my hair, and smile. Thank You, God, for my blessings!

Dear Father, it's good to know that other moms have been through similar experiences. It's so easy to lose my cool when the kids are misbehaving. I'm thankful for the reminder to keep my sense of humor and thank You for my blessings! Amen.

Going with the Flow

Praise be to the Lord, to God our Savior, who daily bears our burdens.
Psalm 68:19

Almost from the moment we found out our first child was on the way my life changed. My energy level dropped, I needed more sleep, and I could no longer drink my beloved coffee ... even the smell of it was nauseating. I got a little crabby (OK, a LOT crabby). I got a little forgetful and even kind of clumsy. What was all that about? My body and hormones were adjusting to growing and caring for this new life that was developing inside me.

Of course I expected changes in our lives once the baby was born, but I didn't expect this. Going with the flow has become the new standard. On the days that I have a lot of energy I do what I can. On the days that I don't ... I rest. I write things down so when I forget stuff I have a check point. When I drop things ... oh well. Through it all, though, I praise God for this child and I do my very best to eat healthy and rest enough so that I can take care of my baby and provide the best "home" I can. What a joy to share in the miracle of a baby!

Dear Father, some days I just don't feel well. Help me to be smart and take care of myself and this baby. Help me to enjoy and anticipate this precious time of pregnancy. I can't wait to meet him or her and see what this baby looks like. Thank You for this joyous privilege! Amen.

Home-Grown Hurricanes

From a wise mind comes wise speech; the words
of the wise are persuasive. Proverbs 16:23 NLT

My house looks as though a hurricane has blown through it. How can one teenage boy possibly have so much stuff? Yesterday I watched my son come in from school and drop his backpack right inside the door. His shoes came off one at a time and lay where they fell. He threw his sweatshirt on the floor, pulled food out of the refrigerator, left a can of soda on the table ... and then he was gone.

His room is so piled with clothes, books and sports equipment that I can't even remember what color the carpet is. My dear son responds to my suggestions to pick up things by saying that I am obsessive compulsive. Just because I worry that something may crawl out from beneath one of these piles and eat him alive??

OK. I'm learning that I must choose my battles. Keeping the common living area of our home tidy and clean is where I'm standing my ground. His room – well, he has now been given the privilege of doing his own laundry. I will be firm about some things and still try to keep communication open between us.

Dear Father, this battle with my son has been tough for me because I am a bit of a clean freak. But my relationship with my son is important to me. Help me know when to battle and when to let go. Amen.

MARCH 20

Praise God from Whom All Blessings Flow!

Give thanks in all circumstances, for this is God's will for you in Christ Jesus. 1 Thessalonians 5:18

Praise You, God, for the blessing of family! I really love being a wife and mother. I don't often take the time to tell you that, though. Thank You for my wonderful husband. Thank You for our terrific kids. Thank You for the privilege of teaching them about You. Every time I get to pray with them or read a Bible story to them I am reminded of the joy of sharing something that means so much to me.

Thank You for their kind and generous hearts that motivate hugs, kisses, silly songs and crayoned pictures. Thank You for the laughter we share as a family. Thank You for the projects we can do together. Thank You for phone calls to their grandma and grandpa. Thank You for holidays together as a family. Thank You for birthday celebrations. Thank You for a family that goes to church together. Thank You, God, for playtimes in the park. Thank You for snow angels. Thank You for snuggle times. Thank You for each and every day we share together; for lessons learned; for memories made; for prayers shared.

Dear Father, I don't often take time to just thank You for the privilege of being a mom. Thank You for my wonderful family! Amen.

What Now?

Those who spare the rod of discipline hate their children. Those who love their children care enough to discipline them. Proverbs 13:24 NLT

I don't know what to do. I've heard of the "Terrible Twos" but, wow, I didn't expect this stage when my son is just eighteen months old. I guess I haven't prepared for how to handle his selfishness and temper outbursts. It's hard enough when it's just our family at home and he wants his way all the time. The temper tantrums are loud and long. I know I'm supposed to just walk away, and sometimes I can, but sometimes it's hard. The outbursts are even more difficult when other people are around.

Usually the other moms laugh and say, "We've all been there," but I don't want people to dread having us around. I need a lot of wisdom in this to teach my son what proper behavior is; to be consistent with discipline; to make sure he knows he is loved even when he is being disciplined. Do the "Terrible Twos" end with the "Terrific Threes"?

Dear Father, I want to be a good mom who teaches my son correct and acceptable behavior. Please, help me first of all to always act in love and with my emotions under control. Help me to be consistent and firm. I love him, Father, and I know You do too. Amen.

Yahoo ... Or Not?

*This is love for God: to obey His commands. And His commands are
not burdensome, for everyone born of God overcomes the world.*
1 John 5:3-4

My son was invited to join a prestigious travel baseball team.
The fact that they asked him to join means they think he is
a great ballplayer. I'm so proud of him! He has worked hard
to perfect his skills and I know he is honored that he was
asked to join the team. But there is a downside. This team
plays all their games on Sundays and many of the games are
away games. This means that Sundays would be completely
taken over by baseball – with no time for church.

Attending church has always been a non-negotiable for
our family; we all go together each week. We believe it is
important to give God that time. Now what do we do? The
season is only twelve weeks. Will it scar our son for life if
he misses church for twelve weeks? Probably not. But what
are we teaching him about honoring and obeying God even
when it's tough? OK, my husband and I need to pray about
this and talk about it with our son. We really need God's
wisdom here.

Dear Father, I know You'll guide us to make the right decision. I
pray that our son will understand and accept it. Help us stay true
to You ... even when it's hard. Amen.

Joy Doubled!

Thanks be to God for His indescribable gift!
2 Corinthians 9:15

My baby had a baby. Yep, I'm a granny now. What pure joy it is to hold my newborn grandson, rocking him gently and singing softly. I love whispering that Granny loves him. He can't understand me now, but he will someday.

What a blessing it is to be close by so I can really get to know my grandson and also be a help to my daughter. While I don't want to be a nuisance to her and my son-in-law, I am available when she wants my help. She has no idea how tiring a new baby is.

Some days she calls early in the morning, asking for a "Granny-Help Day." Some days she calls in the afternoon and some days she doesn't call at all. But the great thing is that she feels free to call when she needs help. I know how tired and confused a first-time mom can feel. I didn't have a granny around when I had my children, so I'm glad that I can calm her nerves and give her a break sometimes. The extra joy is that I get to care for my little grandson. What a joy. What a blessing!

Dear Father, thank You for the birth of my grandson. Thank You for the relationship my daughter and I have. I'm so blessed to be a part of this experience. Father, guide her and her husband as they raise this little guy. Bless this new family! Amen.

MARCH 24

A New Stage of Life

*"Do not worry about tomorrow, for tomorrow will worry about itself.
Each day has enough trouble of its own." Matthew 6:34*

Life will never be the same. My heart is now a large lump in my throat and probably will be for the next several years. This new stage of life will certainly keep me on my knees; figuratively if not literally. Here's the deal, my baby; my little girl, just got her driver's license. Oh my, the worries and fears that flood my mind are countless. There's the danger of driving too fast; the danger of being distracted while she drives; the danger of other drivers being distracted or driving too fast.

She now has the freedom of choosing where to go and has to deal with the pressures of what her friends want. There is a lot of responsibility that comes with driving. I hope we have taught her to be responsible enough to handle this. I'm sure she will think I'm a pain in the neck as I remind her every day to be careful, pay attention and make good choices. Yes, I will do those things but I will also constantly pray for her, asking for God's protection to be like a cloak around her.

Dear Father, I get cold chills every time I think about my daughter driving. It's not that I don't trust her but there are a lot of crazy drivers out there. Surround her daily with a shield of Your protection. Amen.

Protecting My Children

God is our refuge and strength, an ever-present help in trouble.
Psalm 46:1

There is nothing and no one more important to me than my children. I will do anything to protect them. But sometimes I'm not certain how to do that. I worry about their safety when my husband has been drinking. He has terrible temper outbursts and sometimes throws things or punches the wall. He has never hurt me or them ... yet.

The sad thing is that I know my husband loves our children, and I know that deep down inside he loves me too. But when he is under the influence of alcohol he becomes a different man ... a scary man. If he ever did hurt any of us I know he would be devastated once he sobered up. But I have to protect my children, so I'm giving him an ultimatum – get help or get out. I'm worried about him and how he will take this request. O God, I pray that good things will come of this ... for all of us.

Dear Father, this is so hard. It is like being married to two different men. The sober man is wonderful, fun, generous and kind, but the drunk man is ... awful. God, help me to know the right thing to do and give me the strength to do it. Help him get help! Amen.

MARCH 26

The Future

*"Love your enemies! Pray for those who persecute you! In that way,
you will be acting as true children of your Father in heaven.
For He gives His sunlight to both the evil and the good, and
He sends rain on the just and the unjust alike." Matthew 5:44-45 NLT*

Most of the stories on the news are terrible and frightening. I'm constantly amazed at the horrible things one person can do to another person, let alone one country to another country. There is so much hatred from certain groups toward people who are different from them. When did our world get so evil? I'm afraid it is getting worse – what kind of world will my children inherit? Will they be able to clean up the mess – or is this just evidence that we're near or in the end times?

I pray for my children's safety and for that of all children everywhere. I pray that the love of God will permeate civilization once again as people obey God by loving Him most of all and loving their neighbors too. Perhaps that important task can begin with my own children learning to love others and treat even those who are different from them with respect.

Dear Father, the world is scary. I pray for the safety and protection of my children from those who would do them harm, even inadvertently. I pray that Your love in the hearts of my children's generation will make a difference in this world. Fill us all with love. Amen.

Letting Go of the "Supermom" Status

"My grace is sufficient for you, for My power is made perfect in weakness." Therefore I will boast all the more gladly about my weaknesses, so that Christ's power may rest on me.
2 Corinthians 12:9

I've always thought of myself as being self-sufficient. I don't like having to depend on other people in order to get things done. But now with a husband, three children, their activities, a part-time job, parents close by, responsibilities at church and a dog ... I NEED HELP! OK, now that I've said that, the question is, "Will I accept help?"

There is this whole "Supermom" thing going on in my head that tells me I need to be all things for my kids. But when I'm busy being all things, I don't have time to be with my kids. That can't be right. I know people would help me if I asked, in fact, my mom would probably love to be more involved with her grandchildren. I'm the problem. I have to be willing to admit that I need help; even from God (who I tend to push aside too). OK, I'll ask. It's not easy, but it is necessary.

Dear Father, help me to be transparent enough to ask for help, for the good of my children, my husband and myself. Amen.

Bathing in Blessings

Sing praises to God, sing praises; sing praises to our King, sing praises.
Psalm 47:6

Scent is a powerful stimulant; a simple smell can bring long lost memories to mind. I used to adore the scent of lilacs because they reminded me of springtime when I was a child. I think there are few things more homey than the smell of fresh baked bread and chocolate chip cookies right out of the oven. Yummy. Roses from a sweetheart are a fragrance to be remembered. My favorite perfume is a pleasant scent too. All of those fragrances are certainly wonderful and I still enjoy them, but my new favorite scent of all time is ... my baby boy right after his bath!

Oh, that smell of lotion, baby powder, and freshly washed hair ... heavenly! I love to dry his little body, rub the lotion on, wrap him in a soft towel and then just cuddle with him. Who would have thought that I would treasure something as ordinary as bath time? I hold my son close and thank God for the miracle of him and the privilege of being his mommy. I hope that for the rest of my life those scents will remind me of these precious times.

Dear Father, thank You for my precious son. Thank You for the gentle blessing of cuddling his little sweet-smelling body after bath time. Thank You for the blessing of being his mom. Amen.

A Good Listener

He who answers before listening — that is his folly and his shame.
Proverbs 18:13

I consider myself to be a good listener. Since I was a teenager my friends have always come to me with their problems, spilled their stories, cried and then gone on their way feeling better. I didn't have to say a word. I was happy to be a listening ear for them and they have often done the same for me.

But where my middle-school aged daughter is concerned, I'm finding that it's hard to just listen. She doesn't often come to me with her problems, but when she does, I am thrilled! It's nice to be needed by someone you love with all your heart. The hard part, however, is that I don't want to just listen — I want to fix her problems! But she doesn't really want my answers, she just wants me to listen because sometimes it helps to say things out loud. I need God's strength and control to keep my mouth shut. I'm afraid that if I offer advice this time she may choose not to talk with me next time. I don't want to do anything to close this door.

Dear Father, help! I want to solve my daughter's problems and yet I know that I cannot. Help me have the strength to give her problems to You and to trust You with them. I believe You love her even more than I do. Amen.

MARCH 30

The Greatest Blessing

God demonstrates His own love for us in this:
While we were still sinners, Christ died for us. Romans 5:8

My daughter just prayed to accept Jesus! What a joy and honor it is to share this experience with her. I'm so thankful that she has come to know Him early, because now her focus is on knowing God better and serving Him. Hopefully she will stay close to Him as she moves into her teenage and adult years.

I love the simplicity of a child's faith – she just believes. I pray for that simple trust to continue as she meets other kids who do not believe as she does. I pray that she will be a light in this dark world and will not be tripped up by the temptations that will assault her. I will uphold her in prayer as she learns and grows.

I know that temptations are many for teens today and that there will always be those who challenge her faith. I pray that the foundations laid for her by her dad and I will give her strength. I pray that God's Word will become her guide and compass in life.

Dear Father, thank You for the joy of being there when my daughter came into Your family. I commit to uphold her in prayer now as she grows in her faith. I know Satan will do everything he can to prevent her growth. Hold on tightly to her, Father. Draw her closer and closer to Yourself. Amen.

April

A Calling?

*Many, O Lord my God, are the wonders You have done. The things
You planned for us no one can recount to You; were I to speak
and tell of them, they would be too many to declare. Psalm 40:5*

I enjoy visiting with old college friends. We get together once a year or so and catch up on what's been happening in our lives. I used to fight a little embarrassment at these reunions. Some of my friends are so successful. One is a journalist who travels around the world writing for an online magazine, another plays violin in a city symphony and another one is climbing the corporate ladder in the banking industry. Wow, I'm amazed at what they have accomplished. They are talented, driven women.

And me? I'm ... a mom. I'm not complaining. It was my choice to put my writing career on hold and stay home to raise my children. The thing is, though, that my on-hold career may never get off hold. I never really thought that I would enjoy being at home, but I love being a full-time mom. I enjoy my children and I love teaching them things. When one of them learns something new my heart overflows with joy.

Dear Father, thank You for the privilege of being a mom. Maybe someday I'll go back to my writing career, but for now, there is no greater calling than raising my children. I pray for Your strength and love to be a good mom. Amen.

A Mother's Purse

*My God will meet all your needs according to
His glorious riches in Christ Jesus. Philippians 4:19*

When I was young and single I had a cute little purse. It was black with a gold clasp and hung lightly on my shoulder. Then I got married and had my first baby. I have noticed that with each child my purse gets bigger. That's because more and more "stuff" is required to entertain and care for my children.

The purse I carry now weighs several pounds and if you empty it out you will find bags of various cereals, marshmallows, cookies and crackers, mints, small metal cars, Band-Aids, crayons, pacifiers, teething medicines, McDonald's Happy Meal toys ... well, you get the idea.

My purse is no longer my domain; it has become a nice supply bag for mothering. I even carry some things in it for hubby too. It must have been a mom who originally came up with the idea for a woman to carry a purse, because the supplies that a mom needs are numerous. Well, it makes me feel like a good mother each time I can reach into my "magic bag" and pull out something that pacifies, satisfies or entertains my children. Life is good.

Dear Father, it is truly a great joy to be able to meet my children's needs. Thanks for the blessings of purses and for the experienced mom-friends who tell me what to stock in mine. Amen.

APRIL 2

The Gift of Love

"A new command I give you: Love one another. As I have loved you, so you must love one another." John 13:34

Sometimes I don't feel very loving. Of course I love my family; that never changes, but sometimes life just seems to get in the way. I'm tired, I've got way too much to do, the children are impossible, my husband is not as much help as I think he should be, my friends don't get it, and I just can't seem to "find God" anymore. Yeah, the whole love thing is not happening for me.

The good thing about these kinds of days is that even when I can't find God; He can find me. On these bad days I hang on to the fact that the fruit of the Spirit includes love. The Spirit's love is one that I don't have to summon up from within me, it is already there as a benefit of God's presence in my heart. I just need to take a minute and call on Him, asking Him to fill my heart with love for my children; my husband; my friends. It will come ... OK, maybe not right at THAT moment, but it will come.

I've been blessed to ask for God's help in this and then look back at the end of the day and see the small ways He has warmed my heart toward my family.

Dear Father, thank You for Your patience with me; especially when I don't feel very loving. Thank You that Your Spirit loves through me; especially on hard days. Amen.

Forgiveness

*Bear with each other and forgive whatever grievances you may have
against one another. Forgive as the Lord forgave you.* Colossians 3:13

There are times when we all need to be forgiven. All of
us – moms, dads, kids. It's important to remember that.
When my child disobeys, misbehaves or even has an
accident, I need to remember that my reaction is key to how
she will feel about this experience.

I pray that my heart will remember the times when I have
disobeyed, misbehaved or had an accident ... and how
I yearned to be forgiven. I'm sure that my child longs for
forgiveness, just as I do.

I believe that it's important for me to put aside any feelings of disappointment or annoyance and respond with
forgiveness laced with encouragement – the same kind of
response I would hope for. I can also remind my precious
child how important it is to apologize and ask for forgiveness when necessary, because it shows a gentle and repen-
tant heart. I can model that by apologizing to her when I
need to – even though it's hard to do.

Dear Father, thank You for forgiving me over and over. Father,
help my heart to go first to forgiveness with my child rather
than to condemnation or criticism. Help me to give forgiveness
as freely as I expect it. Amen.

APRIL 4

Being a Listening Ear

The heart of the discerning acquires knowledge;
the ears of the wise seek it out. Proverbs 18:15

I care about what happens to my child, I care a lot. Sometimes the most difficult thing is to just listen to her talk through a problem or a major decision she is struggling with. Listening silently without offering unsolicited advice is tough for me. Thankfully I can recall my own teenage emotions well enough to know that my teenage daughter doesn't always want my advice. She wants to figure things out on her own and just wants me to listen so she can talk things over out loud.

Hearing situations explained by her own voice somehow takes away the power from people or things perceived as overwhelming. Talking through the situation and her feelings is all she needs to do. However, I am her mom and I can't help wanting to fix things. I need the strength of God clamping my lips shut sometimes and holding back my advice or answers. The best thing I can do for my growing girl, is listen. Just listen.

Dear Father, those words – just listen – are easy to say but so hard to do sometimes. Help me to be discerning as to when my daughter wants advice and when she wants me to just let her talk. Father, give her wisdom in solving things and knowing which path to follow. Amen.

No Greater Love

*Surely goodness and love will follow me all the days of my life,
and I will live in the house of the LORD forever. Psalm 23:6*

This is really hard for me to believe but deep in my heart I know that God loves my precious child even more than I do. I love my child so much that I would willingly die for her (like Jesus did for us). I love my daughter so much that I want to guide her life in order to protect her from bad decisions and mistakes (God's Word does that for us). I love my daughter and willingly give my time and efforts to make her life better (Jesus is available 24/7 for us).

I've always found it hard to comprehend that Jesus loves her more than I do, but He does. That's the bottom line. He gave her to me and loved her deeply even before I knew about her. Knowing how much God loves her, I should be able to trust Him completely with her. When I pray for her, I should be able to leave her needs with Him, knowing that He will take care of her. This is tough because sometimes it's hard to believe that His love for her can be greater than mine.

Dear Father, I need help here. My head knows that You love my daughter even more than I do, but my heart has trouble believing it. Help my unbelief, Father. Help me to trust You with her and understand the amazing depth of Your love. Amen.

APRIL 6

The Gift of Peace

*"Peace I leave with you; My peace I give you. I do not give
to you as the world gives. Do not let your hearts
be troubled and do not be afraid." John 14:27*

Peace is not a common state of mind for a mom with three young children racing around. Life is noisy, busy and chaotic. Life is ... life. I seldom have five minutes for myself, let alone five minutes to spend with God. I have to lock myself in the bathroom to have a minute of solitude – and even then the children are outside the door, clamoring for my help and attention. Peace? I don't know what that means anymore. And yet, the Bible promises that if I seek it, peace will come. It's a result of the fruit of the Spirit in my heart ... love, joy, peace ... but how do I find it? Slow down.

In the midst of the chaos and noise, seek God. Peace isn't necessarily quiet; it's a state of mind and heart. It's a result of trusting God and receiving His love. Even if I need to get up fifteen minutes before my children to spend a few minutes in God's Word and talking with Him, that will move me forward in the peace process.

Dear Father, thank You for peace. I know my life doesn't often reflect peace, but I know that it's available from You. Help me, Father, to slow down enough to allow Your peace to settle in my heart. Amen.

Climbing the Success Ladder

Give thanks to the Lord, for He is good; His love endures forever.
Psalm 107:1

I thought I'd be glad today, I thought I would celebrate – but I was wrong. Instead I'm filled with anxiety. Today my little son crawled up the staircase for the first time. All the way up twelve steps to the second floor. Yes, it was exciting and yes, we applauded and cheered, but at the same time, I realized that life just changed.

Now I have to watch him even more closely because he can go up but he can't come down safely. Yikes. I know it is important that I celebrate this success with him; it's important to encourage his successes and encourage him to keep learning. But it's also important to recognize how the new things he learns change my life.

I've got to watch him more closely and carefully teach him the next step in the growing up process ... coming down the stairs. His growing up and learning happens so fast. I don't want to miss a thing!

Dear Father, thank You for this new victory in my son's life. Thank You that he is learning new things. Thank You that he is growing and changing. I love every stage of his little life. Thank You for the blessing of him! Amen.

Let It Go

If we confess our sins, He is faithful and just and will forgive us our sins and purify us from all unrighteousness. 1 John 1:9

I messed up yesterday. I didn't exactly display the best parenting skills – I didn't even display the best evidence of living for Christ. The anger I directed at my children – my precious children – just showed my impatience and self-centeredness. I feel so bad. How do I face my precious children today? Will they approach me with fear in their eyes, wondering if the angry mom who put them to bed last night (way earlier than usual), without even a good night prayer, is the same mom who will greet them this morning?

My heart aches that I put them through that ... again. Unfortunately, my bad behavior often breeds more bad behavior – from their side and mine. I have to let it go. I must ask for God's forgiveness and accept it. Then I must admit to my children that I was wrong, ask for their forgiveness and tell them how much I love them. Of course they will forgive me, because their hearts are so gentle. Then, the hardest thing of all, I must forgive myself, let it go and start this day fresh.

Dear Father, I'm so sorry for my behavior yesterday. Please forgive me. Help my children to forgive me. Help me to forgive myself. Father, let's start this day fresh and help me to model Your love and patience this day. Amen.

No Giggles Allowed

Discipline your children while there is hope.
Otherwise you will ruin their lives. Proverbs 19:18 NLT

The funniest thing happened this morning. It was so funny that a giggle started rolling up my throat from deep inside, but I had to stifle it! I couldn't let it escape. My two-year-old son deliberately disobeyed me and began playing in the dog's water dish. I told him twice to stay away from it, but I was busy with the baby so he took advantage of my distraction to go right back to playing.

When the dish suddenly flipped upside down and landed with a thud on his feet, soaking his shoes, socks and even his pants, he looked totally shocked. It was so funny – but I couldn't laugh. He had disobeyed so I had to be firm and put him in time out and ... not giggle! Yes, that took some strength, but I've learned in these two years of parenting that consistency is important and laughing at his disobedience will make him think obedience is a game. So, I didn't laugh ... on the outside anyway.

Dear Father, I want to be consistent with my son so that he knows obedience is not an option. Discipline is not fun, but I know it is necessary for him. Please help me to be free enough to laugh with him when it's appropriate and even sometimes surprise him with my laughter. Amen.

APRIL 10

A Breakthrough!

If you have two shirts, give one to the poor. If you have food, share it with those who are hungry. Luke 3:11 nlt

Kindness does not always come naturally to a three or four-year-old. Too many times I've seen my little girl hit a friend on the head and take away her toy. Today, though, I believe there was a breakthrough. My daughter and her friend began to fight over a toy. Why do they always want the same toy at the same time? My daughter grabbed the toy and struggled to pull it out of the other girl's hands.

But then, to my amazement, my daughter stopped and obviously thought about this struggle. She's been talked to and punished so many times for this behavior. I could almost see the wheels in her brain turning as she put the pieces together. Then she looked at her friend and said, "You can have it," and went to get a different toy!

YAHOO! I feel like we've had a breakthrough where the words spoken to her are connecting with her behavior! One more building block in place!

Dear Father, thank You that my daughter is "getting it" (at least she did today). I know there will still be struggles – I even battle with this behavior sometimes – but I'll celebrate today's behavior and pray for it to continue! Amen.

Groundwork for Parenting

In the morning, O LORD, You hear my voice; in the morning I lay my requests before You and wait in expectation. Psalm 5:3

There is no doubt that parenting is a full-time job. From the moment the kids open their eyes in the morning until they finally close them again at night I feel like I am "on." If I don't shower and dress before they get up, it's a challenge to fit it in! Each moment of the day is focused on caring for the children, serving them, playing with them, teaching them ... there is very little "me" time.

However, I am very aware that the mood of the day, as well as my attitude, outlook and perspective, is set by whether or not I make time in the morning for quiet time with the Lord. It's so easy to push that aside and say that I'll do it later, but of course, later seldom comes. I wonder why something so important gets pushed aside so easily?

I definitely see a difference in myself when I've started my day with the Lord. It makes me a better person and a better mom. It's a groundwork for the day.

Dear Father, OK, I get it ... I need to start my day with You. I want to, but it's so easy to just push it aside when the kids need something. It's kind of like the squeaky wheel (my kids) gets the oil. Father, help me to remember that my days will be better, and I will be better if I begin my day with You. Amen.

APRIL 12

A Need for Consistency

Confess your sins to each other so that you may be healed.
The earnest prayer of a righteous person has great power
and produces wonderful results. James 5:16 NLT

You can't get much past a teenager, especially if he's trying to prove a point. I have learned that the hard way. If I'm going to proclaim the value and necessity of the Christian life, then I've got to live my Christian faith consistently before my teenager. In the heat of a disagreement, he will gladly point out any inconsistencies in my life. That means I've got to truly be careful about criticizing others, judging people's motives, being honest in all things, showing loving kindness to others, and having a servant attitude.

Granted, these things should not be hard because I do seek to follow Christ and live in the way He teaches. However, we all have times when we simply mess up – we make bad choices, behave selfishly and make mistakes.

I long for my life to consistently model Christ's life, but when I fail (especially if my teenager knows that I failed), I must admit it, apologize and pledge to ask the Lord's help to do better. Consistency is important – honesty is even more important.

Dear Father, I want my teenager to know that my faith matters to me and that I don't dismiss it when I fail. Help me to be honest. Help my son to see that I long to live more obediently to You. Amen.

Blessed Conversations

Let your conversation be always full of grace, seasoned with salt,
so that you may know how to answer everyone. Colossians 4:6

The "teenage tunnel" hurts. When my son entered that tunnel and pretty much stopped talking to my husband and I, it was hard. When our daughters began to pull away from us and give us only the most basic of information, it hurt too. It doesn't hurt just because you aren't sure what they are doing when they aren't with you – it hurts because you miss them.

I missed the joking around, the quick catch-ups at the end of the day, I missed the relationship I used to have with them. Now that my children are adults, we have recovered that closeness and I praise God for that! I love it when the phone rings and it's one of my kids just checking in. I love it when one of them stops by the house for a cup of coffee and a chat. I love the conversations! It's fun relating to them as adults.

I'm so thankful that during those "silent" years I didn't do or say anything to damage the relationship and prevent this closeness from being reestablished.

Dear Father, thank You for conversations. As basic as that may sound, I am so glad that my children are talking to me again. I missed them. Thank You that we made it through those silent years and can now laugh, share and talk once again! Amen.

APRIL 14

I'm a Little Nervous Here!

Praise be to the God and Father of our Lord Jesus Christ, the Father of compassion and the God of all comfort, who comforts us in all our troubles, so that we can comfort those in any trouble with the comfort we ourselves have received from God. 2 Corinthians 1:3-4

In just two weeks I will give birth to our second child. I'm nervous for a lot of different reasons. I haven't thought about the delivery process until just this moment. It hurts ... a lot. That makes me nervous. Life is going to be super busy with a toddler and a newborn. It is going to be more expensive to have two children. Will I be cheating my toddler out of "Mommy time" with this second child? I'm nervous about that.

Wow, I could spend all day being anxious and worried, but, at the end of the day, I would just be anxious and worried and still have the same problems.

A better approach is to take my worries to the Lord. I can talk with Him about them and seek His guidance. He has also placed people in my life who can offer advice. Nervousness is OK if it motivates me to learn more and share with those around me!

Dear Father, it takes a lot for me to admit that I am nervous. I want people to think I have everything under control. Help me to be open enough to admit when I need help. Thank You for Your wisdom and for those You've placed in my life who can help me. Amen.

The Village

Though one may be overpowered, two can defend themselves.
A cord of three stands is not quickly broken. Ecclesiastes 4:12

I always wondered about the old saying, "It takes a village to raise a child." It never made sense to me because I always thought it should be the mother and father's responsibility to raise their own child. Then I had a child and it suddenly made a lot more sense. As my daughter grows, I am so thankful for Sunday school teachers who invest in her not to only teach her the truths of God's Word, but also to show her love and concern. I'm thankful for neighbors who play with her and talk with her, letting her know that there is a "village" of people watching out for her and caring for her.

I'm thankful for aunts and uncles who share stories of Mommy's and Daddy's past with her so she can see the heritage of family. I appreciate grannies and grandpas who make cookies with her and take her fishing. All these people help my daughter know that the world is a bigger place than our house and that many, many people in this world love her.

Dear Father, thank You for our "village" of people who love and care for my child. I pray for my own awareness of the children of my family and friends for whom I can do the same. It's wonderful that we can all work together to raise our children to be God-serving people. Amen.

APRIL 16

The Stages of Life

If I speak in the tongues of men and of angels, but have not love,
I am only a resounding gong or a clanging cymbal. 1 Corinthians 13:1

I'm not normally a complainer but something has come to my attention that I just feel is completely unfair – even a little mean. I believe that God is in control of this world, I believe that circumstances like when a child is conceived and born are ultimately in His control. But here's my complaint ... why did He deem it a good idea to have my child enter the moody teenage years at the exact same time I hit the hormonal menopausal years?

OK, it is a test of faith, I will admit that, but there are days when I think my husband probably wants to head for the hills to get away from the two of us. Because I'm the adult I feel the responsibility of remaining sane, but as my daughter's rising hormones make her incredibly moody, my sinking hormones are not making sanity easy. It's going to take God's strength working in both of us to get us through this stage of life. But with God's strength, patience and hormone-leveling power we will make it through.

Dear Father, I feel so out of control sometimes and I know my daughter must feel the same way. Neither of us wants to admit that and maybe we don't even realize when it's happening. Father, help us to keep communication open. Keep us from burning any bridges that can't be rebuilt. I love her and I don't want to lose her. Amen.

A Great Day

I will praise You, O Lord, with all my heart;
I will tell of all Your wonders. Psalm 9:1

It's five o'clock and I haven't even started dinner. In fact, the chicken is still in the freezer. The floors in every room are scattered with toys, I'm still wearing the sweats I threw on after a quick shower, no makeup and barely brushed hair. The sink still has breakfast dishes in it with cereal dried to a crust. Does this not sound like a great day? It was.

My four-year-old daughter and I built a tent with the dining room chairs and blankets. While she stocked it with her favorite books and stuffed animals, I made lunch and then we crawled inside the tent to eat. Then we used a flashlight to make designs on the blanket ceiling. We laughed and talked and even took a little nap together. It was a great day!

Sure, I wish I had gotten all the housework done, but my husband will understand why we're eating frozen pizza for dinner, and the dishes can wait. My little girl will only be a little girl for a while and I want to enjoy it!

Dear Father, thank You for blanket tents and shared giggles. Thank You for precious times like this with my child. Precious memories ... for both of us. Amen.

A Long-Term Investment

Train a child in the way he should go, and when he is old he will not turn from it. Proverbs 22:6

I've prayed and prayed for my son to come to Christ. He is an adult now and I've prayed for his salvation since he was a newborn baby. I've prayed persistently and passionately, I've even gotten other people praying for him too. It has been a long-term investment on my part to pray for my son's salvation. I am so proud of him – of his accomplishments in life; of what a kind and caring person he is; and of his career success.

He is a nice, intelligent young man. But still my heart aches to know that he hasn't accepted Christ as Savior. That is the most important thing of all. He isn't antagonistic to Christianity, he just doesn't seem to need it right now.

I believe that one day my prayers will be answered. In the meantime, I will keep lifting his name before the Lord. I will continue to live out my faith before him without preaching at him. I will keep on loving him. I'm in this for the long term.

Dear Father, I pray for my son to recognize his need for You in his life. I thank You that he is a good, kind person. I pray that somehow he might understand how much fuller life can be with You in it. Father, soften his heart and bring him to Yourself. Amen.

Job Description, Please

Be joyful in hope, patient in affliction, faithful in prayer.
Romans 12:12

I did not sign up for this. Thirteen years ago when I went through labor to bring my little girl into the world, I did not dream of the verbal and emotional abuse she would bestow on me in the future. I love my daughter with all my heart, but I certainly don't understand her right now. Oh, I know she is flexing her "independence wings" and I know that's normal, I just didn't know that it would hurt me so much or that her struggle to grow up would mean she wants to be free from me!

I suppose that deep down she doesn't mean for her words and attitudes to be so hurtful to me. (Actually, she probably doesn't think about me at all.) Right now life is all about her. But ... I miss her and I'd love to share in this growing up experience with her.

I guess for now, I'll just be consistent in how I respond to her. I'll be loving, but not demanding. I will pray for her daily and wait for her to realize that I'm still the same intelligent, funny, loving mom she thought I was five years ago.

Dear Father, I won't deny that this is hard. My daughter sometimes hurts me a lot with her words and attitudes. Please help me to respond with firmness, kindness and love. Help us through these years. Amen.

Chore Time Battles

"I will instruct you and teach you in the way you should go;
I will counsel you and watch over you." Psalm 32:8

Why is it such a battle to get my kids to share in household chores? They've been responsible for certain chores since they were small children, but now that they are teenagers they are suddenly rebelling.

It doesn't seem unreasonable to me to ask them to help around the house – after all they do live here and enjoy the benefits of being a part of this household. I know I must stand firm on insisting that they complete their chores and do them well. If they don't then there must be consequences.

Someday, when they have homes of their own, they will thank me that they know how to do these things. I may not win a popularity contest with them right now, but I'm not trying to. Being a parent means sometimes being unpopular. So, the chore schedule will remain on the refrigerator and I will continue to enforce it.

Dear Father, I don't enjoy it when my children are upset with me, but I want to teach them to be responsible adults. I believe that learning to do laundry, cleaning bathrooms and cutting the grass are a part of that. Give me the strength to stand strong, and please let them realize the benefits of chores sooner rather than later. Amen.

Mommy Is Sick

Cast your cares on the LORD and He will sustain you;
He will never let the righteous fall. Psalm 55:22

When my kids are sick, I take care of them. I clean up their messes, make them soup, fluff their pillows, cover them with a soft blanket, read them stories and whatever else they need. When my hubby is sick, I do pretty much the same – except maybe for reading him stories. The point is that when my family is sick, I take care of them. But when I feel a bit under the weather ... life goes on because Mommy doesn't get sick!

Well, in fairness they try to help me, but they just don't know how. Many times I've had to get out of my sick bed to answer questions and help with projects. I guess it's good to be needed. I am thankful for each sweet "Get well" card my children draw for me. I'm thankful when my husband takes the kids out for dinner and lets me sleep. I know my family loves me and I recognize that they care for me in the best way they know how. I'm thankful that I can show my love for them by caring for them.

Dear Father, OK, I'll admit it, I'd like to be pampered and served when I'm sick, but I also recognize that my family doesn't always know the best ways to do that. Help me notice the ways they do show their love and care. Help me to appreciate those actions. Amen.

APRIL 22

Baseball Games

We love because He first loved us. 1 John 4:19

I never thought I'd hear myself say this, but I love going to my son's baseball games. What's amazing about that is that I don't have an athletic bone in my body. I've spent my life reading books and enjoying movies – my idea of exercise is lifting a stack of books. When my son wanted to play baseball I felt a twinge of anxiety because I knew I would have to support him and attend his games.

The cool thing is that I've actually found a real enjoyment in watching the games. I like watching my son work to perfect his skills. I love seeing his joy at being a part of a team and building friendships with his teammates.

What a blessing to be able to support my son, cheer for his successes and encourage him when he has had a bad game. I enjoy the conversations with other parents and even the opportunity to gently share my faith through those budding friendships. Who would have thought I would end up enjoying baseball? I'm so glad I can share this experience with my son.

Dear Father, what a joy. Thank You so much for this baseball experience. I love sharing this with my son. Driving to the games, buying treats for the team, cheering for him. It's great. I'm so grateful that I can share this with him! Amen.

Blushing in the Walmart

Since we belong to the day, let us be self-controlled, putting on faith and love as a breastplate, and the hope of salvation as a helmet.
1 Thessalonians 5:8

I know other moms have been through this. In fact, most moms have probably had this experience; but that doesn't make it any less embarrassing. I was racing through the Walmart store, picking up a few necessities, when my two-year-old son went psycho. He spied a toy he felt he needed, I disagreed and tried to distract him with something else, but it didn't work.

Before I knew what was happening he threw a temper tantrum to top all tantrums. Everyone in the store could hear him and those shoppers around us simply stopped and stared. Some moms looked sympathetic, some smiled and shook their heads in sympathy, and some made me feel like I was mistreating the poor boy.

How do I teach him that this behavior is not acceptable? What is the proper way to handle a child's temper tantrum? I love my son and want him to learn correct behavior. I certainly need wisdom as to how to handle this.

Dear Father, please help me. I don't know how to handle my son's temper tantrums, in public or at home. Help me, Father, to teach him how to control his anger ... by controlling mine first. This is important, Father. Help me handle it correctly. Amen.

Inherited Characteristics

*Each of you should look not only to your own interests,
but also to the interests of others. Philippians 2:4*

It's fun when a friend comments that my infant daughter has my eyes. My husband beams when someone notices that her chin is like his. Sometimes we study her intently to pick out likenesses to each of us or some of our family members. It will be interesting as she grows to see our characteristics appear in her.

One element of inherited characteristics is a bit sobering, however, she will not only show our physical characteristics, but also our behavior, our attitudes and our habits. It kind of scares me that I may see my short temper displayed in her or my tendency to make excuses for my failures rather than take responsibility for my actions.

I pray that God will keep that in my mind as my little girl grows up. My prayer is that God will help her show some of my better characteristics: a tender heart and a loving spirit. I pray that God will cause her to overlook my shortcomings and develop her own good things. Knowing that your child will learn from observing your actions sure does make a mom stop and think.

Dear Father, help me to remember that I'm modeling behavior for my daughter every day. Father, grow her into a girl who loves You and lives for You, in spite of my shortcomings. Amen.

Disciplining My Son

Let love and faithfulness never leave you; bind them around
your neck, write them on the tablet of your heart. Proverbs 3:3

Well, this was a weird experience. Today my mom dropped in for a visit with me and her beloved two-year-old grandson. We were having a nice visit until my son directly disobeyed me. When I again asked him to do something, he stubbornly refused. The scenario escalated until I felt I had no option but to punish him. My husband and I have chosen to use physical punishment only as a last resort. But I felt the best option here was a slap on his little bottom.

Although it didn't hurt him, the noise of the smack startled him and made my point. What was weird was doing that in front of my mom. I immediately wondered what she would say and how she would feel about me. After all, she adores her grandson. But my mom didn't say a word. She didn't interfere at all. She is an awesome mom who disciplined us when we were children. She taught me to be fair but firm and she reminded me this afternoon that God disciplines us when we need it too. Discipline is an important part of learning to be a better Christ-follower.

Dear Father, I don't enjoy disciplining my son – even though I know it is necessary. Help me, Father, to always discipline in love and only when I am in control of my temper. Amen.

Playing Shop

*Now that you have purified yourselves by obeying the truth
so that you have sincere love for your brothers, love one
another deeply, from the heart. 1 Peter 1:22*

I love this. I can be busy in the kitchen, making dinner or cleaning up and I can hear my children playing in the family room three steps down and around the corner. They don't know that I am listening to them. Three children from ten years old down to three years old and they play so well together (most of the time).

Today I hear them playing shop. Their creative minds make use of the stuff in the house and they call their game David's Store of Mother's Stuff. (I don't know where the David came from since none of them have that name.) I'm so thankful for my oldest child, who is a natural born peacemaker. She bridges the age differences for all three of them. I'm thankful for the high energy and creativity of the middle child, who keeps things moving. And the youngest? Well, I'm thankful that his sisters include him.

My kids like each other, and that is a gift that will continue throughout their lives.

Dear Father, thank You for love. I'm blessed to hear my children play together. I'm blessed that our family loves to be together. Thank You for each of my precious children. Help me to nurture and grow those positive things in them. Amen.

An Awkward Situation

For the foolishness of God is wiser than man's wisdom, and the weakness of God is stronger than man's strength. 1 Corinthians 1:25

I need a lot of wisdom to know how to handle this situation. We have rules in our home about what movies and television programs are appropriate for our children to watch. My ten-year-old is not allowed to watch R-rated movies — ever. She doesn't fight that rule; or at least she hasn't fought it. But I found out that one of her friends doesn't have this same rule, so when my daughter is at her house she can watch movies we would not approve of. I know this family and I like them. I also know this friend is important to my daughter. So how do I handle this?

Do I talk to the other mother, or will that make her feel that I don't think she is a good mother? Do I talk to my daughter? That puts the responsibility on her to come home if an inappropriate movie is being played. Is she strong enough to break up a party or leave her friend when just the two of them are watching a movie? I feel strongly about this and I want to handle it correctly. God's wisdom is needed more and more as my children grow older and face more difficult situations.

Dear Father, HELP! I want to handle this correctly. Guide my words, guide my tone of voice, guide this decision. Thanks for caring about this as much, or even more, than I do. Amen.

APRIL 28

Knowing When to Get Involved

Be on guard. Stand firm in the faith. Be courageous.
Be strong. And do everything with love. 1 Corinthians 16:13-14 NLT

My son has a new friend; a little boy from his class at school. Yesterday he came over to play for the first time. I haven't been able to think about much since then. It was a hot day so the boys pulled out the sprinkler and had fun running through the cool water. I watched from the kitchen window and saw something that made my heart ache. There were ugly bruises on the little boy's back and sides. Lots of them. It looks like this little guy may be a victim of someone's uncontrolled anger.

What is my responsibility here? If this boy is being abused I can't just turn away and do nothing. But what can I do? I don't know his parents, I don't even know his living situation. I spent the rest of the day and evening praying about it and asking for wisdom to know what to do. I feel God has given me an answer and I will proceed – with prayer cushioning every step.

Dear Father, it breaks my heart to think that we actually know a child who is abused. Perhaps we know more such children but just haven't discovered it. Father, guide my steps, my words, and my decisions. Help this little boy to get help and to be safe. Amen.

The Joy of Laughter

A cheerful heart is good medicine,
but a crushed spirit dries up the bones. Proverbs 17:22

Life is pretty hard sometimes. The overwhelming problems of finances, sickness, broken relationships ... well, the list can go on and on. Even the situation in the world is oppressive. These things can easily weigh you down.

Laughter is medicine for the soul. The Bible even says so, so it must be true! The best medicine comes from the laughter of my own children. No matter how bad the day is; the free, joyous laughter of my children lifts my emotions. The unadulterated joy that my children find in the simplicities of life reminds me that no matter how dark things may look, they will get better.

I'm so thankful for laughter and for its healing power. Moments of spontaneous, joyous laughter remind me of the importance of surrounding myself with others who can find joy in life. Of course there is a time to cry as well as a time to laugh, but too often we focus on the crying times. The pauses that laughter brings in the problems of life are truly healing.

Dear Father, thank You for the gift of laughter. I know You understand how important laughter is – You've made so many things for us to enjoy in this world. Thank You for friends and for my children who find joy in moments of life. Amen.

May

What to Wear?

"Why do you worry about clothes? See how the lilies of the field grow.
If that is how God clothes the grass of the field, will He not
much more clothe you, O you of little faith?" Matthew 6:28, 30

After giving birth, finding clothes that fit becomes an issue. After the birth of my first baby I was shocked to discover that my body didn't immediately go back to the shape it had been ten months before. So, as I search through my closet for anything with an elastic waistband, my thoughts went to the verses about not worrying about clothes because God clothes the flowers in the field.

I know I shouldn't worry about something as basic as clothing ... but I can't go outside naked! If I just step outside in faith, will new clothes magically appear to cover up my nakedness? Yeah, I didn't think so. God gave me common sense and that tells me it would not be wise to try that little trick. My common sense also tells me that worrying about how stylish I look is silly. After all, I just had a baby! So if I have to wear elastic waistbands and my husband's shirts for a while, so what? Clothes are not what I should be focusing on right now anyway.

Dear Father, You'll have to help me let go of this. I have always cared about looking put together. Please help me to do the best I can right now. Help me to focus on being thankful for my baby instead! Amen.

Letters from Grandma

Your word is a lamp to my feet and a light for my path.
Psalm 119:105

My kids love to get mail. Even in this digital, Internet-driven, Facebook, Twitter, texting age we live in, they love receiving an old-fashioned paper letter in the mail. I think it makes them feel special that someone took the time to handwrite a note, put it in an envelope and mail it to them. I guess I don't blame them, I feel blessed when I get a handwritten note too – it's so personal.

What a great teaching tool this is. I can explain to my children how special and personal a letter from God is – and we have a whole book of letters. I can show them how the Bible is addressed to each of us and filled with personal messages for specific times in our lives.

I want my children to come to love God's Word at a young age and to see its relevance in their daily lives. They see me reading the Bible and hear me quoting from it so they know it holds an important place in my life. I want to pass that love and appreciation on to them.

Dear Father, I pray that my children will quickly grasp the depth of love revealed in Your Word – love for them! I pray that they will learn its relevance to their everyday lives and come to find comfort and joy in Your words. Amen.

MAY 2

Fighting Bullies

I pray also that the eyes of your heart may be enlightened in order that you may know the hope to which He has called you, the riches of His glorious inheritance in the saints, and His incomparably great power for us who believe. Ephesians 1:18-19

What makes a kid become a bully? Why does one kid find joy in pushing another kid around, belittling him and making life miserable for him? And why do other kids join in this game of picking on a weaker kid? It's hard to understand ... especially when your kid is the one being bullied. I've heard stories of kids who have tried to take their own lives just to escape the constant bullying. That scares me.

I'm asking God to show me how to deflate the power of a bully by convincing my son of his worth and value in this world. I want him to understand that committing suicide at fourteen is a permanent answer to a temporary problem. I know he's miserable right now, but he will grow up and the bully will eventually lose interest in him. Even more than that, I want to teach him that he has value as a person in God's creation. The things these other kids say to him and the way he feels because of those words are just not true. He is a masterpiece of God's creation.

Dear Father, give me the right words to say to encourage my son. If he needs help greater than I can give, Father, intervene and make the bully stop. Amen.

Overwhelmingly Alone

"Do not fear, for I am with you; do not be dismayed,
for I am your God. I will strengthen you and help you;
I will uphold you with My righteous right hand." Isaiah 41:10

It's not easy being a single parent. It is my responsibility to meet my children's every need. It's also my responsibility to earn enough money to buy our food and clothes and pay the rent. I'm the only one they have to help them with their homework and attend their sporting events and school functions. Sometimes I am just overwhelmed with the responsibility.

I don't want my kids to feel cheated that they only have me. I don't want them to feel neglected or like they are an imposition to me. In the darkness of those moments I remember that I am not actually alone. My heavenly Father is always with me. His strength will help me through the long days. His guidance will direct me through financial crises. His love will always surround me. Then, I quietly peek in at my sleeping children and the anxiety fades away as I thank God for them.

Dear Father, it is hard sometimes to do this alone. I don't want my children to feel cheated because they only have me. I'm doing the best I can but I know I wouldn't be making it at all if it weren't for You. Thank You for Your love, presence, wisdom and support. Amen.

Daily Praises

Praise the LORD. Praise God in His sanctuary; praise Him
in His mighty heavens. Praise Him for His acts of power;
praise Him for His surpassing greatness. Psalm 150:1-2

One thing my children are pretty consistent with is asking for stuff. Every commercial they see on television becomes something they MUST have! Their requests become persistent as though they know they can wear me down with their constant barrage. I must admit that sometimes I do give in – just to stop the noise. It reminds me a bit of what my prayer life is like ... how often I bombard the Lord with my requests without once recognizing all that He gives me every day.

It is time to stop my kids' requests and take time to say thanks. We'll look around us every day and recognize the gift of trees, flowers, clouds, puppies, friends, family ... There is so much to be thankful for. I'm going to work on redirecting my thoughts and those of my children toward praise and thankfulness for all that God gives us. Each day we will focus on one thing to be thankful for.

Dear Father, I'm sorry that I'm constantly asking You for things and neglecting to praise You and thank You for all that You give me every day. Father, I praise You for Your love, creativity, grace and mercy. Help me to teach my children to praise You. Amen.

Handling Grief

The LORD is good, a refuge in times of trouble.
He cares for those who trust in Him. Nahum 1:7

I'm not very good at handling grief. It's not something you get a lot of practice at until you actually need it. It's so hard because grief hurts so much. But now I need to teach my daughter how to handle grief. Yesterday the father of one of her good friends died quite suddenly. My daughter is hurting so badly for her friend and wants to help her. She's asking me what she can say and how she can help. This experience has also made her realize that moms and dads do not live forever – there are no guarantees of a long life.

She's grieving with her friend, wanting to help her, but worrying at the same time. How can I help my daughter? What can I say about grief that will make it easier? What can I teach her about compassion and love? The truth of the two greatest commandments comes to mind – remembering how important it is to love God with all our hearts, and to love others more than we love ourselves.

Loving is a two-way street of receiving and giving, and showing others how much we care.

Dear Father, my heart aches for my daughter's friend and for my daughter as she seeks to be a comfort. Help me, to have the right words to share with her. Father, comfort her heart. Amen.

MAY 6

A Work in Progress

*Wisdom will enter your heart, and knowledge
will be pleasant to your soul. Discretion will protect you,
and understanding will guard you. Proverbs 2:10-11*

Why don't kids come with instructions? They could have little printouts on their foreheads that immediately tell you why they are crying. "I'm hungry." "My diaper is wet." "My tummy hurts." It would make life so much easier. I feel like a failure when the books tell me that I should know what my baby's cries mean.

But, I don't always know ... why don't I always know? I guess I need to consider that parenting is a work in progress. The better I get to know my baby, the better I will anticipate her needs and understand her cries. I guess I'll learn what each cry means as I learn her schedule.

The most important thing right now may be cutting myself some slack. I need to let go of some of my perfectionist tendencies. We will learn and grow together and we will be just fine.

Dear Father, I wanted to be a great mom from day one but sometimes I just feel like a failure because I don't know how to meet my baby's needs. Please help me to learn and to be patient with myself as I get to grips with this parenting thing. Father, help me to be a good mom. Amen.

Birthday Giving

"When you give to someone in need, don't do as the hypocrites do — blowing trumpets in the synagogues and streets to call attention to their acts of charity! I tell you the truth, they have received all the reward they will ever get." Matthew 6:2 NLT

My eight-year-old son has a birthday coming and we're planning a party with the whole family and all his friends. He has so much stuff — toys, games, books — that he is having trouble coming up with ideas for a gift list. However, yesterday he came up with an amazing idea: instead of asking for gifts for himself, he wants to ask everyone to come to the party and celebrate with him but to bring gifts for the local food pantry instead of for him. I'm so proud of him! Of course he will still get a few gifts from us, but he won't be overloaded with even more stuff he doesn't need and can't possibly use.

He's always had a tender heart for those who have less than he does but this is the first time that he's voluntarily wanted to do something for someone else. The fact that he wants to do it on his own birthday is amazing. He is even hopeful that some of his friends might copy the idea for their birthdays.

Dear Father, I'm so proud of my son for thinking of others. What a tender heart he has. I pray that his friends will willingly join him in this generosity. Bless him, Father, and always keep his heart tender. Amen.

MAY 8

Handmade Gifts

Now these three remain: faith, hope and love.
But the greatest of these is love. 1 Corinthians 13:13

My daughter takes such joy in making gifts for me. Every few weeks she comes home from church or school with a macaroni-encrusted bowl or a construction paper mobile. She is so proud of these creations! Sometimes at home she will get out her markers and paper and make me countless cards and pictures. Of course she wants each one displayed on the refrigerator – I can't even find the door handle anymore.

Sometimes I get a little annoyed at all these gifts. Finding a place to put them becomes one more thing for me to do. Some days I just want to say ... "ENOUGH!" But then I look at my daughter's face when she presents me with her newest creation and I see her pure joy at being able to give me something that she made for me with her own hands. Wow, the simplicity of her creation and the heart that motivated it straightens my attitude right up.

Who cares about fancy, expensive gifts? Gold? No! Diamonds? Ha! Dinners out? OK, I do still want dinners out ... but I want a brand-new picture from my daughter to greet me when I come home!

Dear Father, thank You for the simplicity of my daughter's heart. Thank You for her pure love. Amen.

Family Reunions

The living, the living — they praise You, as I am doing today;
fathers tell their children about Your faithfulness. Isaiah 38:19

We're traveling west this summer to a family reunion. I'm looking forward to reconnecting with cousins whom I haven't seen in years. Living halfway across the country from where I grew up has separated us from extended family. My children have missed the joy of knowing the family history that would come from having them close by. Some of my relatives will meet my husband and children for the very first time.

My children will no doubt hear stories about my cousins and I growing up and some of the silly things we did. They will meet my aunts and uncles — godly women and men who taught me much about living for God. I can't wait for my children to meet them. I believe they will even see physical similarities between themselves and their cousins. I know my children will love this experience and will come away with a richer heritage of family. I'm so thankful for my extended family and so excited to share them with my children.

Dear Father, family is so important. The history that I share with my family has helped make me who I am today. Thank You for aunts, uncles and cousins. Amen.

The Armor of God

Finally, be strong in the Lord and in His mighty power.
Put on the full armor of God so that you can take your
stand against the devil's schemes. Ephesians 6:10-11

There are days when I literally feel that my life is under attack. On those days it seems like anything that could go wrong does. From appliances breaking, to dogs throwing up, to crabby kids … there is chaos everywhere. I have a choice as to how to respond to this. I can lose my cool and shout and complain. Or I can use the defenses that my Father has provided for me.

Putting on the armor of God will protect my heart and mind from the lies of Satan and the temptation to react rather than respond. This armor will fit me with faith, hope and love and the patience to work through each circumstance of chaos. It is my choice to put this armor on. God has made it available, but I must call on the Holy Spirit to fit me with it. I will stand firm with the armor of God.

Dear Father, thank You for providing this armor. It is my defense against behaving in a way that would not be honoring to You. Wearing this armor will help my children see faith in action – what a model for their own faith. Thank You. Amen.

The Power of Prayer

This is the confidence we have in approaching God:
that if we ask anything according to His will, He hears us.
And we know that He hears us. 1 John 5:14-15

I would do anything for my children. Think for a minute about all the things a mom does for her children. She makes sure that they have food, and clothing. She provides a loving home; chauffeurs them to all their activities; helps with homework; well, the list could go on and on.

Lately, though, I've become aware that, while all those activities are important and certainly play a major role in children's health, safety and development, there is one other thing I can do for my children that is more important and powerful than anything else: I can pray for them.

God promises to hear my prayers and to act on them when they are in accordance with His will. So I will pray for them to know Him, follow Him, love Him and love His Word. I will pray for their safety and protection, and for them to show kindness and love toward others. I'll pray for their future careers and future spouses. Thankfully we have a very powerful God.

Dear Father, I love doing things for my children, but I'm most privileged to pray for. Thank You that I can lift my children up to You and trust You to care for them and protect them. Amen.

MAY 12

Picking Up the Pieces

Because of the LORD's great love we are not consumed,
for His compassions never fail. They are new every morning;
great is Your faithfulness. Lamentations 3:23-24

One of the painful things about parenting is standing by when your child's life falls apart and not being able to stop it. When your child's marriage fails, his career collapses, he gets into financial problems, he runs into trouble with the law ... the possibilities are endless – and you can't do anything to fix it. It's so difficult.

Sometimes the problems are simply too big for a parent to stop them. In those cases, even though your mother-heart is breaking, all you can do is pray, offer a shoulder to cry on, give a hug, a hearty meal ... and be there to pick up the pieces. Love him, just love him, even though it's hard. Problems in our lives should serve to move us closer to God. When all our man-made foundations are taken away, only God is left ... and He is all we need. As a loving, caring parent, encourage your hurting child to turn to God, to lean on Him and to trust Him. Then pray for your child.

Dear Father, You know how much it hurts when your child hurts. You've been there. Father, I pray that my child turns to You for comfort and guidance through this difficult time. Father, show Your strength, Your power and Your love. Amen.

Who Is in Charge?

Submit yourselves, then, to God. Resist the devil,
and he will flee from you. James 4:7

Generally Mom is in charge. OK, when Dad is around we lead as a team, but as far as running the household is concerned, I'm the one who sets the rules and enforces them. I expect my children to respect me and obey my rules.

Once in a while I have to stop and think about that expectation in relation to my own life. I know that Jesus is my Savior, but is He my Lord? Have I submitted to Him to the point that He rules my life?

It's not always easy; in fact, it's a moment-by-moment decision to allow Him that position in my heart. His Lordship gives Him authority over my life and that means I seek His guidance and will. I am completely humble before Him. It means that I don't resist His will the way my children resist me sometimes. The parent/child relationship I have with my kids is a good reminder of the Lord/servant relationship I have with Jesus. In both cases love is the key – the parent's love for her child and the Lord's amazing love for His servant.

Dear Father, I confess that I'm not always submissive. I confess that I fight to have my own way sometimes instead of Yours. Father, forgive me. Help me to love You and trust You enough to allow Your Lordship in my life. Amen.

Changes Ahead

Don't speak evil against each other. If you criticize and judge each other, then you are criticizing and judging God's law. James 4:11 NLT

Life is about change. I'm nervous about how my children will handle this change. After five years of being a single (divorced) parent, I've decided to remarry. I'm sure this is a good thing. My soon-to-be husband loves my kids and they love him. But already they are asking questions about what this means in relation to their "real" dad. I appreciate that my ex-husband and I have maintained a cordial friendship that truly benefits our children and I don't want to do anything to mess that up. He loves his kids and they love him. He's a good dad. I pray that we can cross this new bridge gently.

I pray for the strength to say only positive things about their dad and for him to do the same about me. We never planned on our marriage falling apart, but it happened. Now, with the bright hope for a new future blending with what already is, I pray for love and support for one another to be our focus.

Dear Father, I'm so grateful that my children know they are very loved. I pray that this new marriage will reinforce that more. Father, keep me mindful of speaking well of my ex-husband and including him in our lives as much as is necessary for our kids. Thank You for Your guidance and strength. Amen.

Mood Swings

"If My people, who are called by My name, will humble themselves and pray and seek My face, then will I hear from heaven and will forgive their sin and will heal their land." 2 Chronicles 7:14

Middle school girls have extreme emotional mood swings. One minute my daughter is so happy she is dancing on the couch and the next minute she is on her bed, sobbing uncontrollably. OK, maybe the change isn't that quick, but her emotions do go from high to low very quickly. I don't know how to handle that. I suppose I was the same way at her age. Besides her mood swings, she also swings back and forth from sometimes wanting my help and comfort, and other times not wanting to hear my voice at all. Whew, that's hard too. I have to kind of "take her temperature" before I say a word.

I want to help her and show her that I care, but it seems like the best thing I can do right now is just pray for her. I can do that consistently, regardless of her mood or attitude. I love my daughter and I miss the snuggles we had years ago. I miss giving input into her life. I believe we'll get through this and be close once again, but for now I'll just keep on praying for her.

Dear Father, I miss being close to my daughter. Help her through these difficult years. Give her an assurance of her worth and value, regardless of how others in her age group perceive her. Amen.

Honesty Is the Best Policy

People with integrity walk safely, but those who follow crooked paths will slip and fall. Proverbs 10:9 NLT

The older my children get the more I'm convicted of my need for complete honesty. After all, how can I tell my children that they need to be honest and truthful with me if I am not doing so with them? Not that I'm in the habit of out and out lying to my children or anyone else, but it's the little white lies that trip me up.

Kids notice when I tell a friend who asks to stop by that she can't come now because "we're on the way out the door" ... then I sit down with a cup of coffee and thumb through a magazine. How many times have I come up with some flimsy excuse for not doing something at the kids' school or at church instead of just honestly saying, "Thanks for asking, but I'd rather not do this right now"? Honesty and kindness is all it takes. When I hear one of my children give a veiled answer that isn't completely honest, I know where they learned it. This also applies to my responses to my children. I must be honest with them about the rules I give them and the answers I give to their questions. Honesty is the best policy.

Dear Father, honesty should be easy but it isn't always because I know that sometimes my honest responses will be unpopular. Help me to be honest in my words. Amen.

Building Blocks

For You created my inmost being;
You knit me together in my mother's womb.
I praise You because I am fearfully and wonderfully made;
Your works are wonderful, I know that full well.
Psalm 139:13-14

It is amazing how quickly babies change and learn new things. When my son was born I wondered if he would ever learn to sleep through the night, let alone learn to hold his own head up! But before I knew it he was sleeping all night, then suddenly rolling over, then sitting up and now he's so close to crawling.

It just boggles my mind that he instinctively knows how to do these things. What an amazing God we have! The first time I saw my son stacking his toy blocks one on top of each other, then taking them off and putting them back on, my jaw dropped. How did he know to do that? I thank God for our complex brains that show how our bodies and brains are maturing and growing by the intelligence we show in things as simple as stacking blocks. Praise God for my son. Praise God for stacking blocks!

Dear Father, You are amazing. You've created our bodies in such complex ways that I'm continually amazed. Watching my son grow and develop convinces me more than ever that You are God! Amen.

MAY 18

The Greatest Command

"Love the Lord your God with all your heart and with all your soul and with all your mind and with all your strength. Love your neighbor as yourself." Mark 12:30-31

Children are so trusting. Their little hearts are blank pages, eager and willing to learn. However, from a young age children are often quite self-focused and view much of life only by how it affects them. It's a pleasure and a privilege to have the opportunity to teach children to replace that self-focus with concern for others. God clearly states in the Bible that there are two great commands.

The first thing is to love God with all your heart; think about Him and serve Him. While some of those concepts are a bit "adult," just talking about them with your children will place the seeds in their hearts. The second command is to love others as much as I love myself. Kids get that. When they are exposed to the needs of people who have little, most kids will want to help. When they are reminded to be kind and generous with their playmates, they will try to do that. Of course, it doesn't work every time (just like it doesn't always work with adults either), but the seed is still planted.

Dear Father, thank You for the privilege of teaching my children these two great commands. Help me to plant these seeds in their young minds and hearts so they will grow into loving, kind adults. Amen.

Be Careful, Little Mouth ...

Do not let any unwholesome talk come out of your mouths,
but only what is helpful for building others up according to
their needs, that it may benefit those who listen. Ephesians 4:29

I just heard my son call his friend a bad name. He shouted his angry words at his friend and turned around to see me standing behind him. He looked like he was going to faint. Oh my, I want my son to understand how those angry, demeaning words land on a friend's heart and stay there for a long, long time. The tongue can do such damage.

This reminds me to be careful with my own words, whether I'm frustrated with my kids or with another driver, I must watch what I say. I am an example to my children of how to speak to and about other people. I want to be an example of words filled with kindness and respect for others. (This includes the tone of voice I use in speaking to my children and my spouse.)

If God took the time in the Bible to mention how much trouble our words can cause, I think I should pay attention and teach my children to do the same.

Dear Father, the little chorus "Be careful, little mouth, what you say" is running through my mind. The reminder that "the Father up above is looking down in love" is one that I need to remember when I speak to others. Help me to be honoring and respectful and to teach my children to speak the same way. Amen.

MAY 20

Garbage In … Garbage Out

Above all else, guard your heart, for it is the wellspring of life.
Proverbs 4:23

My faltering culinary skills just gave me a great teaching moment with my children. Gross, but effective. My daughter wanted to help me make dinner. Great, I love the company. I sent her to the pantry to get the bag of potatoes but she came back with no potatoes and her gag reflex working quite well. Some of the potatoes had gone bad and the stench was overwhelming. As I sorted through the bag, tossing the bad potatoes and keeping the good ones, I asked her if I should use the stinky potatoes for dinner or the good ones? Her obvious choice was to use the good ones.

"Well," I asked, "what would happen if we used the bad ones?" My daughter's instant response was that the bad potatoes would make our tummies feel bad and we would be really sick for a long time! This set up a gentle reminder that when we put bad things into our bodies, bad things happen. The same is true of our minds; put bad things in and bad things will come out. I think she got it.

Dear Father, thanks for gentle object lessons like this that create teachable moments. Bad potatoes were a good reminder for me as well as a lesson for my daughter to put good things in my body and good things into my mind and heart. Amen.

Big World, Small World

Religion that God our Father accepts as pure and faultless is this: to look after orphans and widows in their distress and to keep oneself from being polluted by the world. James 1:27

It's so easy to focus only on my surrounding world. There is a constant temptation to get caught up in the world we live in — our own country, state or city. We begin to see everything else that happens around the world only in relation to how it affects us and our country. When this happens we forget that there is a bigger world out there and that much of the people in it live much more difficult lives than we do.

Unless we watch the news we may forget about starving children, warring countries, or places where women and children are kidnapped and forced into lifestyles they wouldn't choose. I don't want my children to live in a bubble that consists only of our town, state and country. I want them to be aware of the bigger world and the needs that are out there. If they know about the world, they can choose to find ways to become involved in the needs of others and help as much as possible. They can only pray for people around the world if they know about them.

Dear Father, I want to be an example to my children. I want my children to be world-wise. Help me find ways for them to be involved in making a difference in the world. Amen.

MAY 22

Giving Birth

My frame was not hidden from You when I was made in the secret place. All the days ordained for me were written in Your book before one of them came to be. Psalm 139:15-16

I had no idea what to expect in the labor and delivery experience. I read all the books and took the classes, but you can't really know what it is like until you actually go through it. The bottom line is ... labor hurts – and it goes on for a long time. I'm thankful for modern medicine and technology.

It's amazing to think what is happening to bring that little baby into the world. What an amazing God we serve! To give birth is such a miracle. I am amazed that God allows us the privilege of sharing in the miracle of bringing a life into this world.

It's amazing that my tiny little baby's body is so intricately and wonderfully made that everything it needs to grow into a full-grown adult is already there, waiting to stretch and grow and develop. I don't know how anyone could experience birth or even look at a small baby and not believe in God. Each time I hold my precious child I will thank God for His amazing plan of birth and growth.

Dear Father, what an amazing plan. Thank You for the miracle of birth. Thank You for the miracle of babies, growing, learning and developing. Amen.

MAY 23

Hit the Pause Button

Come near to God and He will come near to you. Wash your hands, you sinners, and purify your hearts, you double-minded. James 4:8

The older I get the faster life seems to go. I don't know if that's because I'm slowing down or if our lives are really speeding up, but I don't feel that I'm keeping up very well. With three children in the house, plus my husband and I, we have five schedules to keep straight. At any given moment we may have five places too. We have five groups of friends to know and stay in touch with. I have laundry, cleaning, shopping, cooking and chauffeuring duties that keep me running all the time. I seriously want to hit the pause button. I want everyone to freeze right where they are and let me take a breath.

What if I could do that? What would I do while the pause button was on? Grab a glass of iced tea, sit out on the deck, hear the birds sing, enjoy the stillness in my mind and listen for God's voice. I miss the silent times with Him in all the chaos of life. Knowing that that is how I'd spend my "pause moment" makes me realize that I need to make time for that in my life. Time with God is my centering time where I find peace and calmness. It's where I remember that I am loved by the Creator of the Universe.

Dear Father, OK, help me to make the "pause moment" a priority in my day, even if I have to get up early. I need time with You. Amen.

MAY 24

Dreams Lost?

Since we are surrounded by such a great cloud of witnesses, let us throw off everything that hinders and the sin that so easily entangles, and let us run with perseverance the race marked out for us. Hebrews 12:1

I never dreamed of being a mother. My dreams ranged from traveling the world, being a famous movie star, being a nurse, being a writer, changing the world for God, and so on. I wanted to use the talents God gave me to fulfill the passions He placed in my heart. But then ... I had a baby and my hopes and dreams were put on hold. Then, a second baby joined the first one.

Truthfully, in my quiet moments I felt that my life had been put on hold and that I'd never get a chance to realize my dreams. I even resented my children just a little for my lost dreams. How did I get past this place? God did it for me. He reminded me that He has a plan for my life. It's His plan – not mine – and I only need to be obedient to Him.

It's OK to have dreams, but I was actually sinning by not living in the moment where God has put me. I love my children with all my heart and I love being their mom. I'm exactly where God wants me to be right now and that's all I needed to know.

Dear Father, the best thing I can do is love my children and teach them about You. I just want to be where You want me to be. Amen.

Real Beauty

"I have loved you with an everlasting love;
I have drawn you with loving-kindness." Jeremiah 31:3

I'm worried about my daughter. Really worried. I just noticed that she's gotten so thin (why am I only seeing this now?) She has become very picky about what she eats and she exercises for hours every day. I'm afraid she might be struggling with an eating disorder. She's a beautiful girl with a glorious sense of humor, a kind heart, an intelligent mind and a cute figure; but she is falling prey to the lies of the media. How do I stop this? What can I say to her that will make her believe she is good enough; no, not just good enough, but exactly right just the way she is?

I missed whatever started this downward spiral and I feel guilty. I want to convey to her that she doesn't have to live up to the airbrushed images in magazines. She has so much to offer that is good. I'm praying for an opportunity to sit down with her and talk honestly about what she's doing to herself and how she is feeling. This problem may be bigger than my wisdom can solve but I have to know what I'm dealing with.

Dear Father, help! That's all I can say. Help me to know what to do and what to say. Help me to find a way to talk to her that is non-threatening so I don't push her farther into this. Amen.

Realistic Expectations

*Let the peace of Christ rule in your hearts, since as members of one
body you were called to peace. And be thankful.* Colossians 3:15

What do I expect of myself as a wife, mother, daughter, friend, and servant of Christ? If the truth be told my expectations are not very realistic. Like most multi-tasking women I think I can do it all and I don't cut myself much slack when I fall short.

The thing is, I think I should be able to do it all (whatever that is) when, actually, the people in my world – my husband, my children, my parents and my friends – don't really expect that of me. Instead of pushing myself so hard and sometimes feeling like a failure, perhaps I need to have more realistic expectations. Then I will be able to embrace what life has to offer me on a daily basis. I can let go of the "What if I had done this?" or "Why didn't I see that?" questions. I don't want to focus on the failures and not enjoy the life God has given me. I especially do not want to teach my children that way of living.

If I can live in the moment and be realistic about life then I can teach them the same way of living.

Dear Father, this isn't easy for me. I need Your help to let go of the unrealistic expectations I have for myself. Father, help me to appreciate each day, each moment. Help me to focus on the blessings You have given – especially my family. Amen.

Neck Dirt and Sweaty Hugs

Praise the Lord. I will extol the Lord with all my heart in the council of the upright and in the assembly. Great are the works of the Lord; they are pondered by all who delight in them. Psalm 111:1-2

Boys have so much energy! My little son seems to be in high gear from the minute his eyes open in the morning until he collapses into bed at night. I love it! He wears me out sometimes, but I love his energy. One of my favorite times with him is on hot summer days. He and his friends play in the sandbox with their trucks and cars all day long. They run and laugh and get so hot and sweaty. They stop only for a cool drink and a bowl of frozen grapes – yummy, so refreshing. I love listening to them talk and laugh.

Then when his friends go home my son comes inside and ... here it is ... my favorite thing ... he has that little necklace of sweaty dirt around his neck. I love that! Sometimes he will come and throw his arms around my neck and give me a big hug that smells of dirt, sweat and outside air. I thank God for those hugs and for my precious, energetic boy! I thank God that He made little boys with such energy and creativity. I also thank God that at the end of the day my son still gives me hugs and kisses!

Dear Father, thank You for boys. Thank You for energy and laughter. Thank You for sticky hugs and sticky hands. Thank You for every minute with my dear son. Amen.

MAY 28

Honest Prayers

Answer me when I call to You, O my righteous God. Give me relief from my distress; be merciful to me and hear my prayer. Psalm 4:1

Sometimes life stinks. There, I've said it and I refuse to feel guilty about it, even though some church-going people might want me to feel guilty. According to them I'm supposed to say, "Praise God for problems. I trust Him completely to turn bad into good." If I hear one more person say, "Leave your burdens at the cross," I will scream!

It's not that I don't believe it, I do, and maybe I will get to that point, but right now, life stinks. If you've ever had a sick child – really sick (I'm not talking about an earache or a broken arm) – sick like your child has cancer and may not live – then you know it's OK to say that life stinks. Is it fair that my child is fighting for his life but someone else's child is out playing soccer? It's hard to accept.

I believe God is big enough and strong enough and wise enough to handle my honesty. I also believe He will see me through this because He is good and He loves my son. I will give this to the Lord and I will trust His plan – even if my heart is breaking in the process. But right now ... life stinks.

Dear Father, I want my son to be well. Please heal him! I know You understand my pain and You will walk through this with me and with my son. It hurts, God, and I'm scared. Please help us! Amen.

"I Thought I Could Take It"

The name of the LORD is a strong tower;
the righteous run to it and are safe. Proverbs 18:10

My son has been enduring verbal abuse for the entire school year and I didn't know about it. Now, with just two weeks left in the year I learn that one of his teachers has had it in for him all year. He didn't tell me this, my son's friends' mothers all told me that they heard it from their sons. Why didn't anyone tell me? Why didn't my son tell me? When I asked him his answer made my heart ache and swell with pride at the same time. "Everyone knows she picks on a student every year," he said. "If it wasn't me it would be someone else. I thought I could take it," he admitted. He was wrong.

All year we had noticed his withdrawal from social settings. He didn't try out for any sports teams, even though he loves sports. He didn't go to any school functions. He basically went to school and came home. My heart aches that he went through this alone, but I am filled with pride that he tried to protect others. I want to help him realize his worth in this world.

Dear Father, I'm angry that my son was put through this. Help me deal with that anger in a healthy way. He's a wonderful boy with a kind and giving heart. If there is such a thing as a reward for a kind heart please bless him with that now. Amen.

Mental Health Days

Flee the evil desires of youth, and pursue righteousness, faith, love and peace, along with those who call on the Lord out of a pure heart.
2 Timothy 2:22

Not everyone will agree with me on this but that's OK. I allow my children one "Mental Health Day" per school year. Why? Think about it: adults have days when life weighs heavy on us and problems we're dealing with oppress us. Sometimes we take "Mental Health Days" – a day off work or a day away from the family.

My kids love this and here's how it has played out: When they first found out that they could take a "Mental Health Day" they each wanted to take theirs immediately. Once they each used their day it was gone and it did no good to beg for another one. That first year all three kids took their "Mental Health Days", but as time went on they seldom did. As we talked through why they wanted to take it and we prayed together about their issues, they slowly decided they could probably make it through.

Finally, they each reached the point of never taking it – just knowing it was there was enough. They learned that praying about their issues was a better plan.

Dear Father, I pray that as I talk through these things with my children they will find peace from being with You. That's what brings true mental health. Amen.

June

Crossing the Great Divide

The God of all grace, who called you to His eternal glory in Christ,
after you have suffered a little while, will Himself restore you
and make you strong, firm and steadfast. 1 Peter 5:10

When my daughter was a toddler I often felt as though she was attached to my hip. We did so much together – cooked dinner, folded laundry, cleaned the house, and bought groceries. I loved it, but I confess that sometimes it would have been easier to do some of those things alone. Well, now I am doing them alone. My daughter is a teenager now and seems to want nothing to do with me.

I miss her. I miss doing everything together; I miss her following me around so closely that I sometimes tripped over her; I miss hearing about her day … By the grace of God I am trying to be kind to her – even when she's rude to me. I believe that my attitude now will allow us to reconnect once this generational gap is crossed. My heavenly Father is a good model for me in this. He gently waits for me to return when I've walked away from the closeness of our relationship. I will be patient with my daughter as God is with me and tell her that I love her.

Dear Father, my distance from You must hurt even more than my daughter's distance from me does. I'm sorry. I will make every effort to stay closer to You. Please help me to handle my daughter with love. Amen.

Making Choices

I consider everything a loss compared to the surpassing greatness of knowing Christ Jesus my Lord, for whose sake I have lost all things. I consider them rubbish, that I may gain Christ. Philippians 3:8

Women are great at multi-tasking. We can keep three or four projects going at a time. It's a good thing because it means we get so much done. But as with many good things, there is a down side to this gift too. Sometimes I find that I have so many projects going and so many responsibilities with my children that the most important thing gets pushed aside. You may wonder what could possibly be more important than doing stuff with and for my children. Well, God, and time with God.

I need to make time in my day for Him. I will have to make the time because the chaos and noise of all the other stuff tend to crowd Him out. In a sense, God is a Gentleman and will not push His way into my day. He patiently waits for me to come to Him.

All the other things I'm juggling are good things, but I will be better at them and be a better person, wife, mom and friend if I put God first in my day. That may mean making some hard choices and letting some things go.

Dear Father, I want You to be first in my life. I want to start my day with You and keep You in the center of my life. If I have to let some other things go then help me with those choices. Amen.

Did I Do Good?

I pray that you, being rooted and established in love, may have power to grasp how wide and long and high and deep is the love of Christ, and to know this love that surpasses knowledge. Ephesians 3:17-19

My children are tired of me asking, "Was I a good mother? Was your childhood happy?" Their answers are always the same ... "Yes, Mom, you were a great mom and we had wonderful childhoods." Why do I ask? Because I love them and each time one of them makes a bad choice I wonder if I could have done something differently when they were younger that would help them now.

The reality, though, is that I did the best I could, and even though both my husband and I surely made mistakes, the bottom line is that we have always loved our children with all our hearts. One evidence that we did OK is that our children love to be together and love to be with us. Some of their problems now are learning experiences for them, while some are simply bad choices. Regardless, my mistakes as a mom were never made on purpose and my intentions were to teach them and love them. So I must stop asking those questions and move forward, loving them more and more every day.

Dear Father, I want to know that my kids had a happy childhood because I love them so much. Thank You, Father, that the mistakes I made can be covered by Your love. Amen.

Accepting Differences

No one has ever seen God; but if we love one another,
God lives in us and His love is made complete in us. 1 John 4:12

I'm often amazed at how accepting my children are toward those who are different from them. Granted, when they see someone who is challenged in some way, they stare and ask questions. It used to embarrass me until I realized that they were just trying to understand. I learned to pull them aside and answer their questions, trying not to embarrass the person who was the object of their curiosity.

Once my children understand what the situation is — they act as though there is no issue. I admire that. There are physically challenged students in each of my children's classes and they interact with them as they do with other friends. When one of my kids first wanted to invite a friend in a wheelchair over to play, I was nervous about what they would do together and how it would go. My son wasn't nervous at all, "We'll just play, Mom. He's a lot of fun. It will be fine." I can learn from my children to look at people's hearts and not their challenges.

Dear Father, thanks that my children are so accepting — they don't even seem to see differences. I can learn a lot from that. Father, help me to see people as my children do … help me to look at their hearts and not at their differences. Amen.

JUNE 4

Loving the Person but Not the Behavior

I am convinced that neither death nor life, angels nor demons, neither the present nor the future, nor anything else in all creation, will be able to separate us from the love of God. Romans 8:38-39

I learn a lot of lessons about my relationship with Christ through my relationship with my son. Here's one: My son deliberately disobeyed me this morning. He was even belligerent about it, almost daring me to punish him. I was so angry with him that even after I punished him I was still angry. As he was "sitting in his room thinking about what he had done" I sat in the kitchen and thought about it too. I love my son but at that particular moment I didn't like him very much. His attitude was disturbing.

As I sat there God turned my thoughts to my own behavior. Occasionally I get the same belligerent attitude toward Him, and I deliberately do things my own way. As I recognized the similarities between my son's behavior and mine I also saw the need to be able to love the person but not the behavior. God doesn't give up on me. He loves me. I love my son, too, and while I don't appreciate his attitude, I can separate that frustration from my love for him.

Dear Father, thank You for these reminders of Your love for me and how that translates into my relationship with my son. Amen.

JUNE 5

Rotten Apples

*Oh, the joys of those who do not follow the advice of the wicked,
or stand around with sinners, or join in with mockers. But they delight
in the law of the LORD, meditating on it day and night. Psalm 1:1-2 NLT*

Friends are very important to teenagers. When you're a teen it's important to be accepted and to fit in. There is a danger in that, though, and sometimes teenagers can't see it.

If the need to belong is too strong and the self-confidence is too low, then the first sign of some acceptance will be grabbed. That's OK if that group of friends are good kids, but if they don't have good values and morals then a problem develops. Just as one rotten apple can spread its rottenness through an entire bag, the bad values and morals of a group of friends can spread to your teenager. Even though you have raised her with Christian standards, those can begin to be compromised by the influence of friends.

Encourage your kids to choose friends wisely and to be realistic about how strong they can be in resisting temptations. It's a choice to live for God, and it's not easy if someone is pulling you in the opposite direction.

Dear Father, this is a concern as my teenager looks for acceptance. I pray that she will make Christian friends who will help her stand strong instead of friends who will pull her away from You. Amen.

JUNE 6

Planning for the Future

*O Lord, You are my God; I will exalt You and praise
Your name, for in perfect faithfulness You have done
marvelous things, things planned long ago. Isaiah 25:1*

My teenage son is looking at colleges and considering careers. He is dreaming big right now, and why not? Standing at the doorway of the future is the time for big dreams. I would do nothing to discourage him. I can help him, though, by encouraging him to pray and plan, and not just dream.

Great accomplishments, for example, becoming a professional athlete don't just happen. They take dedication, hard work, and planning. My son knows what he enjoys and what career he would like, but my encouragement to him is to make certain that God is leading him that way too.

I've learned that sometimes we think we know where we're going in life, but as we move in that direction, God leads us down another path. It's hard to move a car that's in park, but once it's rolling, steering is possible. I must warn my son to pay attention when God is closing doors, changing passions, and directing his path. What an exciting time! I can't wait to see how it turns out.

Dear Father, I am excited for my son. I pray that he will pay attention as
You direct his path. I know that if he follows You, his life will be blessed
and happy. Amen.

Being Held Accountable

Share each other's burdens, and in this way
obey the law of Christ. Galatians 6:2 NLT

Make time with God. Lose weight. Exercise more. Have date nights with my husband. Spend time with friends. Volunteer in my community. That is my to-do list. Is it realistic? Nope, especially not with three children whose schedules keep me busy. But if I don't start working on these things, they will never happen. I'll end up an overweight, unhealthy, lonely old woman who isn't close to God and thinks of no one but herself. Ugh! So, what do I do? How do I make time for all of these things?

I'll start with one, just one, and I'll work on that for a while until it becomes a habit. However, I know myself well enough to admit that I need to be accountable to someone for this. So I'm enlisting the help of a dear friend. She is choosing one thing on her to-do list and I'm choosing one on mine and together we will encourage and motivate one another and hold each other accountable. Together, we will change and become better people because of it.

Dear Father, thank You for my friend who will help me with this. Please give me the persistence and strength to make these changes in my life. I know they will make me a better person. Amen.

A Hiding Place

*The LORD is a refuge for the oppressed,
a stronghold in times of trouble. Psalm 9:9*

One of the greatest gifts I can give my children is to teach them where to go when life gets difficult. I hope that if they learn this at a young age it will stick with them throughout their lives. They will find out early that the temptations the world offers is to find numbness from problems in alcohol, drugs, sex or even in accumulating more and more wealth.

None of those things work – their problems and loneliness will still be there when they wake up the next day or deposit the next check. That's just the way it is. I can teach my children and model for them that the best hiding place in the difficulties of life is God. His Word offers comfort, and the reality of His love and His plan for their lives is like a warm blanket against the coldness of life. I can't just tell my children this, I must show them that it works by how I live my life and where I turn when I'm hurting. If I don't model turning to God then why should they listen to my words?

Dear Father, this is so important. Help me show my children the truth of hiding in You by how I live. Father, help them to understand and begin to practice this themselves. Keep them from the vices that so many in the world use to numb their pain. Amen.

JUNE 9

The Silver Lining

LORD, You know the hopes of the helpless. Surely You will hear their cries and comfort them. You will bring justice to the orphans and the oppressed, so mere people can no longer terrify them. Psalm 10:17-18 NLT

There have been times in the past when I was so busy that I would have kissed anyone who said I had to stay in bed for a few days. What a gift – I could read books and watch old movies all day – sounds awesome, right? Yeah, not so much. A few weeks into my second pregnancy, I've been ordered to bed rest. Seriously? How do I stay in bed all day when I have a two-year-old running around? And the whole read-a-book-or-watch-a-movie thing? It's not going to work. My brain is so busy being concerned about the baby growing inside me that I can't concentrate anyway.

Is there an upside to this bed confinement? Actually, it depends on my attitude. If I use this time to pray for God's protection over this child and seek His peace and comfort rather than worry and fret, then that's good. I can also invite my two-year-old to climb up on the bed and read books with me or color pictures. Always look for the silver lining that is only found in discovering God's peace.

Dear Father, I'm a little scared. I just want my baby to be OK. Give me a peaceful assurance that You are taking care of things. Help me to make good use of my quiet time. Amen.

Mentor Magic

A word aptly spoken is like apples of gold in settings of silver.
Proverbs 25:11

One of the greatest gifts God has given me is a mentor friend. She is a woman several years older than me who has already lived through a lot of the experiences I am dealing with right now.

Her guidance and wisdom is so valuable. She has saved my children's skin a few times by calming me down when I'm frustrated and assuring me that things will get better. It is so helpful to have a friend to talk to about parenting issues who has already been through the same things – and survived.

Her wisdom and advice on teenagers has helped me many times. Plus, her walk with Christ is an incredible example and so motivating that I strive to know Him better too. She talks through spiritual issues with me, too, as I learn and grow in my faith. What a gift this friend is. After a good hard cry she will hold my hand and pray with me and soon have me smiling or even laughing – what a stress-lifter! This friend is a gift from God.

Dear Father, thank You so much for this friend and the wisdom You have given her. Thank You that she cares for me and shares her wisdom and advice so generously. I really love my friend. Amen.

The Highest Goal

Do nothing out of selfish ambition or vain conceit,
but in humility consider others better than yourselves. Philippians 2:3

When my children were teenagers they were very concerned about what other people thought of them. It was unacceptable to be uncool. Admittedly I had some pressures in that area too. I wondered sometimes what other moms thought about me and my parenting and how I chose to spend my time. One of the benefits of the wisdom gained from getting older is that I now care less about what other people think. In fact, I have realized that others aren't really thinking about me that much at all.

As I've become comfortable in my own skin my highest priority has become to glorify God in all I do and say. I care more about what He thinks than what people think, and that's the way it should be. His Word encourages me to seek to glorify Him through every thing I do. That occurs by the way I interact with my children – the respect with which I speak to them and the fairness with which I treat them.

He is glorified by my honesty in caring for others as I allow myself to be transparent and vulnerable. He is glorified by my humility in thinking of others before myself.

Dear Father, I want my life to glorify You. I pray that my children, husband and friends will see Your love in my life. Amen.

JUNE 12

Anger Management

In your anger do not sin. Do not let the sun go down while you are still angry, and do not give the devil a foothold. Ephesians 4:26-27

Help! The terrible twos have hit! Seriously, my son went to bed one night a sweet, fun-loving little boy and woke up the next morning a two-year-old monster. OK, that's a bit strong, but he suddenly has a terrible temper and no understanding of how to control it or how to express it appropriately. It's going to be a long year.

I realize that I must teach him the proper ways to manage his anger ... while controlling mine. Anger at any age usually stems from self-focus, such as not getting your way in a situation or if someone hurts your pride. That's not so hard to understand about a two-year-old, after all, a two-year-old's entire world is all about him.

The truth is that I struggle with it sometimes too; I get angry when his tantrums interrupt my life. As the adult in the situation, I must convince my son that the world is bigger than his needs and wants. I can model that by letting him see that I don't get my way all the time. This is going to be a journey and I'm going to need a lot of strength and patience from God.

Dear Father, I've kind of been dreading this day. I've heard so many horror stories about the terrible twos. Help me to teach my son control. Help me to model control by the way I treat him. Amen.

Beauty Contests

"Don't judge by his appearance or height. The Lord doesn't see things the way you see them. People judge by outward appearance, but the Lord looks at the heart." 1 Samuel 16:7 NLT

Television, magazines, movies, the Internet ... the images fed to my pre-teen girl of the world's opinion of true beauty make me crazy! It's not difficult to see why so many girls suffer from eating disorders, want to spend bazillions of dollars on the "right" brand of clothing, and spend hours on their hair and make-up. Everything the media feeds girls today is so superficial. I want my daughter to understand that true beauty comes from within – inside – from a kind, generous, caring heart.

That kind of beauty shines through the eyes and facial expressions. Physical beauty is a wonderful thing, but focusing on that to the extent that inner beauty is ignored is not a good idea. Of course I want my daughter to take care of herself, wear nice clothes and look pretty, but true beauty is deeper than that. God says He looks at a person's heart. He cares about who we are on the inside.

I want my daughter to understand that – even though it goes against all that the world is shouting at her.

Dear Father, help me to explain inner beauty to my daughter. Help her to believe it, and while she takes care of her outer self, encourage her to also work on being more Christ-like. Amen.

Life Stages

We have come to share in Christ if we hold firmly till the end the confidence we had at first. Hebrews 3:14

I understand that the stages of life are a series of opportunities to start over again. But just because I understand it, doesn't mean I like it. My baby is heading off to college; following in the footsteps of her older siblings. Now it will be just my husband and me. Gulp.

What will we talk about? Do we still have stuff in common after twenty-five years of being so child-focused? It's kind of scary. I'm still learning how to relate to my children as adults and they can, for the most part, make their own decisions.

I don't always agree with their choices and I'm sure they know that, but while I can worry and pray (OK, I know that should just read "pray," but let's be realistic, sometimes moms worry), I realize that this stage of life is a new beginning for them too. A part of new beginnings is making mistakes and learning from them, so I must let them do so. This empty nest stage feels a little weird ...

Let's see, I could call one of the kids or I could ask my husband to take me out for a nice romantic dinner. Hey ... I think I'm going to like this stage!

Dear Father, I'm looking forward to reconnecting with my husband. Bless this time for us as we sort of get to know each other again. Amen.

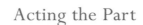

Acting the Part

Faith by itself isn't enough. Unless it produces good deeds, it is dead and useless. James 2:17 NLT

Making my words and behavior match is very important because eight and nine-year-old kids notice when they don't. My boys will be all over it if, for example, I give them a lecture on honesty and how God doesn't approve of cheating, but keep the extra change I'm mistakenly given at a fast-food restaurant. Yes, they notice.

When I encourage them with, "If you can't say something nice, don't say anything" and then they hear me criticizing a friend or even making fun of someone ... they notice. A mom should always be thinking and listening to herself and watching herself with ears and eyes that match an eight-year-old's. It's not easy sometimes, but if we moms want to show that the precepts of the Bible are important to us, then we have to live them.

Otherwise, why would our children pick up on them and even want to incorporate them into their lives? If God doesn't change us, He may not get the chance to change them!

Dear Father, this is a big responsibility. However, with Your help and strength, I know it isn't impossible. Help me to think about what I say and how I act so that my words and behavior match. I want my children to see Your love and values in action. Amen.

It Feels Good to Belong

*The eternal God is your refuge, and underneath are
the everlasting arms. Deuteronomy 33:27*

Watching my six-year-old son play with his older brother makes me smile. I'm not smiling just because they are having fun. It's not just because they are playing instead of arguing either. It's not even because I'm getting some me-time while they play together.

My pleasure is because my six-year-old son knows that he belongs with us, in our family. It took a while for him to feel that way. We adopted him from another country only a year or so ago. He didn't even speak English. It only took a couple of days before my older son began enticing his new younger brother to play with him.

Then, a word at a time, he started picking up English. He learned games, he tussled with his brother and now he knows he belongs to our family. He snuggles with me to read a book, stretches out on the floor by his brother to watch TV, and even has responsibilities in our home. I enjoy teaching him about God and pray that he comes to know Him soon. He is a member of our family and we love him.

Dear Father, I thank You so much for our new son. I'm glad we can offer him a loving home and a comfortable life here. Help him as he continues to adjust to our family. Bless him, Father. Amen.

Grateful Security

We have this hope as an anchor for the soul, firm and secure.
It enters the inner sanctuary behind the curtain, where Jesus,
who went before us, has entered on our behalf. Hebrews 6:19-20

I'm so thankful that I belong to God. I know I don't deserve His wonderful, unconditional love, but I'm thankful that He gives it to me anyway. I know that the Holy Spirit's presence in my life makes me a better person, a better wife, a better mother and a better friend. There is such complete security in knowing that even if I mess up and become totally self-focused or even downright mean ... God still loves me.

He won't throw me out of His family; He won't turn His back on me. God is willing and eager to forgive my failures and to help me overcome the weaknesses that make me stumble. He loves me and wants to help me become more like Christ in all I do. Knowing how much I love my family makes me even more amazed at how much God loves me.

The security of knowing that I am firmly settled in God's family gives me incredible peace.

Dear Father, thank You for the security of Your love. It makes me a better person. I long to pass that security on to my children. Help me to live my life in such a way that they see Your love. Amen.

JUNE 18

Bitter Youth

Get rid of all bitterness, rage and anger, brawling and slander, along with every form of malice. Be kind and compassionate to one another, forgiving each other, just as in Christ God forgave you.
Ephesians 4:31-32

Bitterness is a terrible thing. Unfortunately I'm beginning to see its effects in my teenager; she is perpetually unhappy with pretty much everything and everyone in her life. It breaks my heart to see her so sad. I don't even know what has made her so bitter, but it definitely is consuming her thoughts, attitude and relationships. She is angry with all of us; in fact she can barely say a civil word to any one in our family. She has only a few friends left who want to be around her.

She committed her life to Christ when she was just a child and until recently she sought to live for Him. I suppose the bitterness and her distance from God came at about the same time. My heart aches for my daughter. I just don't know how to help except to pray for her and be available to talk or listen. I know that she must reconnect with God, so I will focus my prayers there.

Dear Father, it is hard to see my daughter so angry and unhappy. I want to help, but her help should only come from You. Father, help her get rid of the bitterness. Father, fill her heart with Your love and remind her of how much You care. Amen.

Did I Do That?

Do not exasperate your children; instead, bring them up in the training and instruction of the Lord. Ephesians 6:4

I admit that I have control issues. I'm not proud of it and I'm working on it ... but it is a work in progress. It's always been an issue for me because, well, let's face it ... my opinion is usually right! But I'm realizing that my forceful way of stating my opinions is causing a problem with my almost-teenage daughter. I am pushing her away rather than encouraging her to talk with me.

I don't mean to do that, of course, but she is beginning to stretch her wings a bit as she longs for independence and my attempts to control her are frustrating her.

She is a trustworthy young lady and I should be allowing her to make some of her own decisions. If I don't allow her that freedom, how is she going to learn to make decisions at all? I want her to have a process in mind of how to think things through and look at the benefits and consequences before she gets to bigger decisions.

I'm frustrating my daughter and God's Word specifically tells me not to do that. I'd better pay attention.

Dear Father, OK, I think I know what's best for my daughter — she must begin to make some of her own decisions. I know it's a good idea, but it's hard for me. I want to teach her and protect her. Please help me to understand the balance. Amen.

Painful Blessings

God blesses those who patiently endure testing and temptation.
Afterward they will receive the crown of life that God has
promised to those who love Him. James 1:12 NLT

Some people say that Christians should never admit to having problems – we should give everything to the Lord and trust Him to handle things. I don't disagree with that in theory, but in reality it's not always that easy – sometimes life is hard! I think it's OK to say that some things really stink – like losing my job, my house burning down, or my husband leaving me. I want my children to understand that even when life is hard, God is with us. He can handle it if I tell Him I'm upset about things. He can handle my complaints and whimpers.

The rest of the story, though, is that sometimes we see God's blessings in the sufferings life brings. We may not see the blessings right at that moment, but usually as we look back we can see the prints of God working through our hearts, lives and situations. The experiences may be painful but the blessings of what we learn are wonderful.

It makes going through hard times a little easier.

Dear Father, this is such an important lesson for my children to learn. Difficult things do happen to us in life, but I want them to know that You are always with them in hard times. I want them to know that they can learn valuable lessons from those difficult times. Amen.

I'm Bored!

Let us not become weary in doing good, for at the proper time we will reap a harvest if we do not give up. Galatians 6:9

What mother has not heard the frustrating, unbelievable whine, "I'm bored!" from her children? Summer school break or even a short holiday break is generally only a few days old before the kids have exhausted virtually everything on their to-do list. Then it becomes a mom's "job" to find things to entertain her children with.

One criterion, however, for this entertainment is that the activity cannot in any way resemble a chore. When children are bored they want to be entertained, not put to work.

The truth is everyone gets bored sometimes, right? Even moms. Your children's boredom can be an opportunity to teach them to entertain themselves. Encourage your bored children to come up with projects to occupy them. Encourage them to work together, to go outside and enjoy God's marvelous creation, exercise, and play with friends. In fact, get outside yourself and have some fun with your children! Work can wait; children grow up so fast!

Dear Father, I must admit that sometimes I'm bored, too, even with the busyness of my life. Maybe that boredom means it's time to have some fun with my children. Guide our boredom antidotes! Amen.

JUNE 22

Looking Around

"Do not store up for yourselves treasures on earth, where moth and rust destroy and where thieves break in and steal. But store up for yourselves treasures in heaven. For where your treasure is, there your heart will be also." Matthew 6:19-21

"Life isn't all about me." It is a revelation when we learn that lesson – no matter what age we are when we learn it. God's Word encourages us to look at the people around us and care about them. The challenge for an adult is two-fold. I must keep my eyes open to notice when someone needs help in the form of friendship, a conversation, carrying groceries inside, shoveling snow or cutting the grass. No one wants to go through life alone, but we must look around and notice who needs help.

The second part of the challenge of God's instruction to me is to teach my children to care about others. Children have such tender hearts, it doesn't take much to get them to notice when they can help others. I can offer them some practical guidelines on how they can befriend lonely people, help our neighbors or even take on big projects to help people in need. Looking around to love and care for others is obedience to God.

Dear Father, I want to be obedient to Your Word and in the process teach my children that the world is bigger than what happens to them. Help me to show them practical ways to help others. Amen.

JUNE 23

Family Celebrations

Shout for joy to the LORD, all the earth, burst into
jubilant song with music. Psalm 98:4

One of my all-time favorite things is family celebrations. Whether it is a birthday, Christmas, Thanksgiving, Independence Day or even Flag Day – I enjoy it when we are all together in celebration mode! When our children were still small, they used to get so excited they could barely contain themselves. It was such fun to decorate the house, plan the parties, and anticipate with them.

I enjoyed their joy as much as anything. Now that my kids are adults, the exciting part for me is that they all come home. We have such fun being together!

I love the pleasure my children find in one another, sharing their stories and remembering the past. We've even been stopped by other patrons in restaurants who notice how much fun we have together. It's awesome!

Now, as I sit back and listen to them chatter I realize that whatever mistakes I've made as their mom are really OK. My children had a happy childhood. They like my husband and me. They like each other. It's truly a celebration of love to be together!

Dear Father, thank You so much for these celebrations. I love hearing the stories of what my children remember from childhood. Thank You for my family! Amen.

A Celebration of Praise

*Praise the LORD, all His works everywhere in His dominion.
Praise the LORD, O my soul. Psalm 103:22*

It is so easy to take the good things of our lives for granted, or even to come to expect them as if we deserve them.

I've realized that when I pray with my children, our prayers are filled with requests of things we want God to do and intercessions for other people. There is nothing wrong with that, of course. I want them to understand that they can take anything to God; I want them to believe that God cares about the concerns weighing on their hearts.

But on the flip side, I also want to teach them to celebrate all He does for them. The Lord's Prayer, which is our example of how to pray, begins with praise so I'm guessing God enjoys our praise. Once I reminded my children to notice all the good things God does each day, the praises rolled out of them. They thanked God for everything from, "Thanks for my family," to "Thanks for roly-poly bugs." It has been a joy to celebrate God's daily, common gifts as well as His unique and "just for today" gifts.

Dear Father, this has been so good for me too. Thank You so much for the lessons I learn from my kids. Thank You for this world, my home, my family, sunshine, rain, flowers, running water … thank You for all that You do for us! Amen.

JUNE 25

Accepting Changes

We know that in all things God works for the good of those who love Him, who have been called according to His purpose. Romans 8:28

Change is never easy and there are not many people who actually like change. I sure don't, because change changes things. Profound, huh? It's a challenge to teach my children to accept change with a positive attitude when I have so much trouble with it myself. When our family had to move to a new town it was difficult for all of us. It was hard comforting my children who missed their friends, because I, too, desperately missed my friends.

We all experienced the "adventure" of learning where things were in the new town; getting used to the new schools, church and house, as well as trying to make new friends.

I'll say it again ... change is never easy, but we're learning to accept the constant changes of life as adventures and opportunities to meet new people and learn new things. We're also learning that it's acceptable to grieve and miss what we've left behind. Those emotions are affairs of the heart and we need to face those to move forward. So face them, embrace them ... then move forward.

Dear Father, I suppose if things always stayed the same life would get boring, but at times a little boredom sounds appealing. Continue to teach me through change. Help me to manage my emotions and help my children learn to manage theirs. Amen.

JUNE 26

Actions Speak So Loud

For you are a people holy to the LORD your God. The LORD your God has chosen you out of all the peoples on the face of the earth to be His people, His treasured possession. Deuteronomy 7:6

How many times do we tell our children, "actions speak louder than words"? Yes, we attempt to drill into their moldable little minds that the things they do, together with the words they speak shows what kind of person they really are inside. Actually, it's an important thing for all of us to remember. How other people speak about us is a good measure of what our character is.

Do they perceive us as kind, helpful, caring and honest; or as mean, selfish and dishonest? Character is in the eye of the beholder, but it is created by the actions and the words of each of us. One important job we have as mothers is to model good character for our children. If my words say, "Be humble, be kind, be loving," then my actions better back those things up. Unfortunately sometimes they don't. So we all have work to do in becoming men and women who reflect God's character to others.

Dear Father, I long to be a woman who reflects You to all I come in contact with — especially my children. Help me to slow down and think before I act or speak. I want Your Holy Spirit to control my actions and my words. Amen.

JUNE 27

Dealing with Cheating

"Whoever can be trusted with very little can also be trusted with much, and whoever is dishonest with very little will also be dishonest with much." Luke 16:10

Why do kids cheat? Is it so important to win a game or ace an exam that they have to cheat? It must seem like it to them, at least at the moment. Of course, the world is constantly throwing a philosophy at them that says if you aren't the winner ... you're the loser; if you're not on the top of the heap then you're nothing. I've even heard a coach say that coming in second place is really just being the first loser.

OK, those kinds of philosophies help explain why kids feel compelled to cheat. Winning is everything – at any cost. It is going against the grain to teach my children that winning is not as important as the character they develop. Coming in second or even last is OK, if they've played with honesty and integrity. I can model this for them in my own honesty with everything from obeying the speed limit to how I do my taxes. Cheating is not acceptable in God's eyes, but honesty always is.

Dear Father, cheating makes me sad. I don't want my children to get in the habit of cheating for any reason or to ever feel that it's acceptable. Father, help me teach them that trying their best at something is the most important. Help me to model honesty for them. Amen.

Cut Backs

In God, whose word I praise, in the LORD, whose word I praise — in God I trust; I will not be afraid. What can man do to me? Psalm 56:10-11

My husband lost his job. We're all scared, even the kids. In one split second it feels as though everything in our world has changed. Suddenly we need to be even more careful about every purchase we make. Eating out is a thing of the past and we're cutting back on luxuries that we used to consider necessities. My husband is so consumed with finding another job that it feels as though we've lost him too. He doesn't really participate in our family conversations or activities anymore.

It would be nice to find a way to put my children's anxieties to rest, but since I'm scared, too, that's going to be difficult. I think we'll have a family meeting to brainstorm ways we can cut back on expenses. We'll also pray ... a lot.

These kinds of experiences are when the "rubber meets the road" ... times when we see whether our claim to faith really means anything. It's an opportunity to model to my children that I truly do trust in God to take care of us and provide for us.

Dear Father, I'm scared. I'm scared we may lose our home. I'm scared that my children won't have what they need, let alone what they want. Father, help my trust in You to grow as I see You taking care of us and providing for us. Amen.

JUNE 29

Pleasure or Addiction?

"No one can serve two masters. Either he will hate the one and love the other, or he will be devoted to the one and despise the other. You cannot serve both God and money." Matthew 6:24

There may be a fine line between enjoying something that gives me pleasure and being so consumed by it that it becomes an addiction. I think of some simple pleasures such as chocolate. It seems like a simple pleasure but if I must have it every day without fail, then it becomes an addiction.

There are countless things to be addicted to and most of them are good things if treated properly; phone conversations with a friend, food, and exercise are a few examples. There are, of course, bad things to be addicted to like alcohol, drugs, pornography or shoplifting. Why does something become an addiction? Control? Power? What can I do about addictions in my life?

I don't want these kinds of things to impact my children. So I'd better try to break addictions – through prayer and conscious effort. If necessary, I can get professional help.

Dear Father, I'm aware every day of the ways I influence my children's lives – both in positive and negative ways. Father, I want to teach them to live for You, lean on You, trust You and let You control their lives. I can't teach them those things if I'm not practicing them. Amen.

JUNE 30

July

Christ-like?

We, who with unveiled faces all reflect the Lord's glory, are being transformed into His likeness with ever-increasing glory, which comes from the Lord, who is the Spirit. 2 Corinthians 3:18

The ultimate goal of my life is to become more and more like Christ. This means that my attitudes, actions, words and purpose should be as His would be. But sometimes I feel like I'm running the race blindfolded. It's hard to always know what to say and do.

Oh, I know the bottom-line stuff of love your neighbor, be kind, watch your words ... those sort of things. What I don't understand is why the hardest place to do that is right here in my home with the people I love the most. I can put on a good show when I'm outside these walls, but keeping my temper in check and being patient with my children ... not always. Or, being patient and encouraging to my husband and doing things for him purely out of love instead of waiting on him to serve me? Not very often. I really need to let God work on my heart so that I can be Christ-like at home as well as in public.

Wait, I don't just need that ... I want that!

Dear Father, my family are the people I care about the most. I want them to see You in me. I want to model Christ-likeness for my children. Please help me to live out my faith here where it matters so much! Amen.

My Old Bathrobe

*The LORD comforts His people and will have
compassion on His afflicted ones. Isaiah 49:13*

My old bathrobe is super soft. It used to be super fluffy, too, but now the fluff has kind of flattened out. It's stained in places, it has a torn pocket, and the color is faded. It's just plain ... old. However, I stubbornly refuse to replace it even though there is a new one, which my family gave me, hanging in the closet. Why? Because it's soft and warm and I love to wrap it around me and snuggle on the couch. The stains on it remind me of times with my kids and memories flood into my mind.

There is a strange sense of security in that old bathrobe. Many cold mornings and late nights I have worn my old robe while I cried out to God for His comfort as I prayed for my children or my parents. It's almost a holy ground place of connecting to God.

My real comfort – my soul comfort – comes from God. When I'm frightened, worried, anxious – I go to Him and He is always there. His love comforts and consoles me. His love wraps around me like an old, warm bathrobe.

Dear Father, I'm so thankful for Your comfort. There have been many times in my life when I simply wouldn't have made it without Your comfort. I pray that my children will go to You for comfort too. Amen.

JULY 2

In for the Long Haul

So do not throw away your confidence; it will be richly rewarded.
You need to persevere so that when you have done the will of God,
you will receive what He has promised. Hebrews 10:35-36

There is an old saying that the greatest gift a father can give his children is to love their mother. I like that, but I don't believe that all the pressure should be on my husband. We both want to show our children that we are in our marriage for the long haul; regardless of what difficulties or trials may come along. We are committed.

Too many areas of life today lack commitment. So, when things get tough in a marriage, a husband or a wife bails out; when a friendship hits a rocky patch, one friend walks away; if God doesn't do what you want ... how committed are you? Commitment begins with my relationship with God. I'm committed to it – even when I don't understand or like what's happening.

Commitment to my husband is next. I'm in this marriage for good – no matter what. I'm also committed to my children. I will love, support, encourage, protect and be there for them as long as I have breath. All of these ... for the long haul.

Dear Father, thank You for "sticking strength." There have been times when it would have been easier to walk away, but I'm glad I didn't – not from You, my marriage, my kids or my friends. Amen.

Staying in Touch

Acknowledge the God of your father, and serve Him with wholehearted devotion and with a willing mind, for the LORD searches every heart and understands every motive behind the thoughts. 1 Chronicles 28:9

Most women are great at communicating. We just love to sit down over a cup of coffee and talk about everything from our husbands, kids and parents to what color to paint the living room. We talk. We listen. It's called communication. Men are not quite so good at communicating, although they do, admittedly, have other strengths.

I'm finding it difficult these days now that my teenage son has dropped into the pit of non-communication. I miss hearing about what happened in his day and what's going on with his friends. I know this is part of the growing up process, but it kind of hurts.

Even as I say that I think about how it must hurt my heavenly Father when I behave the same way sometimes. Just as my son pulling away and being independent hurts me, the times I pull away from God – whether intentionally or because I simply let other things crowd Him out – must hurt Him too. I will take this reminder to stay in touch with God and keep the lines of communication open.

Dear Father, I miss talking with my son. Help me to be patient until this stage passes and we reconnect again. Help me to remember how I feel now and use that to remind me to stay in touch with You. Amen.

Power Struggles

I can do everything through Him who gives me strength.
Philippians 4:13

The question is ... who is in charge – me or my two-year-old? I know the answer is supposed to be me, but we are having some major power struggles these days. I sometimes feel as though I'm in competition with my child!

It amazes me that at two years old she can be so stubborn and so persistent and so LOUD. Sometimes I give in just to make her be quiet even though I know that it is important for her to begin to understand authority and obedience. She must learn to trust my judgment for her and to know that I'm simply trying to protect her by my decisions.

I really need God's strength and wisdom to help me handle this. I want to do this right but some days, really, I don't have a clue. I'm thankful for the friends God has given to me who have already been through this and share their experiences and wisdom with me. It's interesting that a child so young keeps me on my knees pleading for God's wisdom!

Dear Father, I do need and want Your wisdom. I want to be a good mother and teach my daughter proper behavior. I want her to be pleasant so that others enjoy being around her. Father, show me how to stop the power struggles. Teach me how to love her through this! Amen.

Healthy Competition

Whatever you do, work at it with all your heart, as working for the Lord, not for men, since you know that you will receive an inheritance from the Lord as a reward. Colossians 3:23-24

My son is a great sportsman and he loves to win. I love it when his team wins, too, especially if my son played well and really contributed to the victory. I must admit that I'm pretty competitive myself and I cheer a little too heartily sometimes. There is kind of a fine line between doing your very best with the talents God has given you, and being a good winner.

A healthy level of competition doesn't lose sight of God's command to love others. I'm not sure I can teach my son where that line is, but I can pray for God to show it to him.

I don't want my son to become so competitive that he stomps over others just to win or becomes so arrogant that he is obnoxious. The nature of competition is that one person wins and another loses but both can be handled with grace and kindness – that's what I pray for.

Dear Father, I'm so competitive myself that I guess I'd better pray for You to teach my heart before I can pass along wisdom to my son. Remind me to be kind to others and to care about them more than I care about winning. Amen.

Rev Up the Motor!

"I know your deeds, that you are neither cold nor hot. I wish you were either one or the other! So, because you are lukewarm — neither hot nor cold — I am about to spit you out of My mouth." Revelation 3:15-16

I'm a pretty passionate person. When a project grabs my attention and I decide I want to get involved in it, I give it two hundred percent! That's just the way I'm made. So now that my teenager seems to have slipped into the mode that most of life takes too much energy to engage in ... it has made me crazy!

She has the energy to stay in touch with her friends but not for much else. Her complacency just baffles me. What bothers me most (and scares me a lot) is that recently she has become very complacent about her relationship with God. I wonder if this new "whatever" attitude stems from friends who think faith is dumb. I always thought she would stand up to that, but I know it must be hard.

My prayer is that somehow God will grab her heart again; that the passion she used to feel for His Word and His work would grow again. Without nagging her, I want to urge her to move forward in life with energy and purpose.

Dear Father, it looks as though my daughter has become luke-warm towards You, but I realize that You are the only one who can fix it. I just pray that she will pay attention to You and let You awaken passions in her heart. Amen.

No More Complaining

Do everything without complaining or arguing, so that you may become
blameless and pure, children of God without fault in a crooked and
depraved generation, in which you shine like stars in the universe.
Philippians 2:14-15

This is what I tell myself: "Take a deep breath. Count to ten, thirty if necessary. Speak kindly and patiently. Take another deep breath." What brings on this mantra? Complaining. My children complain about everything from whether it's too hot or too cold outside to chores they must do to not having the "right" clothes to wear ... the list is endless.

I worry that my children have come to believe they deserve certain things, so moaning when they don't get what they "deserve" leads them right into complaining.

I want to teach them to celebrate life – the big, incredible gifts of God and the everyday common things too. As they learn to do that, they will celebrate people in their lives and the things those people do to bless them. Noticing those things will inevitably cut down on their complaining.

Dear Father, first, I must ask You to forgive my complaining and help me to model celebrating life. Father, I pray that my children's complaints will be turned to joyful celebration. Amen.

Peace

Do not conform any longer to the pattern of this world, but be transformed by the renewing of your mind. Then you will be able to test and approve what God's will is — His good, pleasing and perfect will.
Romans 12:2

Peace is not possible in our home without the essential ingredient of compromise. My two boys both like to win. They will fight battles and have shouting arguments to the bitter end (unless I intervene) with no resolution. How do I make them understand that they cannot both win every time?

Compromise means that once in a while you have to give in and let the other person win. You can't always get your way. They would have much more fun playing if they learned this, and our home would be much more peaceful.

So what do I do? I can continue to model the idea of compromise, continue talking with them about it and pray for ways to make that message stick in their minds. It's a lesson I long for them to learn because their lives will never be peaceful without compromise.

Dear Father, this is a hard lesson for two competitive boys. Help me to find ways to demonstrate compromise and please let it sink into their minds and hearts. I know their lives will be much happier once they learn to compromise. Amen.

Making Things Right

I acknowledged my sin to You and did not cover up my iniquity.
I said, "I will confess my transgressions to the LORD" —
and You forgave the guilt of my sin. Psalm 32:5

Hiding things from God is just not possible. I don't know why I keep thinking I can slide things by without Him noticing. Even when I do confess my failures to Him I always have a justification to cause my actions to make perfect sense. Isn't it funny that I insist on my children confessing when they have disobeyed, but I do pretty much everything in my power to avoid confessing things to my heavenly Father?

Part of my reticence stems from embarrassment. I don't like to admit my failure. However, my history with God reminds me that once I have confessed my sins, He readily and eagerly forgives them. After that, the burden of failure is lifted from my heart and I have a fresh start ahead of me. I willingly do the same for my children when they regretfully confess. It's what love does.

So look at confessing to God as an opportunity; a gift of a new beginning.

Dear Father, I'm sorry confession is so hard for me. Thank You for Your forgiveness and for the many, many fresh starts You have given me. I'm so thankful for Your love. Amen.

JULY 10

Knowing Who I Believe

*Blessed are those who trust in the LORD and have made
the LORD their hope and confidence. Jeremiah 17:7*

There are many things I want to teach my children, but the most important legacy I want to leave them with is being able to know who they can trust. Now, of course, I can't always guide them through the process of knowing which friends or coworkers can be trusted – especially when they get older. However, right now while they are children, I can teach them the most important foundation of trust – God.

I'm trying to show them by my own relationship with Him that God can be trusted. Even when life gets pretty tough – I trust Him to make it better and teach me through the problems. When I don't understand what He is doing – I trust Him, because I believe He loves me and will do what is best for me. When I can't see His hand at all and I wonder if He is paying attention – I trust Him, because He promised to always be with me.

My prayer is that my children will learn to trust God completely throughout their lives.

Dear Father, I'm thankful that I have reached this point in my relationship with You. I still have so much to learn but I'm growing every day. Father, start my children on the path of trusting You too. Help them learn that the foundation of their lives must be in You. Amen.

Believing in Yourself

God created man in His own image, in the image of God
He created Him; male and female He created them. Genesis 1:27

Why is it so difficult to have good self-esteem? It's true that there is a fine line between good self-esteem and being so proud of yourself that no one wants to be around you, but self-confidence is important.

Knowing who they are and what their values are will help children stand strong against temptation. Temptations are going to fly at them from all directions, including from schoolmates and friends, to do things and try things that they really don't want to. If my kids believe in themselves and feel good about themselves they will be better equipped to stand strong.

My children know they are loved by their family. They know God loves them. They have been raised with Christian values and taught to trust God. They have been taught that they are created in the image of God Himself.

Their skills and talents have been recognized and appreciated. I hope all these things pour into their self-esteem.

Dear Father, I want my children to have good self-esteem. Father, help them to believe in themselves and appreciate the gifts and talents You have given them. Help them to stand strong. Amen.

Out of Control

"Therefore, if you are offering your gift at the altar and there remember that your brother has something against you, leave your gift there in front of the altar. First go and be reconciled to your brother; then come and offer your gift." Matthew 5:23-24

What began as a little misunderstanding with my daughter has blown way out of control. We're barely speaking to each other now and I feel terrible about it. I take the blame because, although I didn't start it, I'm the adult and should have stopped it.

Conflict is so hard. I really don't like it when people are angry with me, especially my precious daughter. It is true that some conflict is justified and, if handled correctly, is fine. However, often conflict comes from a place of self-centered, all-about-me feelings. When someone doesn't do what you want or expect then you get bent out of shape and conflict is the result.

The key to a positive result is the manner in which the conflict is handled. God instructs us, all of us, whether parent or child, to respect others and speak with kindness. In resolving conflict we must be fair, unselfish and even-tempered. This is hard to do without God's help.

Dear Father, I want to resolve the conflict with my daughter in a way that shows I respect and honor her. Help me to be kind and gentle. Help my words to be loving and even-tempered. Amen.

JULY 13

Little Voices

I strive always to keep my conscience clear before God and man.
Acts 24:16

Thank God for consciences. My son's conscience is that little voice in his head that encourages him to make a good choice, even if it isn't the popular choice, and he has to take a stand before his friends.

That little nagging thought in the mind is sometimes God's way of communicating with His children or at least reminding them of His teachings and will. It's His way of keeping His children on track with the commands and teachings of His Word.

I'm thankful that my son listens to his conscience and that sometimes it turns him back from making foolish choices. I know it's possible to ignore that little voice so often that pretty soon you don't even hear it anymore. Then it seems to become inactive as evil and selfishness take over a person's life.

I encourage my son to spend time in God's Word and to talk with God so that he is sensitive to the twinges of his conscience, because it might just be God speaking to Him!

Dear Father, thank You for speaking to Your children. Sometimes it is hard to know whether the voice we hear is You speaking or our own subconscious. Help my son to recognize Your voice. Amen.

JULY 14

Paying the Price

If you repay good with evil, evil will never leave your house.
Proverbs 17:13

One of the most painful things about parenting is when I have to punish my child for disobeying me. I know it's important because she needs to understand that her actions have consequences, but it is still difficult. I must constantly keep in my mind that enduring the consequences of her actions will help her learn and thus become a better person. It makes a difference in how a person behaves when she understands that every action has a consequence.

Putting that truth together with God's command to love others as you love yourself means paying attention to actions and words so that the consequences of what you say or do are not painful to anyone else. I also want my daughter to understand that disobeying God has consequences and punishments.

Obedience to God's Word is important for both parents and children. So, of course, I must consider the consequences of my actions too.

Dear Father, I don't want to do anything that causes unnecessary pain or angst to my family or to my friends. Help me model a life that is aware of the consequences that are caused by words and actions. Amen.

Contentment

I am not saying this because I am in need, for I have learned to be content whatever the circumstances. Philippians 4:11

Contentment has two prongs ... one good and one not so good. On the one hand it is good to be content, or at peace, with our families, in our relationship with the Lord, our neighbors and even with ourselves. On the other hand we should never be so content that we stop looking forward and striving to learn and grow.

This is an interesting concept to teach children: Be happy with where you are but DON'T be happy with where you are. We should be content with where we are to the point that we live "in the moment" and enjoy the experience, but we must always be anticipating what God has next for us.

If we are too content, we may miss chances to have new experiences and allow God to use us in new ways. Basic contentment comes from knowing that God is in control and is directing our steps, and then trusting Him and where He is leading.

Dear Father, help me to teach my children this dual concept. In fact, help me to understand it too. Help me to find the right balance of being content right now without being consumed with what the future holds. Guide my children to understand it too. Amen.

JULY 16

The Comfort of Control

"Do not let your hearts be troubled. Trust in God; trust also in Me."
John 14:1

My children say that I have control issues. I respectfully disagree of course. I do give input into their lives and decisions based on the wisdom of my years, but that's not controlling ... is it? I hope not because I have come to the point where I know who is in control of my life ... and it isn't me.

With all the struggles of choices and those times when life throws a curve, there is great comfort in knowing that ultimately it is God who is controlling things. Not that I always bow immediately to His will or His direction ... I'll be honest, I fight Him sometimes. But when I finally relax in my trust of Him and submit to His control, I find great comfort and peace.

This is what I want to teach my children – peace is found in trusting God's control. The basis for this peace is believing that God loves me unconditionally and completely, and therefore, will bring peace through frustrating and unpredictable circumstances.

Dear Father, it's easy to believe You love me and that I can trust You when things are going well. Help me to grow to the point of trusting Your control in my life even in difficult times. Help me to teach my children this too. Amen.

Working Together

"He went to him and bandaged his wounds, pouring on oil and wine. Then he put the man on his own donkey, took him to an inn and took care of him." Luke 10:34

Being a single parent is a lot of work! Everything is my responsibility, from earning money to support us to fixing broken things to taking the garbage cans out to the curb. I'm always thinking about what I need to accomplish in each day so I seldom feel like I can relax.

On top of the multitude of things I must do ... I'm lonely. I miss my husband and I know my children miss their father. I'm so thankful for the people God has brought into our lives who care for us and love us. They show me that we aren't really alone in our pain or in creating what our new normal is going to be.

Cooperation is the only way we're going to make it through this. My children are willing to do more chores, my family and friends are willing to help fix the broken things, and they let me cry and even cry with me. I'm more aware than ever before of my place in God's bigger family. By caring for each other and working together we can help one another through this life.

Dear Father, thank You for my friends and family who want to help my children and me through this adjustment. I know we will make it because You have placed these caring people in our lives. Amen.

Strong Backbones

My soul is weary with sorrow, strengthen me according to Your word.
Psalm 119:28

The pressures on kids today begin earlier than they used to. More and more statistics show that children as young as elementary school age are facing pressure to take drugs, drink alcohol and even experiment with sex. This is a scary statistic. It's enough to cause parents to stay on their knees interceding for their children.

I pray for my children to stand strong against temptations. I pray for their openness to talk with me about what they are facing. I pray for their wisdom to discern when something presented so positively to them has underlying bad things at its base. I pray for them to know that God's strength is available to help them stand strong in doing good and being kind and loving. His strength will help them fight off temptation. I pray for their courage to come from His presence in their lives.

My children have been taught from a young age to trust God and to turn to Him in trials – this is where the rubber meets the road.

Dear Father, I pray that my children will understand that Your strength is available to them. Your strength is greater than anything else in this world. You love them and will help them stand strong against schoolmates who push temptation at them. Amen.

New Creatures

Anyone who belongs to Christ has become a new person.
The old life is gone; a new life has begun! 2 Corinthians 5:17 NLT

What an amazing God we have. His patient love for each of His children changes us from self-centered, self-focused beings to creatures who are becoming more and more like Christ with the focus of glorifying Him and loving others.

God's imagination is so clearly seen in creation. His strength and power is evident in the oceans, mountains, canyons, waterfalls and majestic trees, so I shouldn't be surprised that His power is great enough to change me from a self-centered woman into a more loving, caring and sensitive person; one who shares God's love by caring for her husband with a less selfish attitude and one who willingly gives her time, energy and focus to her children.

It is an amazing privilege to be able to teach my children about God's love by letting them see the things I'm learning about myself. I know that my life is a work in process, but I pray that the changes are beginning to show to my family!

Dear Father, I pray that the new creature I'm becoming is evident to my family. I pray that the changes in me will cause them to want to know more about You. Amen.

Stop the Criticism!

The tongue is a small part of the body, but it makes great boasts.
Consider what a great forest is set on fire by a small spark.
The tongue also is a fire, a world of evil among the parts
of the body. It corrupts the whole person. James 3:5-6

If someone has ever criticized you then you know that ugly words spoken lie on the hearer's heart for a long time. For some reason, even if the speaker has apologized and confessed to being frustrated, tired or overwhelmed, the seeds of criticism take a long time to go away.

What a lesson for moms! Constant criticism tears down a child's self-esteem and belief in himself. Each critical word you say is like a brick that slowly builds a wall between you and your child. After a while he will believe that you aren't proud of him and that he will never be able to please you, regardless of what he accomplishes.

Of course, this may not be true; it may simply be that you spoke without thinking, hoping to motivate him, or because you were tired or whatever. Regardless, critical words can do a lot of damage!

Dear Father, help me to remember this. Help me to think before I speak, even if I'm trying to motivate my child. Help me to find positive ways to do that instead of criticizing. Amen.

Who Do You Think You're Fooling?

The heart is deceitful above all things and beyond cure.
Who can understand it? Jeremiah 17:9

You've heard the expression "trying to pull the wool over someone's eyes," haven't you? These people are very good at spinning a story so they always look good. They can justify any behavior or words to make people believe their intentions were actually good.

These wool-pulling experts are quite effective at convincing people to believe what they want them to believe. So, when they are unkind or dishonest, they are very good at giving reasons that make their actions look good. The problem is that, although these people may be successful at pulling the wool over our eyes for a while, eventually their lies catch up with them. Then any trust that people may have had in them is destroyed and it will take a long time to rebuild it.

There is also the more important truth that they have never for a moment fooled God. Wool pulling may work for a while with people, but it never works with God!

Dear Father, my children need to learn that in the long run deceit never works. Help me to teach them to always be honest and not deceitful with people or with You. Amen.

JULY 22

Making Decisions

Show me Your ways, O Lord, teach me Your paths;
guide me in Your truth and teach me. For You are God my Savior,
and my hope is in You all day long. Psalm 25:4-5

Making decisions doesn't come easily to some people ... like me for instance. Why is it so difficult to make a decision? Actually, this inability to make a decision is something that I'm concerned about because I don't want to pass it on to my children.

I know there is a process of thinking through the options and considering the consequences of each decision. I must also think about how my decisions will impact others. Maybe all those steps are why it's so frightening. I worry about those very issues – how my decisions will affect others and whether they will be adversely affected by my choices. Maybe I over think things. I want to teach my children the steps involved in making a decision.

I want them to know they should pray before making a decision and trust God's leadership in the choice. Then when it is made, live with it.

Dear Father, making a decision is so hard sometimes. Help me to seek Your guidance, make my decision and stick with it! Help my children to learn to do the same. Amen.

Dealing with Depression

I waited patiently for the LORD; He turned to me and heard my cry. He lifted me out of the slimy pit, out of the mud and mire; He set my feet on a rock and gave me a firm place to stand. Psalm 40:1-2

How do you make someone be happy? If only we could, huh? I've tried very hard to cheer up my daughter. Her depression seems so pointless to me; after all, she is a beautiful girl with many talents, lots of friends and a family who loves her so much. My mother heart wants to "fix" her depression so she will just be happy.

It's taken me a while to understand that it doesn't work like that. I know that some depressions must be treated by a professional, so if it looks like she needs help I'll take her to a doctor, but I also understand that there are times in life when teenage girls are just ... sad. As their hormones change and mature it just happens.

So what can I do for my daughter? Love her. Just be there for her if she wants to talk. Do fun things with her when she's willing. But mostly, just love her and remember that, truthfully ... I get sad sometimes too.

Dear Father, it's hard to see my daughter so sad. Help me to consistently just love her and not try to fix her problems. Father, reach out to her and remind her of Your love for her! Amen.

JULY 24

Desires of the Heart

*The plans of the LORD stand firm forever, the purpose
of His heart through all generations. Psalm 33:11*

Most children are asked hundreds of times what they want
to be when they grow up. Of course it's fun for them to
dream that they can be anything they want to be, but as
children grow older the actual desires of their hearts come
to the forefront.

From the time my son was quite small, my husband and
I told him that he could be anything he wanted to be. We
wanted him to believe that. Of course he went the gamut of
fireman to president. However, along with our encouragement, we also taught him that God loves him very much and
has a wonderful plan for his life.

My prayer for my son is that as he grows, the desires of
his heart will be the same as God's plan for his life. I know
that as he gets to know God better and better, the gifts God
has given him will become evident and I pray that he will
long to use them in service to God. What a joy to know your
children are serving God and fulfilling the desires of their
hearts at the same time!

Dear Father, I pray that You would take hold of my son's heart
so that as he grows up and makes plans for his life, Your goals
will be the desires of his heart. Father, lead him! Amen.

JULY 25

Dependence

"I lay a stone in Zion, a tested stone, a precious cornerstone for a sure foundation; the one who trusts will never be dismayed." Isaiah 28:16

When my children were very small they were pretty much completely dependent on me. As they have grown up they have become less and less dependent and more and more independent.

I know that's a natural process and I encourage it, however, it has also been a lesson to me. Their independence from me has become a reminder to me to check where my dependence lies. If my foundation – the strength and steadiness that keeps me going through life – is not on Jesus Christ, then there is always the danger of everything crumbling and falling away. It is so tiring to live my life when my foundation is not on Christ; why do I do that?

I want to strive to model for my children that the only sure foundation is Jesus. Friends and family are certainly important and are true blessings but none of them should ever be more important than Jesus. Standing on the foundation of His love and power will make each of us better people and help us through the storms of life.

Dear Father, thank You for the foundation of Jesus. I know I can always depend on Him and stand strong because of Him. Thank You for Your love and power that guide me through life. Amen.

Positive Words

Humble yourselves before the Lord, and He will lift you up. James 4:10

Being an encourager is really a gift because, if we're honest with ourselves, we all get discouraged once in a while. Being an encourager does not mean you have to have all the answers. It means sticking close when someone you care about is going through a difficult time. Having a friend or family member who walks through painful times with you is such a blessing. Honest encouragement lifts the spirit and gives hope.

An encourager does not always have to say positive words – sometimes that isn't appropriate. Often an encourager sits beside someone in pain and is just ... there. A friend who can offer hope through her presence and gentle reminders of God's presence and His plans can bring a ray of light.

Even without the spiritual gift of encouragement, this is a reminder to me to offer encouragement to those I love and sometimes to just be with them. It is an opportunity to point our loved ones to God's Word and the encouragement that comes from it.

Dear Father, thank You for the people in my life who can bring encouragement either through their presence or through their words. Father, help me to be sensitive to my children, my husband, my friends and to see ways to encourage them. Amen.

Childlike Enthusiasm

Shout for joy to the LORD, all the earth. Worship the LORD with gladness; come before Him with joyful songs. Psalm 100:1-2

My little children enjoy life! It's so much fun to see life through their eyes. They get so excited about something as ordinary as a butterfly or a tiny yellow flower.

There are times when their enthusiasm makes me smile and reminds me to stop and appreciate the world around me. But, truthfully, there are also times when their joy and desire to stop and admire things slows me down. I want to pull them forward and get on with the tasks of my day.

My prayer is that for once, I will learn from my children and slow down, "Stop and smell the roses" so to speak. God has given us such a wonderful, creative world. If I don't slow down and appreciate it then I am in danger of missing everyday blessings. Have I come to expect things like sunshine, birds, flowers? I don't want to do that. I want to appreciate all that God gives. I want to celebrate life with enthusiasm as my children do!

Dear Father, thank You for the enthusiasm my children share for life. I am so very thankful for all You do for us each day. I'm thankful for this beautiful, creative world. Help me appreciate it even more as I see it through my children's eyes! Amen.

JULY 28

Little Eyes Are Watching

If you want to enjoy life and see many happy days, keep your tongue from speaking evil and your lips from telling lies. Search for peace, and work to maintain it. 1 Peter 3:10-11 NLT

Parents don't always pay attention to how much their children notice what is going on around them. The truth is that their little eyes are watching ... closely. They notice whether their parents' actions match their words. They notice whether their parents practice what they preach.

This makes me pay attention to my actions and my words. Since I tell my children to pray about their problems, seeking God's guidance and help, then I had better be doing that too! Since I tell my children to be quiet if they can't say something nice about others then I'd better watch my own words. Since I encourage my children to give generously of their time and money to God's work, it is important that I model that for them.

My children are watching all the time so it is extra important for me to honestly live my life before them.

Dear Father, I want to live my life for You. The fact that my children notice if my words and actions match makes it even more important that I live honestly. Help me to be diligent in following You. Amen.

No Excuses

*Since you call on a Father who judges each man's work impartially,
live your lives as strangers here in reverent fear. 1 Peter 1:17*

Here's an interesting observation ... when my children disobey or do something wrong, I will not accept any excuses they make for their behavior. My philosophy is that they know the rules so there is no excuse for disobeying them. If they do something wrong it is because they didn't think before acting. However, when I make a mistake or do something that really is not right ... my excuses count.

Shouldn't I either offer my children the same right to justify their actions as I have or do away with my own excuses? If I'm honest with myself then I should believe that what's fair for them should be what's fair for me.

What am I teaching them about honesty if I make excuses for my actions instead of facing the consequences or even just apologizing? Now, while they are young, is the time to teach them to take ownership of their choices. I must model that.

Dear Father, I really don't like to admit it when I'm wrong or when I've messed up. Help me to be honest enough and courageous enough to do so. Help me to remember that I'm teaching my children good things by being honest. Amen.

Believing in Christ

*All have sinned and fall short of the glory of God, and are justified
freely by His grace through the redemption that came by Christ Jesus.*
Romans 3:23-24

The greatest privilege I have had as a parent was being able to pray with my daughter as she accepted Jesus as her Savior. What a joy! It was interesting to see how God used everyday experiences in her life to move her to this decision for faith. Her simple six-year-old explanations of why she believes Jesus came to earth, lived, died and rose again all for her was precious.

It reminded me of how simple God's love for each of us really is. Adults make it so complicated and put such parameters on the Christian life. God must just shake His head at us sometimes.

It is going to be a pleasure nurturing my daughter's faith and helping her grow in her understanding of God's plan and in living her life for God. I'm sure I will be reminded to simplify my faith walk too. As my young child learns to simply trust, I will be reminded to push away some of the ways I've polluted the simplicity of my walk with Christ.

Dear Father, thank You that my daughter has come to know You early. What a joy to be able to celebrate that with her! I pray that her faith will grow and that her walk with You will be strong. Amen.

August

Now What?

Don't be misled — you cannot mock the justice of God.
You will always harvest what you plant. Galatians 6:7 NLT

I'm facing a situation I never expected to face and I'm not sure how to handle it. My daughter was caught red-handed defacing school property. What was she thinking? I'm totally baffled as to why she did this. She likes school.

I want to blame this on her friends' influence, but that's not fair. She must take responsibility for her own actions, regardless of what her friends were doing or encouraging her to do. She must take whatever punishment the school gives her, along with the punishment her father and I will give her. She must also make restitution to the school from her own savings for the damage done.

The lesson I want her to learn from this is that every action has a result. Actions have consequences and I want her to learn this now. It's a hard lesson but a necessary one.

Dear Father, I feel like I've failed as a parent, yet I've tried to teach my daughter right from wrong. I never expected something like this. Make this a learning experience for her – one that makes such an impression that she never wants to face it again. Amen.

Secret Joy

As for me, it is good to be near God. I have made the Sovereign
LORD my refuge; I will tell of all Your deeds. Psalm 73:28

Don't tell my children, but I love it when they are ill or afraid. Does that sound mean? I don't intend for it to be. It's just that when they are sick or scared, they need me.

Since they've gotten older and a little more self-sufficient, they don't voluntarily snuggle on the sofa with me or lie on the bed and talk and talk or sing silly songs – all the things we used to do when they were toddlers. But when they get sick or scared, they still come running to me. I love that. I love meeting their needs, calming their fears, protecting them. I love to be needed.

Wow, I just realized the comparison of that situation to my relationship with God. I'm so much more likely to run to Him when I'm scared or have problems. I bet He misses me too.

Just as I long for connections with my kids, I know God longs for them with me. So I'll make time for Him in my day and sit on the sofa and talk with Him. I guess I just learned something from my kids again!

Dear Father, thank You for the reminder that You enjoy spending time with me just as I enjoy being with my children. Father, I enjoy being with You too. I'll make time for You in my day. Amen.

True Confession

These commandments that I give you today are to be upon your hearts. Impress them on your children. Talk about them when you lie down and when you get up. Deuteronomy 6:6-7

I was never one of those girls who dreamed of becoming a mommy some day. I wanted to travel the world and see all the places I had read about. I wanted to start a career and make a mark in the world. I wanted to "be somebody." But then I met this wonderful guy who I just couldn't get off my mind. Before long we were married ... and then the babies started coming.

Nine years and three children later and I still haven't been out of the country. Pretty much all I've seen are children's museums. My career dreams are packed up in boxes in the attic. And I ... have never been happier.

I wanted to make a mark in the world and that's exactly what I'm doing. I'm making a mark in three young lives by teaching them to be responsible people, by teaching them about God's love for them, and how Jesus died for them. I might not "be somebody" in the eyes of the business world but in the eyes of my children I'm pretty wonderful!

Dear Father, it's funny how my dreams have changed over the years. I can honestly say, "Thank You" for the privilege of being a mom to three wonderful children. I can't imagine doing anything else! Amen.

Persistent Prayers

"Ask and it will be given to you; seek and you will find; knock and the door will be opened to you. For everyone who asks receives; he who seeks finds; and to him who knocks, the door will be opened." Matthew 7:7-8

How long, O Lord? I've prayed and prayed for my son to return to You. My heart aches for him. As a child he gave his heart to the Lord, he went to church with us and was active in a youth group all through high school. He seemed to take his faith seriously, but when he left for college I think he left his faith here at home.

Ever since his college days he has had no use for God at all. He doesn't care about what Jesus did for him. He just isn't interested in anything related to Christianity. I pray for him every day, many times a day, to return to the faith of his childhood. I claim God's promises about children returning to Him.

However, I also know that my son has free will and it's his choice. So, I pray and pray. I love him and I won't let this become an issue between us. I know I can't bring it up each time I see him. I don't want to do anything to push him farther away. So, I pray.

Dear Father, I pray for my son to return to You. I'm worried about what he may have to go through in order for that to happen, but I must trust You. The most important thing is that my son's heart returns to You. Amen.

Prayer Time?

"I am the vine; you are the branches. If a man remains in Me and I in him,
he will bear much fruit; apart from Me you can do nothing."
John 15:5

Somehow I don't think that God's intent was for my prayer time to be reduced to the fifteen minutes I have while I'm waiting in the carpool line or waiting for gymnastics lessons to end. Now that I think about it, that kind of makes my time with God seem like an intrusion in my life; like I fit it in wherever I can instead of making it a priority. Wow, that's just wrong.

Yes, my life is super busy, but do I really want to relegate something as important as private time with God to stoplights and parking lots? Yes, I can certainly pray at those times, too, but personal, dedicated quiet time should not be shared with watching for the car line to move or the stoplight to change.

So what am I going to do about this? I'm going to start realistically with fifteen minutes of by-myself-alone-with-God quiet time each day. I'll carve it into my day. Then the parking-lot prayers will be bonus time!

Dear Father, I confess that I've been lazy about spending time with You. You are important to me so I want time with You to be a priority. Help me to protect my time with You and not let other things crowd it out. Amen.

Communicating

"He calls his own sheep by name and leads them out. When he has brought out all his own, he goes on ahead of them, and his sheep follow him because they know his voice." John 10:3-4

I love that my toddler is learning to communicate. Oh, he doesn't use actual words yet, but he is definitely communicating. I have to hide my smile when he stands straight and tall and babbles on and on about something that is obviously very important to him.

Oddly enough, I can often figure out what topic his babble is about. How do I do that? I guess the simplest answer is that I know my son. I know him so I can look into his eyes, listen to the inflections of his voice and often figure out how to respond to him. There's a lot to be said for knowing someone that well.

I wonder if I know my heavenly Father well enough to know His voice and figure out what He is saying? Jesus said that the sheep would know their Shepherd's voice, but I guess that can't happen if I'm not spending enough time with Him to hear His voice.

Dear Father, I'm continually amazed at the things I learn about my life with You through the experience of being a mom. Thank You for teaching me through the everyday things of life. Amen.

AUGUST 6

Birthday Parties

Finally, all of you, live in harmony with one another; be sympathetic,
love as brothers, be compassionate and humble. 1 Peter 3:8

I'm so very proud of my son. What he did today showed me the condition of his heart ... and it's in really good condition. There is a boy in my son's class at school who is, ummm, neglected might be a good word. To my knowledge his parents have never attended a school program and his mother has never volunteered for holiday parties. He doesn't seem to have many friends and he pretty much keeps to himself.

Somehow my son found out that this little boy has never, ever had a birthday party. Never. My son came right home and announced to me, "We're having a birthday party!" He had already made arrangements with the teacher. He spent the evening making plans for decorations, cupcakes and punch. He even spent his own money to buy a small present. I'm proud of his sensitive heart and of his sacrificial investment in this project.

The little boy to be honored is going to be so surprised!

Dear Father, thank You for the kind and generous heart my son has. Planning a party is one thing, but spending his own money on it and getting his buddies excited about it shows that he is committed to it. Bless him and bless the little boy for whom the party is held. Amen.

Thinking about the Kids

Search me, O God, and know my heart; test me and know my
anxious thoughts. See if there is any offensive way in me,
and lead me in the way everlasting. Psalm 139:23-24

When my husband and I got married we took our commitment seriously. The vows we made were to be for life. Divorce was never an option. But through the years something has happened. We argue and fight all the time now; we can barely say a civil word to each other. I see the fear in my children's eyes as our arguments escalate into shouting matches. I know we should just stop and have a civil conversation about whatever it is we're fighting about, but we don't seem to be able to do that.

I don't want my children to be afraid of having Mommy and Daddy home at the same time. I don't want them to worry that our family is going to break up (though I'm worried about that too). So I'm going to ask God to examine my heart and reveal to me where I've become self-centered and impatient. I'm going to ask God to restore my love for the man I married; to show me again the man I fell in love with. Maybe he will do the same and our marriage can be saved.

Dear Father, divorce is not an option I want to consider. Remind me of why I once loved my husband. Renew that love. Please save our marriage. Amen.

AUGUST 8

New Mom Thoughts

The Spirit helps us in our weakness. We do not know what we ought to pray for, but the Spirit Himself intercedes for us with groans that words cannot express. Romans 8:26-27

I'm a mom. We waited nine months, planning, dreaming and preparing, and now the baby is here. We did everything we could to prepare for this baby. The nursery is painted, the crib is up, the mobile is hung, the dresser is filled with freshly-washed clothes, diapers are on the changing table. Everything is ready. Everything except ... me. I don't know how to take care of a baby. How will I know when she's hungry? What if I don't know why she is crying? How will I know what her routine is?

I don't even know how to hold a baby. I'm scared! Is it really instinctive to know how to care for my baby? Even if it isn't, I know that my mother, my mother-in-law and my friends will help. I guess God has taken care of me already by surrounding me with people who can give me advice and share their wisdom. This will be the most important job I will ever have and I don't want to mess it up!

Dear Father, thank You for the people in my life who can help me learn to be a good parent. Thank You for their wisdom. Help me to be a good mother. Amen.

Respecting Elders

"Rise in the presence of the aged, show respect for the elderly and revere your God. I am the LORD." Leviticus 19:32

Teachers who have been working with students for a long time often say that respect is disappearing from our children today. The way students treat their teachers makes being a teacher very difficult. I do not want that to happen with my children. While encouraging them to be independent and to explore their talents and their interests, it would not be acceptable for them to stop treating their elders with honor and respect.

I believe it is my responsibility as a parent to teach my children to speak with respect, to be obedient, and to honor those who are older than they are — whether it is a teacher, grandparent or neighbor.

This simple act of respect is the right way for a child to treat those who are older and more experienced than they are. Being respectful will show their understanding of the wisdom of those who are older and the fact that they can learn much from them.

Dear Father, help me understand how to teach this element of respect to my children in a world that is pulling in the other direction. Father, help my children to embrace this teaching and may respect flow from their hearts. Amen.

Protection

Don't let anyone look down on you because you are young, but set an example for the believers in speech, in life, in love, in faith and in purity.
1 Timothy 4:12

I am amazed at the garbage on television, I am appalled at the smut on the Internet and I am even upset at things that are in some books.

"Some people" have made the decision that my children should be exposed to all kinds of junk in order for them to know what the world is really like and what voices should be heard. I disagree. I hold this opinion I am determined to pay attention to what kinds of things are being fed into my children's brains.

While some may think I'm overprotective or super conservative, I feel that I'm protecting my children's minds and hearts. You see, I believe that what goes into a child's mind and heart definitely affects what grows there.

My desire is for the grace, kindness and love of Jesus to grow in their hearts and minds, so more than ever it is important to monitor what they see and hear.

Dear Father, I know I'm sometimes unpopular because of the limits I put on my children's viewing, gaming and Internet time, but I really want their minds to be filled with positive and Christ-honoring things. So help me to be diligent in this. Amen.

Quick Meals

Then will I go to the altar of God, to God, my joy and my delight.
I will praise You with the harp, O God, my God. Psalm 43:4

Is it really a big deal if I don't cook dinner that often for my family? Oh, we eat together pretty much every night, but it is seldom something that I've actually cooked and not just heated up or microwaved. I don't really enjoy cooking. In fact, I'm not much for housework at all these days. I would much rather spend my time playing in the yard with my children or listening to them as they talk together and dream big.

Someday, when my kids are grown up, I'll have time for the chores I don't get done now. I can cook gourmet meals, make sure my house is spotless and do all the domestic goddess things I'm skipping now. But my joy right now is playing with my children; making memories with them – and if that means we eat bologna sandwiches for dinner, so be it.

I never want to forget that these children are a gift from God. I want to enjoy every minute of their young lives. Chores can wait … children won't.

Dear Father, my children are growing up so fast. Some days I wish I could put life on hold and just soak in the joy of the stages they are at. Help me to enjoy every moment with them. Amen.

Seeing the Joy Each Day

Let them sacrifice thank offerings and tell of His works with songs of joy.
Psalm 107:22

I have a confession ... some days I am not very joyous. And ... part two of my confession is that I resent the Christians around me who make me feel guilty for part number one. OK, now I can face this head-on. The Bible tells me that the fruit of the Spirit is love, joy ... so I should be joyful.

Why does my joy sometimes disappear and become so difficult to discover again? I believe it's because I take my eyes off the Lord. I notice the joylessness most when I'm caught up in the busyness of life and how everything affects me and how my children are not obedient.

How do I pull the joy back in? Well, I'm taking baby steps by stopping each day to thank my Father for the gift of that day. Then I thank Him for the gift of my children, my husband, and my friends. Thankfulness is the foundation I'm building on. I believe that joy will follow. I can't be truly joy-filled if I'm not first thankful.

Dear Father, I take so many of Your gifts for granted and that's when my joy disappears. Thank You for Your love and patience with me. Fill me with the joy of thankfulness for all that You give me. Amen.

Focused Worship

The LORD your God is a consuming fire, a jealous God.
Deuteronomy 4:24

I'm amazed at how subtly things change in my life. Once again I've learned an important life lesson by listening to my children. I was driving my son and his friends somewhere yesterday and listening as they talked about their favorite sports teams and favorite professional athletes.

I was struck by the awe in their voices as they spoke about these people – it almost sounded like worship. I made a mental note to talk with my son about it later.

As I thought about it, I realized how easy it is to change the focus of worship from God to other things. God spoke to my heart about the importance of my home. I take great pride in decorating my home and spend a lot of energy, thought and money on it. Has it become the focus of my worship? I wouldn't have thought so, but as I measure the time I spend on it versus the time I give to the Lord and my attitudes about Him, I think I need to readjust things.

I will still have a conversation with my son, but it will be a lot more honest than I first thought.

Dear Father, I don't want to allow anything in my life to crowd You out. My worship should be focused only on You. Forgive me, Father, and give me the strength and focus to keep You in first place. Amen.

Worry vs. Trust

"Do not worry about your life, what you will eat or drink; or about your body, what you will wear. Is not life more important than food, and the body more important than clothes? Who of you by worrying can add a single hour to his life?" Matthew 6:25, 27

People say worry and trust can't live in the same heart. So when I learn that something awful has happened, like a child being kidnapped in our area; I should not worry for my child's safety? That sounds very spiritual, but not very realistic.

What is realistic for me is that too much worry denies God's presence and control in my life and that of my child. I try to use the energy that worry produces to be more diligent in caring for my child and being aware of the world around us. But the first twinge of worry causes me to turn to God and pray diligently for His protection and wisdom. I don't believe worry is a bad thing if I let it be my motivation for turning to God.

As much as I would like to be, I'm not in control of what happens to my child. However, God is in control. He has told me that He loves me and my child. I can trust Him. Worry? A little. Trust? A lot.

Dear Father, worry can become consuming and pull me farther away from You. I don't want to ever let that happen. So when worry creeps into my heart, remind me immediately to turn to You. Amen.

A Woman's Work

Whatever you do, work at it with all your heart, as working for the Lord, not for men. Colossians 3:23

The old saying, "A woman's work is never done" is ringing through my head because it is true. Three young children keep my house ... a mess. There is so much to be done! Cooking, cleaning, laundry, ironing, chauffeuring, school projects and shopping are only a few of my chores. Plus there are the things I do for friends and church and school clubs.

To keep my sanity I approach work from two directions: one is to just be thankful that I can work. I am grateful that I am physically able to accomplish the things I want to. Secondly, I am teaching my children to work. I want them to see the benefit of starting a project and seeing it through all the way to the finish.

I want them to understand that God actually cares about their work because the choice to do work well, with perseverance and honesty, brings glory to Him.

Dear Father, thank You that I can work. I'm sorry that I sometimes complain about it. I'm thankful that I can contribute to the world around me and that there is purpose in my day because of my work. Help me to teach my children the blessing of work. Amen.

AUGUST 16

The Gift of the Word

All Scripture is God-breathed and is useful for teaching, rebuking, correcting and training in righteousness, so that the man of God may be thoroughly equipped for every good work. 2 Timothy 3:16-17

I'm so thankful to have the Word of God available to read whenever I want to. I'm so thankful that God gave us His Word and that I can learn to know Him better and serve Him more faithfully through reading it. The Bible never fails to speak to me and challenge me to serve Him more faithfully, obey Him more diligently and love Him and others more fully.

I'm also thankful for children's Bibles and Bible storybooks. Because these books make God's Word understandable and relevant to children at such a young age, I believe they will grow up with an appreciation for the Bible. Of course, as they mature, they graduate to more mature versions of God's Word.

The Scriptures ... God's words to His people are also for my children and I appreciate that they can learn from the Bible even at their young ages.

Dear Father, thank You for Your words to us. I so appreciate that I can read Your Word and know that it contains a message You want me to know. Thank You that my children can also read Your Word in a way that speaks to them. Teach us, Father, always teach us. Amen.

Sharing the Good News

"You will receive power when the Holy Spirit comes on you;
and you will be My witnesses in Jerusalem, and in all Judea
and Samaria, and to the ends of the earth." Acts 1:8

Once again I've learned something from one of my children. It was my nine-year-old son this time. Kids can be so uninhibited sometimes. My son and a friend were playing in the backyard and through the open window I heard my son say, "Dude, you should come to my church with me." His friend mumbled something, but my son picked it right back up.

"Yeah, 'cause you're a sinner who does bad things. It's OK, though, cause we all do bad things. God will forgive you. Seriously, you should come and learn all about it."

Wow. My son is witnessing – actually witnessing. I have to admit that I'm too inhibited and nervous to be as direct as he is, but the fact is that we Christians have the best news ever – God loves you – so we should be sharing it with everyone we meet. I'm going to take a lesson from my son and share the wonderful and urgent news of God's love with my friends and family.

Dear Father, the truth that You love me and all people is incredible. Father, please give me the confidence and courage to willingly share this good news. You instructed Your children to do so and I want to be obedient. Thank You for my son's example. Amen.

Sharing Wisdom

She speaks with wisdom, and faithful instruction is on her tongue.
Proverbs 31:26

Teenagers think they know everything about everything. I know – I apparently lost my intelligence this year (according to my daughter). My daughter is a junior in high school and is beginning to look at colleges and careers. She's pretty sure that she has all the answers, but I'm not sure she even knows what the questions are.

I'd like to be able to share things that I've learned through the years and impart some of my hard-earned wisdom to her, but dumping it on her without her asking for it just means it will run off like rainwater on a rock.

What can I do? Well, one of the bits of wisdom I've gained is the understanding that true wisdom comes only from God. So I can diligently pray for her as she makes choices and plans for her future. I can be available to talk with her when she does ask for my view on something, and I can think before I speak so I don't push her away. Sigh ... there's that message of self-control again. It seems to be a guide word for parenting!

Dear Father, I love my daughter so much and I want the best for her life. I pray that she will seek Your guidance and wisdom. I pray that she will be comfortable enough to talk with me about her plans. Amen.

Strong Kids

*If you are wise and understand God's ways, prove it by
living an honorable life, doing good works with
the humility that comes from wisdom. James 3:13*

AAAHHHHH! I'm going to scream. I've read a gazillion books about parenting a strong-willed child and listened to the experts' advice on the radio. I don't know whether my daughter is exceptionally strong-willed or whether I'm a slow learner, but none of the answers are working!

I sometimes wonder what life holds for my little girl that made God think she is going to need to be so strong-willed. That kind of scares me. Our battles are so frequent and so powerful that I'm emotionally drained most of the time.

Sometimes I give in just because I'm tired of fighting. I know it isn't the right thing to do. I don't want her to be an obnoxious kid who others don't want to be around, but I'm out of ideas. I simply can't deal with this child without God's patience, wisdom and strength. I know I must be consistent in my dealings with her and I must also convey to her that I love her with all my heart.

Dear Father, help me to know how to parent my daughter. Help me to be consistent with her and give me wisdom and discernment in knowing how to deal with her powerful and strong will. Amen.

AUGUST 20

Keeping Up

Each one should use whatever gift he has received to serve others, faithfully administering God's grace in its various forms. 1 Peter 4:10

We live in one of the wealthiest counties – the US – even though we're not particularly wealthy. Our children struggle with the dichotomy of their friends driving brand-new convertibles to school while they ride the bus. They wonder why we can't spend spring break skiing in the Alps instead of visiting grandma in the Midwest. The bottom line is that we can't keep up with the financial levels of their classmates – we just can't.

The thing is, even if we could, we might choose not to. We try to teach our children the futility of living beyond your means. It's hard when we're competing with such excesses. Our kids are ... kids ... and they don't always understand what we're saying, but we are consistent about it. We explain the instructions from God's Word to share what we have with those who are less fortunate.

We have what we need, if not what we want, but there are others who do not even have what they need. We don't judge anyone else's choices, we just choose to live within our means and share what we can with others.

Dear Father, help my children to understand our decision to stay within our means rather than keeping up with others. Help us to think about others and give as much as we can to help them. Amen.

Undergirding My Child

So this is what the Sovereign LORD says: "See, I lay a stone in Zion,
a tested stone, a precious cornerstone for a sure foundation;
the one who trusts will never be dismayed." Isaiah 28:16

The pressures bombarding my adolescent daughter keep me on my knees. I'm amazed at how young the pressures begin. How does the age keep creeping down as to when the temptations toward drugs, drinking and such begin?

It began so quickly that I wonder if we have prepared our daughter for it. Does she have the foundation and the information to stand firm against such temptations? I didn't expect this for a couple of years yet so I am a little stunned that it has already begun.

At least my daughter is telling me about the conversations she has had with classmates and some of the "offers" they made her to have "fun." I'm thankful that I have a chance to talk things through with her. I am diligently praying for my daughter. I'm calling on God to surround her with His angels, fill her with wisdom, and just protect her in general. I want her foundation … her undergirding … to be God and His love for her.

Dear Father, this is the scary part of parenting. Keep my daughter safe. Give her wisdom and discernment in the choices she makes. Keep the communication between us open. Amen.

New Kittens!

*My frame was not hidden from You when I was made in the secret place.
When I was woven together in the depths of the earth, Your
eyes saw my unformed body. All the days ordained for me were
written in Your book before one of them came to be. Psalm 139:15-16*

What a great learning experience! Our cat just had kittens
and my young children had lots and lots of questions about
the baby kitties. It was a joy to explain God's plan of babies
being formed inside their mother's body.

Of course they had even more questions so we pulled
out pictures of each of them when they were newborns.
It was fun. When they saw the tiny kittens with their eyes
closed my children were worried that the kittens were blind.
We went right back to their own pictures and they saw how
their own eyes were opened wider in each picture.

It was an amazing opportunity to explain how, even as a
newborn person or kitten, everything that little body needs
to become a full-grown adult is already inside it. What a
creative God with such an incredible plan. My children were
amazed. In fact, so was I ... all over again!

Dear Father, I am amazed at Your creative plan for forming new
life. You are amazing. Thank You for the opportunity to share
this plan with my young children and for the wonderful miracle
of brand-new kittens! Amen.

Homebound

Do not be overcome by evil, but overcome evil with good. Romans 12:21

We raise our children to mature into adulthood, start a career, find a spouse and move into their own homes to start a family. That's the plan. So, why is my twenty-seven-year-old son still living at home, working at a part-time job with no leaving in sight?

Maybe I've made it too easy for him to be at home. I thought I was just being a mom or showing my love for him when I cooked his meals, did his laundry, paid for his gas and even gave him a few dollars when he was a bit short on cash, but perhaps I've been putting him off growing up.

Whew, this is hard. I want him to become the man God has always planned for him to be and I know the seeds are there for that to happen. Somewhere along the line my son lost his drive for independence and forgot who he is in God's eyes. It makes me sad, but I know it isn't hopeless. I'll pray for him with lots of energy and do all I can to encourage him to take some risks.

Dear Father, my son has so much potential. I know You can do amazing things in his life. Father, help him find the drive to move forward in his life. Help him overcome whatever has paralyzed him in the last few years. Amen.

Learning from Failure

*Then the LORD said to Joshua, "Do not be afraid;
do not be discouraged." Joshua 8:1*

When a child first experiences personal failure it is hard for a mom to know how to handle the child's emotions. My fifth-grade daughter failed a test. It's the first time she has ever failed anything so she's not sure how to handle it. I think she is embarrassed, frustrated and afraid that this might be opening a door to more failures. My job is to help her learn from her failure. I've even read her stories of some of our biggest biblical heroes and their failures.

As seen in many of their lives, one failure doesn't mean a ruined life or a string of more failures. There are lessons to be learned from failures that will ensure no more failures in the future.

The subject that my daughter failed is one that doesn't come easily to her so we will study it together for a while. She will be diligent in studying for the next exam. We also discussed some of her successes so she doesn't just focus on her failure. The reality is that failure is a part of life. This is a good chance for her to learn how to handle it and move forward.

Dear Father, give me wisdom in facing my daughter's emotions with regard to failure. Help her to understand there are lessons to be learned from failing. Amen.

Wedding Planning

Then Jesus told His disciples a parable to show them
that they should always pray and not give up.
Luke 18:1

My daughter and I planned her wedding together. It was such fun to work on it with her. Shopping and making things and looking through magazines … We made a lot of memories.

Now my son is getting married and I … don't have much to do. I love my son and I adore my soon-to-be daughter-in-law so it's hard not to be in the middle of all the planning. However, the most important thing is to keep a good relationship with both of them and not be pegged as a pushy, problem-causing mother-in-law.

So, I'm focusing my energy on praying for them. Every time I start to feel left out, I just stop and pray for the process of planning a wedding. I pray for their unity in the plans. I pray for the family they are establishing. I pray for their ministry as a couple. I may not be helping to plan a wedding, but I'm playing a part in the planning of their life together!

Dear Father, thanks for this insight of how I can participate in my son's wedding. I do pray for them as they start a new life together. Bless their new family. Use them for Your purposes. Amen.

A Full Heart

*I have no greater joy than to hear that
my children are walking in the truth.*
3 John 4

Like so many other little girls, when I was young I dreamt of being a mom someday. I thought it would be so much fun to have a noisy house full of children running about.

From the moment I learned I was pregnant with my first child, I anticipated and enjoyed every step of the process. I loved being pregnant and, amazingly, I even enjoyed labor and the delivery. The long sleepless nights of having a newborn in the house weren't even all that bad.

When my little ones were toddlers I loved teaching them and seeing the world through their discovering eyes. It has been a joy to see their personalities develop and notice how they are like me or like their father. I've loved reading Bible stories with them and sharing my faith so that they can understand.

My heart is truly filled with the joy of parenting. I'm so grateful to God that my dream came true!

Dear Father, thank You for the privilege of being a mother to these amazing children. Thank You for the joy of teaching them and sharing with them. Thank You for the thrill of telling them about You. My heart is truly filled with joy! Amen.

Don't Give Up

Consider it pure joy, my brothers, whenever you face trials of many kinds, because you know that the testing of your faith develops perseverance. Perseverance must finish its work so that you may be mature and complete, not lacking anything. James 1:2-4

Some people have a natural drive to work hard. They find the obstacles of a project motivating and enjoy the challenge of overcoming them. Others are quite willing to just give up.

My son is more in that last group. Challenges seem to knock the drive right out of him. It has become my project to encourage him to get creative in finding ways to overcome obstacles and keep going forward.

I'm more aware than ever of the many verses encouraging perseverance and persistence and the offers of God's strength and power. Once my son saw a little glimpse of the end result of sticking with something to the end, whether it was learning a new sports skill, finishing a chore or working through a problem with a friend, he was motivated to keep trying. Now his motto is "Keep on keeping on!"

Dear Father, this has been a challenge for me. I don't want my son to miss the feeling of accomplishment when he overcomes an obstacle. It's an amazing feeling. Help me to motivate him. Help him understand the joy of working hard to achieve something. Amen.

Self-Control

The fruit of the Spirit is love, joy, peace, patience, kindness, goodness, faithfulness, gentleness and self-control. Galatians 5:22-23

I'm not good at self-control. I know it's one of the fruit of the Spirit, but it's not one of my strong points. I'm working on it, but for now, when my almost two-year-old throws a classic temper tantrum, my self-control is not very good. The experts say that when this happens I should just walk away from him and ignore the tantrum. In theory, when he sees that his tantrum isn't working, he will stop and get on with life.

This has become a matter of prayer – how to react to his tantrums, strength to have self-control, actually knowing (and believing) what is the best way to handle his tantrum.

Admittedly I don't always do the right thing, but sometimes I do. There is a lot at stake here. If I react in anger then I'm teaching my child that is the correct way to respond. If I don't react at all, though, am I teaching him that tantrums are OK because sometimes he might get his way? Big responsibility that I can only handle with God's help!

Dear Father, I want to do the right thing. Fill me with Your Spirit so that self-control flows from me. Father, help me to react and respond in a way that honors You. Amen.

Know When to Stop

*Out of the same mouth come praise
and cursing. This should not be.* James 3:10

Most parents teach their children that honesty is the best policy. We even tell them that they will not get in trouble for what they say if they tell the truth. Whew! That's all true, but there is another element to honest speaking that we also need to impress on our children.

We need to teach them when to speak and how much to speak. Even when the truth is spoken, it must be done with kindness and respect. For example, there's little kindness in telling an overweight woman that she is fat – especially in public. There is a point where we all have to reign in our tongues and think about how our words may affect the other person – or how our children may hear them and then repeat them to others.

So the lesson is, "Think before you speak." Think about what you're saying and whether it needs to be said. Think about how your words will make another person feel. Think about how your children will hear your words. Just think.

Dear Father, this is a lesson I need to be reminded of even as I teach it to my children. I must think before speaking – think of others and whether my words will be perceived as filled with kindness and respect. If not ... be quiet! Amen.

Modeling Obedience

Bear with each other and forgive whatever grievances you may have against one another. Forgive as the Lord forgave you. Colossians 3:13

We are quite strict about obedience from our children. My husband and I have been firm on this because we feel our rules are fair and are there to protect our children. The rules are in place because we love them.

Yes, we did adapt that process from the way our heavenly Father cares for us. He has set rules and standards for us to obey to make us better people, better followers of Christ, better spouses, better parents and better friends. Sometimes they are just to keep us safe.

Do we always obey? No. Just as our children disobey our rules sometimes, we disobey God too. Sometimes our actions are flat – out rebellion; sometimes an accident; sometimes just lack of thought, but disobedience is disobedience. What we are challenged to remember is how God handles our disobedience. Yes, there is discipline involved, but there is ALWAYS forgiveness and a second chance. God is a pure example of forgiveness and second chances for our children.

Dear Father, thank You for Your constant forgiveness. It makes me feel so loved and I strive to be more obedient each time I realize how much You love me. Help me to model that forgiveness with my children when they disobey. Help them see Your love in me. Amen.

September

Mother/Daughter Time

Though one may be overpowered, two can defend themselves.
A cord of three strands is not quickly broken. Ecclesiastes 4:12

I'm always on the look-out for special ways to connect with my teenage daughter. We have a good relationship but she is often so busy with her friends and school activities that it's easy to lose touch with her. However, we've created a special mother/daughter time that we try to schedule every few weeks: we go for pedicures together!

It could be considered an extravagance, but for me it is a connecting time. We sit next to each other and for an hour or so just chat and laugh with each other and with the lovely technician. These mother/daughter times are such a treat and have really helped us reconnect.

God reminds us often in Scripture to stay connected with one another. There is strength in numbers. I know that if I can keep the lines of communication open with my daughter, I will have more opportunities to encourage her and challenge her and just simply love her. Besides ... pedicures are fun!

Dear Father, thank You for this simple way of providing a connecting time with my daughter. It is such a silly little thing, but I enjoy being with her and talking with her so much. Help me to continually be looking for ways to keep our communication flowing. Amen.

SEPTEMBER 1

Passing Along the Joy

*We have different gifts, according to the grace given us. If a man's
gift is prophesying, let him use it in proportion to his faith.
If it is serving, let him serve; if it is teaching, let him teach;
if it is encouraging, let him encourage. Romans 12:6-8*

My children are adults now and I'm not going to lie; it was a
long road to get here. Although we had our difficult times,
as most families do, we made it through. We all still love
each other. What I mean is ... we did OK as parents.

Now, what should I do with all this wisdom tucked away
in my brain? According to Scripture, I should share it. I know
plenty of young moms who are just beginning the parenting
process and some who are struggling through the teenage
years. They could certainly use the gentle encouragement
of one who made it through successfully.

I won't "dump" answers on them, but I can listen to
them, tell them that things will get better one day, and offer
advice when they ask. I'll be there for these young women
and help, because I have been there.

Dear Father, I know Scripture says to encourage the younger
women. Show me how to do that so that I'm not perceived as
some know-it-all old woman. Father, give me wisdom and the
right words to speak when opportunities arise. Amen.

A Boy?

If I speak in the tongues of men and of angels, but have not love, I am only a resounding gong or a clanging cymbal. If I have a faith that can move mountains, but have not love, I am nothing. 1 Corinthians 13:1-2

OK, I'm a girl ... obviously. I had no brothers. I wasn't close to any of my boy cousins. In short, I don't know much about boys. So, of course, I have a son.

There is no doubt that God has a great sense of humor. I like pink, frilly, nice-smelling stuff, dolls, hair things and nail polish. My son does not like any of those things.

So how am I going to relate to a boy? What will we have in common? What will we do together? Well, I want to learn to do things that he enjoys. He's a big baseball fan and loves to play so I'm going to learn to play catch. He enjoys practicing his game and this will be a great way to connect with him.

Where do I get my example for this? Jesus. He always met people where they were. He often used illustrations from the work that His listeners were involved in. He made sure people understood what He was talking about by identifying with them. What a great idea!

Dear Father, I want to stay connected to my son and make some memories with him. Father, show me ways to connect with him. I love him so much. Amen.

A Fussy Baby

In my distress I called to the LORD; I cried to my God for help. From
His temple He heard my voice; my cry came before Him, into His ears.
Psalm 18:6

Newborn babies cry – I know that. Newborn babies wake up a lot at night – I know that. Newborn babies don't do much except eat, sleep and mess their diapers – I know that too! What I didn't know is that newborn babies cry ... all day ... without really taking a nap longer than fifteen minutes. I'm exhausted. I'm so tired that I sometimes don't know what I'm doing. This afternoon I put the phone book in the freezer!

I'm frustrated that I can't make my own baby stop crying. I feel like a failure. How am I going to get through this? What do I do? I've prayed for God to make her stop crying. He hasn't done that yet, but what He did do was urge a friend to call this afternoon to see how things are going. It helped to tell her and to cry about it.

God has given me a lot of friends and family nearby who are more than willing to help me. I guess He never intended for any of us to try to make it through life alone. That's why He puts people around us.

Dear Father, thank You for help. Thank You for people who care about me. Thank You that they will help me and then I can help them when they need it. Thank You for community. Amen.

Toddler Trials

Worship the LORD with gladness; come before Him with joyful songs.
Psalm 100:2

Some people call children little people, which makes them sound like compressed adults. That certainly explains why a toddler can have SO MUCH ENERGY – it's all that adult energy compressed into a little body! My goodness, my little guy goes non-stop from the time he gets up in the morning until bedtime. I work and work to get a nap in his day; mostly for my benefit. I have to catch my breath some time!

His curiosity keeps him exploring everything. His energy keeps him moving. I love it though. I love the joy and abandon with which he attacks life. He has so many questions and he'll ask them over and over until he gets an answer that makes sense to him.

He's quite the entertainer; he's so funny that he just keeps me laughing and laughing sometimes. He likes that. He's a snuggler too. When he senses I'm sad, he will often climb up on my lap with his sweet smile and just be with me. What a joy my little guy is. What a gift from God!

Dear Father, I can't imagine life without my energetic, inquisitive son. Thank You so much for him. Give me the energy to keep up with him and to enjoy his energy, care and laughter! Amen.

School Daze

May our Lord Jesus Christ Himself and God our Father, who loved us and by His grace gave us eternal encouragement and good hope, encourage your hearts and strengthen you in every good deed and word.
2 Thessalonians 2:16-17

I knew this day had to come but I don't have to like it. My baby is starting school today. She's only five years old. She can't possibly be old enough to go into that big building for several hours a day! OK, fine, she is big enough and she is very excited. She has no idea how much I'm going to miss her!

The day she starts school everything changes and will never really be the same again. Friends will become more important in her life. Her teachers will have a powerful influence over her. She won't need me as much as she used to. How can she be so excited about this change while I'm so nervous?

I have to keep reminding myself that this is the natural, normal process. My baby can't stay a baby forever. God has been growing her body and mind and preparing her for this. I've been teaching her things and now ... she's ready to go to school. She's going to do well and will love it!

Dear Father, this is hard. Take care of my daughter, Father. Help her to choose good friends. Give her good teachers. I can't wait for her to come home and tell me everything that happened. Amen.

SEPTEMBER 6

Peer Pressure Poverty

A friend loves at all times, and a brother is born for adversity.
Proverbs 17:17

I never thought I'd say this, but I kind of wish my daughter was struggling with peer pressure. Crazy, huh?

I guess what I'm saying is that I am concerned because my junior-high daughter doesn't have many friends. She doesn't seem to fit in anywhere. She's not super athletic, musical, or a brain. She's just a nice kid who really cares about others.

I wonder how her self-image is handling this. I worry that she's lonely and I want to fix it! I don't really want her to suffer from peer pressure, I just want her to have a group of friends who see how charming and sweet she is. I want her friends to appreciate her quirky sense of humor and fun-loving nature. I want my little girl to be happy.

Dear Father, I realize that happiness is a fleeting emotion. No one is happy all the time, but You understand how I'm concerned for my daughter. I remember being in junior high and I know that friendships are so important. Father, give her a good friend or two who will appreciate her and enjoy her ... and not pressure her. Amen.

High-School Parties

Though I walk in the midst of trouble, You preserve my life;
with Your right hand You save me. Psalm 138:7

My son is so excited to be in high school. He made the basketball team and is in the drama club. He's also made a lot of new friends. I'm excited for him, but also a little concerned about the opportunities he may have. His dad and I have taught him good moral standards and we've modeled how to make good choices. Now, I just pray that those things will guide him through these days.

It is inevitable that some of the kids he is friends with may pressure him to join them in activities that he normally wouldn't do. Peer pressure can be so strong – everyone wants to fit in and not be considered weird by their classmates.

I know my son may make a few choices I wouldn't want him to make, but I will be surrounding him with prayer every day. I will be praying for his choice of friends, for his strength to withstand temptation, for his faith in God to remain a strong guiding light in his life. I do want my son to enjoy high school.

Dear Father, please protect my son from the pressures of high school. Help him make good choices with his friends and activities. Father, I pray that he has a great experience in high school but that he stays true to his walk with You through these years! Amen.

An Empty House

*LORD, You establish peace for us; all that we
have accomplished You have done for us.*
Isaiah 26:12

I remember how sad I felt when my daughter first started kindergarten. I thought my world had ended because she would never need me again in the same way. I was right; nothing was ever the same once she started school, although she did still need me, just in a different way. Those elementary years were wonderful, junior high was a bit harder and high school had its ups and downs.

Now we're at another crossroads: she is leaving home for a college several hundred miles away. My husband and I are anticipating being empty nesters, but my heart is aching at the same time.

I've heard that sometimes when kids go away to school, they end up staying near the location of the school as their careers begin. So my relationship with my precious daughter is going to change once again. I'll take a deep breath, pray with all my heart, and smile in love as she packs her car and leaves.

Dear Father, I'm going to miss my daughter a lot. I pray that college will be a great experience for her. Bless her with good friends. Keep her safe and guide her class choices and career plans. Bless our new relationship. I know it can be a great one and I look forward to it. Amen.

Taking Care of Business

"Love each other as I have loved you. Greater love has no one than this, that he lay down his life for his friends." John 15:12-14

No doubt every parent prays that their children's lives will be even better than their own has been. I certainly have that hope. Not that my life hasn't been wonderful, it has, but I hope for even more happiness, love, purpose and contentment for my children.

As I've grown more mature I've learned that one of the best things I can do to help my children is to treat their father with kindness, love and respect. Does that sound strange? Think about it, though. If I speak kindly to him (even when I'm frustrated), if I go out of my way to do kind things for him and acts of love (even when he hasn't done that for me) and if I respect his opinions, his career, his parenting style (even when I don't agree), if I thank him for all he does for me, then I'm teaching my children to do the same for their spouses, co-workers and friends.

Treating others with love, kindness and respect will certainly take them a long way to having a good life. That's what I want.

Dear Father, my actions and attitudes impact my children more than just "telling" them what to do. I want to show love and kindness to my husband, after all, I love him. It's just that "I" get in the way sometimes. Help me to get out of the way and just love him. Amen.

SEPTEMBER 10

Battling the World

I have hidden Your word in my heart that I might not sin against You.
Psalm 119:11

My husband and I established our home on the values found in God's Word. It is the foundation for our individual lives and for how we choose to raise our children. However, as our children are growing up we've had to fight to stand firm with our values as the values of the world try to creep in. It's a daily exercise to explain to our children why we believe as we do and why we believe some things are right and some things are wrong based on what we read in God's Word.

At some point our children will decide for themselves what they believe, but we want the foundation of God's Word to have a strong hold on their hearts as they make those choices. At the same time, we strive for them to understand that God's Word and His relationship with His children is not a list of rules, but is a relationship of love and concern for them as individuals and for the world as a whole. We teach them that Jesus lived and died ... for them ... and that He rose again and intercedes for them all the time because He loves them.

Dear Father, the pull of worldly values is so strong and so constant. Help our children withstand them. Father, I pray that their understanding of Your love for them will pull them back to You. Amen.

Red Rover, Red Rover

The LORD is my rock, my fortress and my deliverer;
my God is my rock, in whom I take refuge. He is my shield
and the horn of my salvation, my stronghold. Psalm 18:2

I remember a game we played as children. It was called Red Rover and there were two teams. The members of each team stood shoulder to shoulder, with their arms linked tightly, to withstand the attack of an opposing team member who ran toward them at top speed to try and break through the linked arms of two people. If that person succeeded then they got to capture a member of that team and take her to their team. If the crasher was not successful, he had to stay with the strong team. The goal was to get all the players on your team.

Do you wonder why I'm thinking of this game? Sometimes when the stuff of life is attacking my family I picture us standing shoulder to shoulder, arms linked to withstand the attacks of busyness, worldliness, selfishness, pain ... any problems or negativities that might try to wedge between us. We will stay united and strong ... together with God leading the way before us!

Dear Father, thank You for my family. Help us to stand strong together. Help us to encourage and protect one another. Help us to pray for one another. Help us to love one another. Amen.

SEPTEMBER 12

Crossing the Generation Gap

May the God who gives endurance and encouragement
give you a spirit of unity as you follow Christ Jesus.
Accept one another, then, just as Christ accepted you.
Romans 15:5-7

"You don't understand!" my teenager screams at me as she runs into her room and slams the door. The sad thing is that she's right. I do not fully understand what she is feeling, the pressures on her or the choices before her.

While some things about being a teenager have not changed since my day, the world has certainly changed and that makes for different pressures and different choices. What I do understand is basic ... I love my daughter with all my heart. So I've got to find a bridge across the generation gap. That bridge is built of love – God's love.

I will ask Him to help me understand – to see things from her viewpoint instead of mine. I'm not going to compromise my values or beliefs, but with God's help I will understand hers a little better. Then we can work together to keep communication open and I can encourage and help her through the difficult things. I want to be her ally, not her enemy.

Dear Father, I love my daughter so much, but I don't always understand her. Help her to turn to You for help. Help her to be patient with me as I am patient with her. Father, help us to stay connected. Amen.

The Whole Truth

*Do not lie to each other, since you have taken off your old self with
its practices and have put on the new self, which is being renewed
in knowledge in the image of its Creator.* Colossians 3:9-10

I'm having a "where the rubber meets the road" parenting moment. It's related to telling the truth, the whole truth and nothing but the truth. My young son has figured out a way to answer my questions with only a portion of the truth in order to get what he wants or to keep himself out of trouble. I can't really accuse him of lying to me but I want him to understand that just a portion of the truth is not acceptable either.

I must be careful to be an example on this point though. It's sometimes a struggle to be completely honest if truthfulness will make me look bad. It's so easy to tweak the truth or just reveal a part of it in order to protect myself. However, I must be completely honest if I want my son to be too.

Of course, truthfulness must be robed in kindness and sensitivity to others, too, which is where some of the problem comes in. Combine truthfulness, kindness, and honoring God – we all need His help in doing this.

Dear Father, help all of us understand how to be completely truthful but also kind and sensitive to others in how we state the truth. Whew, this is not always easy. We need Your help. Amen.

Trusting God

To Him who is able to keep you from falling and to present you before His glorious presence without fault and with great joy — to the only God our Savior be glory, majesty, power and authority. Jude 24-25

"Trust God" my children hear at church and Sunday school. I, too, tell them to trust God. It's so easy to say that we should trust God. The words just flow out of our mouths because it is the "Christian" thing to say. Some Christians even think that believers should never have problems because, after all, we "trust God." Sorry, but I don't think that sort of viewpoint is always realistic.

When I have problems I do get to a place of trust, but sometimes I start from the problem place. Hopefully that journey to trust will show my children that learning to trust God is sometimes a process and that, once you have trusted Him and seen His care and His plan in action, then it is a little easier to trust the next time.

Of course, the goal is for full trust all the time, but I don't want them to struggle with guilt when the trust isn't quite there. It's a work in process — we are a work in process.

Dear Father, help me to honestly model trust for my children. Help them learn that You love them and You have a plan for their lives. Help them learn to trust ... step by step. Amen.

Facing Tragedy

*"When you pass through the waters, I will be with you; and
when you pass through the rivers, they will not sweep over you.
For I am the LORD, your God, your Savior." Isaiah 43:2-3*

"God loves me. God loves my family. God is in control."
I keep repeating these words over and over. By repeating
them I am hoping that my heart will accept them. Right now
my head knows these words are true, but my heart is struggling.

How does a parent deal with the death of a child? How?
Parents are not supposed to bury their children. It just isn't
right. And yet, it happens. In the midst of this pain and
agony I'm hanging on to God tightly. Even as my own heart
is breaking, I am aware that my other children are watching
to see if my faith means anything to me in this, the most
difficult experience I've ever had.

Does it? Yes. I believe God understands my pain and
sense of loss ... He's been there Himself. I know He is
holding me close, helping me through this, and that He can
handle the pain and disappointment I feel. God loves me
and He loves my child very much too. I believe with all my
heart that God Himself is sad right now, just like me.

Dear Father, my heart hurts so much. I don't know how I'm
going to get through this. I know that I can't without Your help
though. Father, strengthen me and my family. Love us through
this. Amen.

Tithing Training

*Remember this — a farmer who plants only a few seeds will get
a small crop. But the one who plants generously will get a
generous crop. "For God loves a person who gives cheerfully."
And God will generously provide all you need.* 2 Corinthians 9:6-8 NLT

Our children get an allowance each week. They are encouraged to save some but they can do what they choose with the rest of it. However, we are also teaching them the concept of tithing.

Sometimes our children get quite excited about giving money to God's work. When they become aware of a specific ministry, they want to give generously because they feel their gift can make a difference. Giving is a believer's responsibility. We share Scriptures with our children that encourage members of God's family to give a tithe at the least and give above and beyond that as they can.

My children's small tithe or gift here at home gives them a part in God's work around the world; from missionaries in Africa to relief aid helping tsunami victims in Indonesia. We're working together with all of God's children to make a difference in the world.

Dear Father, it is a privilege to teach our children about tithing and giving to Your work. Thank You that they are excited about giving and do not selfishly hold on to their money. Thank You that we can all be part of the big family that gets Your work done on earth. Amen.

Small Steps

We are hard pressed on every side, but not crushed; perplexed,
but not in despair; persecuted, but not abandoned;
struck down, but not destroyed. 2 Corinthians 4:8-9

There is an old saying, "How do you eat an elephant?" The answer is "One bite at a time." The logic of that answer is what I'm holding on to as I deal with the chaos of life.

A full-time job, running a household, raising two children and all that that entails is wearing me out. I don't have a husband to help me with any of this so all the financial pressures are on my shoulders too.

Late at night when I'm sitting at the kitchen table, paying bills and trying to magically stretch dollars, I often feel like I just am not going to make it. Those are the moments when I cry out to God for help. "I can't do this alone," I cry. "You aren't," He gently reminds me, "I'm with you. I haven't forgotten you." With that reminder I go back to the elephant logic. I can only get through the chaos of my life right now by taking things one step at a time. Being organized, intentional and disciplined, and remembering that God has not abandoned me, will get me through these years.

Dear Father, I don't know how people, especially single moms, make it without You. Thank You for the gentle reminders that I am not alone. Thank You for Your help. Amen.

SEPTEMBER 18

Learning Thankfulness

Give thanks to the LORD, call on His name; make known among the nations what He has done. 1 Chronicles 16:8

I want my children to be thankful people. We live a middle-class lifestyle in North America where the standard of living is pretty good compared to other places. I've traveled to some places around the world and seen what the lifestyle of people in developing countries is like. I'm embarrassed when I come home, not so much because of what we have, but because of what we expect.

I've been as guilty as my children at times of feeling that I "deserve" a good lifestyle and the luxuries that are continually available here. On top of that, how often do I honestly and sincerely thank God for what I have? I mean thank Him with all my heart ... really meaning it.

Will my children learn true thankfulness if they do not see it coming from me? I take this responsibility very seriously. We are blessed ... so very blessed ... and we need to be truly thankful for all we are continually given.

Dear Father, You are so generous to us. Our lives are so good and so easy. As I've seen how people live in other countries, I have felt very blessed. Thank You for all You give us and do for us. Father, help us look for opportunities to share what we have and help others. Amen.

Remembering to Say "Thank You"

Let the word of Christ dwell in you richly as you sing psalms,
hymns and spiritual songs with gratitude in your hearts to God.
Colossians 3:16

My five-year-old daughter has just got on my last nerve. Today we visited some friends, which meant a play date for my daughter and a good chat over coffee with my friend.

When we were ready to leave, my friend gave my daughter a small gift. Of course my daughter's response should have been to say, "Thank you," but she adamantly refused to say those two simple words. After a few exchanges of, "Say thank you" – "No," I was ready to explode. Thankfully my friend's little son saved the day. He stepped up, put his hands on my daughter's lips; moved them up and down and said, "Thank you" as if she were a puppet. Of course, we all dissolved into laughter.

Why is it sometimes so hard to simply say "thank you"? Perhaps we get so caught up in ourselves that we can't allow ourselves to thank someone else. Whatever the reason ... it's wrong. It's important to say thanks.

Dear Father, thank You. Thank You for my friends. Thank You for my family. Help me as I continually try to teach my daughter to express thankfulness to those who do kind things for her. Amen.

SEPTEMBER 20

Tumbling into Temptation

Be self-controlled and alert. Your enemy the devil prowls around like a roaring lion looking for someone to devour. Resist him, standing firm in the faith. 1 Peter 5:8-9

We all struggle with temptation at one time or another. So it is unrealistic to think that my children will avoid temptation to try something they know they shouldn't. There is often a pull of curiosity that feeds temptation; curiosity about what it would feel like to do that thing, say that word or taste that drink.

What will keep my children from giving in to temptations? Well … a lot of prayer on my part won't hurt. Jesus fought off temptation by quoting Scripture verses, so putting God's Word in their hearts will help them.

I know that when I fail to stand strong against temptation I feel like such a failure. I can encourage my children to get over that feeling quickly, pick up the pieces and move forward. We're all human and we all make bad choices sometimes. Succumbing to temptation is not the end of the world. They will recover and can choose to stand stronger next time. Through their victories their faith will grow stronger.

Dear Father, help my children to stand firm against temptation. Remind them of the words of Scripture they have memorized and may those words encourage them and strengthen them. Amen.

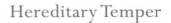
Hereditary Temper

Better to be patient than powerful;
better to have self-control than to conquer a city.
Proverbs 16:32 NLT

This is weird ... My daughter has an incredibly powerful temper: she screams, she throws things and she hits. What's so weird about that? I have the same kind of temper.

So the question is: Is she modeling what she has seen me do? Not completely. I've gotten a pretty good handle on my temper as I've matured, but I will admit that there have been times when I've lost control. I'm not proud of that. Or, is it possible that my daughter inherited the tendency to this kind of temper? I don't know the genetic answer to this question, I only know that I don't want her to have to deal with it her whole life as I've had to.

If she can get her temper under control while she's still young, her life will be so much easier. God tells us to keep a handle on our tempers; to think of others before ourselves; to resolve arguments before we go to bed so they don't have a chance to smolder overnight. God really knew what He was doing when He wrote the Bible, didn't He?

Dear Father, I pray that my daughter will learn to control her temper and think of others before herself. I pray that her temper will not control her but that kindness and love will rule her heart. Amen.

Hurting Hearts

"Be merciful, just as your Father is merciful." Luke 6:36

I love the tender hearts of children. Seriously, why do we lose that spontaneous compassion as we grow older? My children care so much about things – like the struggles of our elderly neighbor; they want to help her with gardening, carrying groceries in and even walking her little dog. They care about her.

When they see news stories of people who are struggling through natural disasters, they want to help. When someone we know personally is hurting because of a loss or an injury, they want to do something tangible to help.

Their tender hearts remind me to look around me to see who may need help, and then take the time to help them whenever I can. It's fun to find projects my children and I can do together that will show compassion and care to others. Working together to help others shows my children the love that God intends for us to share. It shows His merciful heart. We have the privilege of being His hands and feet to those around us.

Dear Father, You mean for us to help one another and care for those who are hurting. Thank You that my children see that. Show us ways we can work together to be actively compassionate to those around us. Amen.

The Hard Questions

"My thoughts are not your thoughts, neither are your ways My ways," declares the LORD. "As the heavens are higher than the earth, so are My ways higher than your ways and My thoughts than your thoughts." Isaiah 55:8-9

"Help, God!" Wow, I've cried out to God for help so many times when my son asks me questions that don't have easy answers. Questions like, "How come the children in Rwanda have to be hungry?" "Why did God let the hurricane kill all those people?" "How come God doesn't stop bad people from hurting children?"

I don't have answers to those questions. In fact, I want to ask them myself. I don't want my son's trust in God to be damaged by these unanswered questions, but my answers of living in a sinful fallen world seem to be a little over the top for his simple questions. I will simply tell him that God is sad, too, when people hurt. Then we can pray together for things to get better.

We can take advantage of the chances we have to help others and we can share the message of God's love as often as possible.

Dear Father, these are hard questions. You know that. Give me wisdom in how to answer my son and how to point him to You in this whole process. Amen.

Steel Will

*Be very careful to keep the commandment and the law that Moses
the servant of the LORD gave you: to love the LORD your God,
to walk in all His ways, to obey His commands, to hold fast to Him
and to serve Him with all your heart and all your soul. Joshua 22:5*

My daughter is incredibly stubborn – and she is just three years old! Sometimes her stubbornness is a problem; for example when she refuses to obey or to do something as simple as pick up her toys. Sometimes her stubbornness is good; like when she works over and over and over to learn something new. When she falls down she gets right back up and tries again.

If her persistence can be channeled into good things, then she might accomplish great things in this world; her drive and tenacity could be a blessing. I say "could be" because it's not so much fun from the parenting viewpoint to teach and train someone who is so stubborn.

This keeps me on my knees praying for wisdom, discernment and patience. I also pray for the joy to enjoy my daughter's energy and celebration of life!

Dear Father, channel my daughter's persistence and drive into positive things so that she can serve You with energy and passion. Use her in positive ways. In the meantime, please show me how to parent her with wisdom and love. Amen.

Praising Always

Praise the LORD. Praise the LORD, O my soul. I will praise the
LORD all my life; I will sing praise to my God as long as I live.
Psalm 146:1-2

What takes my breath away? The Niagara Falls; the Himalayan peaks; the Grand Canyon; killer whales; hummingbirds; oceans; butterflies; kangaroos; rainbows; ants; dolphins; roses; orchids; clouds; thunderstorms; the different seasons; shooting stars; snowflakes … Ahh, we live in an amazing world. Our God is the creative Master.

I'm reminded by the writers of Psalms to praise God often for this amazing planet and universe. It is truly a gift from Him. I'm embarrassed to admit that my prayer times are so often spent asking for things. I'm always quick to ask for God to do this or that. I often "tell" Him what to do. The psalmists remind me to stop asking and start praising God instead; to tell Him how much I appreciate all He has done.

I love sitting with my children and praising God. We each take turns saying things we are thankful for. I love hearing my children praise God. They are learning to give God praise and celebrate His gifts instead of making their prayer times just a list of requests.

Dear Father, You are amazing. What a creative and incredible world You made for us. I praise You and thank You for every bit of it! Amen.

SEPTEMBER 26

Family Member

*"Put your trust in the light while there is still time;
then you will become children of the light."*
John 12:36 NLT

I would do absolutely anything to protect my children; I would even die to keep them safe. That's true of most mothers. I give myself, my time and my energy each day to make their lives as pleasant and productive as possible. I love my children with all my heart.

When I step back and think of myself as a member of God's family ... a daughter of God ... and realize that He feels the same way about me as I feel about my children (and more so) ... I'm speechless. I am a child of God. His Word tells me that God thinks about me, the members of the Trinity talk about me, the Holy Spirit prays for me, Jesus intercedes for me. They love me. How amazing is that?

What a great truth to pass along to my children! As they understand how much I love them and how much I do for them, I can explain that God loves them EVEN MORE. How special we are to Him! What a privilege to be called His children.

Dear Father, I'm humbled and can find no words to thank You for Your amazing love and care. Thank You for giving so much to make my life better and to provide eternal life for me. Help my children grasp how wonderful this is. Amen.

Love from God

Whoever does not love does not know God, because God is love.
1 John 4:8

A lot of a mother's teaching time with her children is spent on relationship things: being kind, being respectful, obeying and showing love. This is not an accident; a good deal of God's instructions to His children are on the same topics. He commands us to love others – a theme that is repeated over and over in His Word.

Loving others is not an option; He even says that His children will stand out from other people because of their lives of love. This is great when you already love the people around you, but there are some people in all our lives who are just not easy to love. God's Word says that anybody can love their friends, which is not hard, but loving our enemies, well, that's a different story.

How do you teach your children to love people who don't really love them back? It is done by opening our hearts to allow God's love to flow through us. It's His love that makes the difference. Loving others isn't an option, it's a command ... so we must do it even when it's hard.

Dear Father, loving our friends is easy. Loving those who aren't so lovable is another story. Help me model this persistent love that comes only from You. Help my children learn how to allow You to love through them. Amen.

SEPTEMBER 28

Controlling Emotions

Hatred stirs up dissension, but love covers over all wrongs.
Proverbs 10:12

My ex-husband makes me so angry! He chose to leave our children and me. He started a new life and hardly has anything to do with us. He seems to enjoy flaunting his elegant lifestyle and freedom to me while I struggle to care for our children and create a family for them. At least it feels that way to me. He hardly sees his kids and they miss him so much. Anger and frustration build up inside my heart and, if I'm not careful, it spills out in nastiness. I do try to stop it, though, because I don't want my children to hear such negativity about their father.

I am calling on God to fill me with His strength to control my emotions and watch my tongue. I tell my children that their father loves them very much and that he is just busy. In the meantime I just pray that he will come into their lives more and more often. If I can control my words perhaps we can have a more peaceful relationship in the future ... for our children's sakes.

Dear Father, I pray that my children's father will want to participate in their lives more. I pray that he will let them know that he cares for them. Father, help me to control my words and not say things about my ex that will influence the children's feelings toward him. Amen.

Encouraging
My Daughter

Encourage one another daily, as long as it is called Today, so that none of you may be hardened by sin's deceitfulness. Hebrews 3:13

Since my daughter entered middle school I've noticed that she gets discouraged often. I know that a lot of that is due to the hormonal changes her body is experiencing, but even if there's a reason for her negativity, we must still find a way to help her deal with her emotions. She doesn't really understand that the major source of her discouragement is simply from growing up.

I could react to her discouragement and negativity with frustration, I could dismiss it as childish pratter. Or, I could find ways to lift her up and encourage her. I choose the last option. I look for things to admire, praise and encourage her in, which isn't hard to do since my daughter is a beautiful young woman with many talents and abilities.

I know that Satan could slide into her life while she's discouraged and pull her farther down. I don't want to let that happen. Everyone needs encouragement some-times and being able to offer that to my daughter is a real privilege.

Dear Father, I know things can be difficult for girls my daughter's age. I don't want to dismiss that. Help me to find ways to encourage her and lift her up. Father, help her to see the good in herself, help her to focus on the positives of her personality and talents. Amen.

SEPTEMBER 30

October

The Sandwich Years

My purpose is that they may be encouraged in heart and united in love,
in order that they may know the mystery of God, namely, Christ, in whom
are hidden all the treasures of wisdom and knowledge. Colossians 2:2-3

I'm in the sandwich generation. That means that on one side of me are my aging parents. They need more of my attention and help than they used to, so I help them with things like driving to the doctor, helping with things around the house, managing financial things for them, and just spending time with them.

On the other side of this sandwich are my own children, who need a lot of those same things plus teaching and training and the general tasks of parenting.

Usually the middle of the sandwich is the best part, but I have to say, this particular sandwich middle is running on empty. I'm pulled in both directions because I feel such a responsibility to both my parents and my children.

However, I must find some time for peace and refueling myself. Moments of stillness to reconnect with God and feel His care for me are vital to maintaining an attitude of love and care for my parents and my children.

Dear Father, I'm glad I can help my parents, but I don't want to cheat my children of my time and energy. Fill me with Your peace and care so that I can serve my parents and my children. Amen.

I'm Pregnant!

I will extol the LORD at all times; His praise will always be on my lips.
Psalm 34:1

My husband and I have wanted to start a family for a long time, but we just haven't been able to get pregnant. The longer our struggle has gone on, the stronger our desire to be parents has become. We've prayed and prayed about this and have been to doctor after doctor; all to no avail. Just when we were about to give up – I'M PREGNANT!

I can't believe it. I'm filled with the anticipation of feeling the movements of my baby, choosing names, preparing the nursery and buying clothing and diapers. We've dreamed about this for so long … my heart is filled with thanksgiving and praise to God. This precious baby will be very, very loved. We are already praying for him or her to come to know God at an early age. We're excited to teach our baby the truths of God's Word and help our precious child know that he or she is even more precious to God.

The next few months are going to be so exciting! My husband and I can't wait to meet our child face to face!

Dear Father, thank You for this precious child who we've waited so long for. Father, we give this child right back to You. We know he or she is Yours and is only on loan to us for a while. We'll do our best to be good parents and will come to You often for guidance and help. Amen.

Peacemaker

*"God blesses those who work for peace, for they will
be called the children of God."* Matthew 5:9 NLT

Three children keep me hopping. Don't get me wrong, they
are fun kids with great personalities and I enjoy them very
much. But, like any kids, once in a while they argue and fight
and my patience begins to wear thin.

Interestingly, my help on those tough days with my kids
comes from ... my kids, well, one of them, my oldest daughter. That girl is a natural born peacemaker. God has given
her a patience and calmness that often diffuses arguments
between her siblings. She gently redirects their attentions
to activities that will occupy their interest and stop the fighting. I'm so thankful for this daughter and the gifts God has
given her.

I'm often humbled by her peacemaking abilities. After
all, I'm the adult, but she even calms me down. I step back
from my frustration, take a deep breath and remember
that these childhood years will go by so quickly so I need
to enjoy them. A little arguing doesn't hurt anyone, it actually makes you appreciate the peaceful moments more!

Dear Father, thank You for my peacemaking daughter. I really
believe that she has a gift from You that promotes peacefulness in
those around her. Bless her and use her to establish peace all around
her. Amen.

OCTOBER 3

Cleaning Up

I lift up my eyes to the hills — where does my help come from?
My help comes from the LORD, the Maker of heaven and earth.
Psalm 121:1-2

The most terrible words a mom can hear are, "Ma'am, this is the hospital. We have your son here." My son overdosed on drugs and was rushed to the ER. I never would have believed that my son takes drugs. I thought I knew my son pretty well, but maybe I've just had my head buried in the sand. I thought I was aware of what was going on in his life; I didn't notice a personality change, his grades didn't drop, he wasn't acting strange ... But the whole time I thought things were great, he was taking drugs.

Now I have the guilt of wondering whether I wasn't paying enough attention. I wonder if he did it because I failed him somehow or because he is unhappy. I don't understand why this happened. Maybe he doesn't understand either. I don't know. I just know that now we must get him help to put this part of his life behind him.

For my part, I will not bombard him with criticism or tears, I will tell him that I love him, believe in him and will help him in any way that I can.

Dear Father, my heart aches for my son. I admit I'm afraid too. Father, help him get clean and stay clean. Protect him from himself and from the temptation to do drugs. Make him strong. Amen.

Baby Steps

"I will forgive their wickedness and will remember their sins no more."
Hebrews 8:12

My daughter is just beginning to learn how to walk. She pulls herself up by a table, steps away and stands alone, wobbly and unsure. Then, with great concentration, she takes a single step. She looks at me with such pride and waits for me to cheer. Then she usually falls down, plopping onto her bottom. So cute! She pulls herself up again and tries once more. This process happens over and over. After a while she will be able to take two or three steps, then several and, finally, she'll be off and running.

This learning process is such a spiritual lesson for me. Learning to walk closer and closer to God is much like the physical process of learning to walk. I pull myself up, take a step and fall right down. Each time I fall I experience God's love and grace as He forgives me and encourages me to try again. The next time I take a couple of steps before falling again. Always, His love and forgiveness encourage me to get up and try again. I can almost picture the smile on His face as I get up and walk again – the same way I smile at my daughter's first steps.

Dear Father, thank You for loving me so much. Thank You for Your forgiveness and grace. I'll continue learning and growing – getting up each time I fall – by Your strength. Amen.

OCTOBER 5

Unwanted Pregnancy

Whether you turn to the right or to the left, your ears will hear a voice behind you, saying, "This is the way; walk in it." Isaiah 30:21

OK, I'm pregnant and I'm not married. I never planned for this to happen, of course. The father wants nothing to do with the baby or me so I'm on my own. These are my choices: I could have an abortion and no one would ever know; I could carry the baby and give it up for adoption, or I could have the baby, keep it and raise it myself.

Well, number one is not an option; I just can't do that. So I can either give up my baby or raise him myself … both of these options have positive and negative implications. I want to accept the responsibility for giving this child life. I don't know, though, whether that means keeping him and struggling to provide a good home for him or giving him to a couple who can't have children but really want to be parents. If I did that then my baby would have both a mother and a father.

I don't know what the future holds for me, but I'm seeking God's guidance and wisdom for this decision. Strangely enough, I already love this child growing inside me and I want to do the best thing for him.

Dear Father, forgive me for what I've done, I'm truly sorry. Give me the wisdom and strength to do the best thing for this child and be with me each step of the way. Amen.

Searching and Searching

"I know the plans I have for you," declares the LORD, *"plans to prosper you and not to harm you, plans to give you hope and a future."*
Jeremiah 29:11

When my son was eight years old his dream was to grow up and be a professional baseball player. When he was thirteen he wanted to be a firefighter. His ideas and dreams have changed a multitude of times through the years. It has always been fun to hear what he was thinking and to dream with him.

Now he is halfway through his college years and needs to select a major and begin settling in to prepare for a career. And ... he doesn't have a clue what that career should be. When you think about it, it's kind of crazy that a kid who is eighteen or nineteen should be making such a major life decision. We're just too young and too inexperienced at that age to make such a big decision.

It's a stressful time for my son, but it's also fun to think that he has his whole life ahead of him – a blank page waiting to be written. I pray for his wisdom every day and in the meantime I love talking with him about the possibilities – I love reinforcing his gifts and sparking interest in his passions. What fun this stage of life is!

Dear Father, guide my son into the career You want him to work in. I know You have a plan for his life. Amen.

OCTOBER 7

Choices

Direct your children onto the right path, and when they are older, they will not leave it. Proverbs 22:6

What happened? Why does a girl who was raised in a Christian home with high moral standards make choices that place her lifestyle in direct opposition to those values? Did I do something wrong? Could I have done a better job as a mother?

My heart is breaking because my daughter has chosen to live with her boyfriend. I don't even know what to say to her. I believe she knows how I feel about her choices because she doesn't call often and hardly comes back home. She hasn't even given me a chance to get to know her boyfriend. I know that the attitude of the world is that there is nothing wrong with living together. But it is scripturally wrong and I just can't get beyond that.

The most important thing to remember, though, is that I love my daughter. I will not turn away from her because of this choice. I still want to be a part of her life and even get to know her boyfriend. I will pray and pray for her to change this choice but I will love her no matter what.

Dear Father, I pray that my daughter and her young man will get married. Regardless of what choice she makes, help my relationship with her stay strong. I love her and I don't want to lose her. Amen.

Step-Mothering

I waited patiently for the LORD; He turned to me and heard my cry.
Psalm 40:1

I sort of feel like I'm in a no-man's land, I recently married the man of my dreams; he's terrific and I love him very much. Besides getting a husband, I also am blessed to now have two stepchildren. They are really nice kids and I enjoy them very much, but the problem is that I don't really know my place with them. I'm not their mother (they made that very clear to me from the beginning), so they don't want me telling them what to do. But there are rules in our home that they must obey and I must also do whatever I can to protect them. So, in some ways I have to "mother" them even though I am their stepmother.

My husband and I talk about this often and try to stay united in our approach to parenting. Beyond that though, I guess I need to be patient in waiting for these children, whose lives have been shaken up lately, to understand that I love them too. They can have three parents who love them. Hopefully they will soon see how awesome that is!

Dear Father, I need Your wisdom to know how to parent as a step-parent. I am not trying to take the place of their mother; I love them, too, and I want them to understand that. Show me how to convey this to them. Help me to be patient. Amen.

Be Clear

"If you remain in Me and My words remain in you, ask whatever you wish, and it will be given you." John 15:7

When I start a job it helps me to know exactly what that job entails. I like having a job description and a detailed plan of what is expected of me. It kind of makes me crazy to have a manager who just gives me partial information on what she expects from me. I don't know if I'm doing a good job or not because there is no way to measure what I've done.

This is probably a good model for parenting, too. If I'm clear with my children about what is expected of them, it will be easier for them to meet those expectations. How can they obey rules that aren't clear? How can they do chores well if they don't know what "well" means? I suppose I thought that being wishy-washy meant I was a little less strict so my children might like me better, but it makes sense to me that it is fairer to be clear with them.

I don't want to be a rule-wielding mom who is continually laying down the law, but as I help them understand this world, I do have expectations of them.

Dear Father, this was a revelation to me — that it's fairer to my children to not be wishy-washy but to be concise and clear about my expectations. Guide me in how to explain things to my children and in being fair with expectations and rules. Amen.

Yippee Time!

Instead, speaking the truth in love, we will in all things grow up into Him who is the Head, that is, Christ. Ephesians 4:15

A pat on the back always feels good. I know I appreciate it when someone tells me that I've done a good job or that they appreciate my efforts or work. It motivates me to do more, try harder, give 200%.

This is a good thing to remember where my children are concerned. Often good behavior is encouraged by punishing bad behavior, but it makes more sense to reward good behavior. What a wonderful way to increase my child's self-esteem and motivate her to want to be more obedient, positive and loving. Here's a confession ... as my life got busier and busier, I found myself slipping into negative reinforcement; complaining about the bad things and hoping that would bring about good things.

I'm glad to be reminded to encourage good behavior with good rewards. It is a lot more loving way to live and a much better example to my children of God's dreams for them and His love. I may need to be reminded of this every so often, but it's definitely my goal.

Dear Father, help me to remember to slow down on jumping on negative behavior and reward good behavior instead. Help me build my child's self-esteem and motivate good behavior by rewarding it. Amen.

OCTOBER 11

Winning Team

God did not give us a spirit of timidity, but a spirit of power,
of love and of self-discipline. 2 Timothy 1:7

We won! We won! I am a fanatic fan of my son's basketball team! I mean fanatic! I wear the team colors to every game. I've recorded all his games on DVD. I cheer loud and long! Oh, I love it.

Would I love it as much if my son wasn't on the team? I've always loved basketball so, yes, I'd still enjoy the games, but the major draw is cheering for my son. I love watching him succeed. He is a good athlete and he works very hard at perfecting his skills. I like telling him I am his biggest fan; he just smiles and shakes his head. What I love is that he isn't just a great athlete; he is also a good team player who cheers for his teammates when they have great games or make fantastic plays. He is also a good sport, which is always appreciated by opposing teams.

It is great to be able to support my son in the sport he loves so much and spends so much time and energy on. I think being his biggest cheerleader is a great thing!

Dear Father, I'm so proud of my son. He works so hard at being a good athlete as well as a good sport. Thanks that I can share in the joy of his games by attending and cheering. What a great thing to share. I'm so proud of him! Amen.

She's Engaged!

May the God of hope fill you with all joy and peace as you trust in Him,
so that you may overflow with hope by the power of the Holy Spirit.
Romans 15:13

My daughter got engaged last night. She is so excited, so in love and just knows that life will be wonderful with this young man. I ... have mixed emotions. Her young man is a nice guy who seems to really love her; but I see some red flags in their relationship, and that scares me.

She thinks I'm just holding back because I'm going to miss her and that's why I have these reservations. OK, I'll admit that I am going to miss her a lot. Truthfully though, marriage is such a big step and with about 50% of all unions ending in divorce, I just want her to slow down and be absolutely sure this is right – that this is what she wants. It's so easy to get caught up in the romance of being engaged and the idea of marriage and ignore any feelings of doubt.

I love my daughter and I want her to have the best marriage ever. I know I can give her my opinion once, then I need to be quiet and support her decision. My place is to just love and support her.

Dear Father, I'm so concerned for my daughter. Father, help her to be sure about this decision. If it isn't right for her, give her the courage to stop. Protect her from the pain of a bad marriage. Amen.

OCTOBER 13

Labor and Delivery

Give thanks to the LORD; make known among the nations what He has done. Sing praise to Him; tell of all His wonderful acts.
Psalm 105:1-2

I enjoyed being pregnant so much. I loved feeling the movements of my child within me. I loved "playing tag" with him as I gently pushed on him and he pushed back. I loved it when he got the hiccups. It was wonderful.

I enjoyed being pregnant so much that I didn't really think about what it was going to be like to bring this baby into the world. So, when my contractions began, I was just a little bit shocked because ... it hurt! OK, I knew it was going to hurt, but the pain kept getting worse and worse. After about ten hours I definitely understood why it's called labor.

Bringing a baby into the world is a lot of hard, hard work! Pushing my son out was the most wonderful, painful feeling I've ever had. But the minute that little guy was out of me and into this world ... it was so awesome that I was ready to do it all over again! What a miracle! What a joy!

Dear Father, what an incredible joy. Thank You for allowing me the privilege of bringing this baby into the world. I just shared in a miracle with You! Now please help me, Father, to be a good and loving mom. Amen.

Breathless

He who dwells in the shelter of the Most High will rest in the shadow of the Almighty. I will say of the LORD, "He is my refuge and my fortress, my God, in whom I trust." Psalm 91:1-2

If you've ever had the experience of running as hard as you can and suddenly falling flat, then you may know what it feels like to have the air knocked out of you. It's a terrible feeling – you think you're going to die because you simply can't get any air in. If you know that feeling then you know how I felt last week when my daughter told me she is pregnant. She's only sixteen! How ... why ... what now?

I haven't been able to take a good deep breath since she told me. I can't seem to think about anything else, and yet I don't want to think about it. I'd like to rewind life back a few weeks to see what I could have done to stop this.

Whether she decides to keep this baby or give it up (how can I let her give up my grandchild!) her life will never be the same. Neither will mine. Right now I have to figure out how to help her and support her. Together we will get through this, but only by hanging tightly to each other and to God.

Dear Father, I don't know what to say to my daughter. I don't know how to help her. Give me the right words; give me understanding; give me hope. Get us through this together, Father. Amen.

OCTOBER 15

Sticking Together

"Therefore I tell you, whatever you ask for in prayer,
believe that you have received it, and it will be yours." Mark 11:24

Could life get any crazier? I'm so busy that I actually file my nails at stoplights. Really ... multi-tasking is an absolute necessity. I don't have time to do just one thing at a time, my job, husband, children, church and friends all keep me running.

However, I recently began making time in my week for an activity that is probably the most important thing I can do in my life. Once a week I meet with other moms I know. We meet for about an hour or two ... alone ... no children allowed. What do we do? We don't go for pedicures or facials, we don't meet to talk about books we've read or to do crafts – although there is nothing wrong with any of those things.

These moms and I meet to pray. We spend an hour or two each week just praying for our children. It's a wonderful time. We don't chitchat or gossip, we sit down, share requests and pray. It's dedicated prayer time for our precious children.

Dear Father, I'm so thankful to be connected with these other women who care so much for their children. Praying together for our kids binds us together. We celebrate answers to our prayers and we cry together over the hard things. Thank You for this wonderful group. Amen.

Creative Children

Set a guard over my mouth, O LORD;
keep watch over the door of my lips. Psalm 141:3

What possesses a two-year-old boy to think it's a good idea to take my car keys out of my purse and hide them? I've turned the house upside down; I've even moved the furniture, lifted up the mattresses and dug through my houseplants. I CAN'T FIND MY KEYS. My son thinks it's funny. Each time I ask him where he put them he laughs and runs away. Times such as this, when my son shows such creativity, make me crazy!

What to do ... I could go berserk, scream, punish, insist that he give me the keys ... but that wouldn't go anywhere. Rational conversation doesn't go far with a two-year-old, and irrational conversation is even less productive. So I will patiently and persistently ask him where he put my keys.

These are the moments when I so need God's guidance and wisdom to know how to handle a situation. Somehow, with God-given patience guiding me, I will convince him that this is serious and I need his help.

Dear Father, I'm not the most patient person and this is making me very frustrated. Please help me to remember that my little boy is a little boy. He doesn't understand things the way an adult does. Help me to be reasonable in pursuing my lost keys. Amen.

OCTOBER 17

Judge Not, Lest …

People with understanding control their anger;
a hot temper shows great foolishness. Proverbs 14:29 NLT

When I saw that my flowerbed had been completely destroyed, I blamed my son. Oh, I'm sure he had some help from his friends, but the responsibility was all on him. He knows that I take great pride in my garden; I spend hours and hours working in it and I thoroughly enjoy the fruits of my labors. My son adamantly declared his innocence but I ignored him and punished him by grounding him from pretty much everything except meals.

A few days later I glanced out the window and saw a large dog in the remains of my flowerbed, rolling on his back in the soil. As I watched him finish off the last few flowers, I suddenly realized that my son may have been telling the truth – perhaps he didn't wreck my flowers.

Now what? I had only one option … apologize to my son and ask for his forgiveness. That's not easy, but it is certainly how God asks me to handle such situations. So I will apologize and ask for forgiveness and hope that my son understands that I love him and am learning to live my life the way God asks.

Dear Father, forgive me for being so quick to make judgments. Help me to be less quick to judge and more willing to listen. Amen.

Obedience and Love

This is love: that we walk in obedience to His commands. As you have heard from the beginning, His command is that you walk in love.
2 John 6

I want my children to obey because they want to obey. I would hope that even when they really don't want to obey, they will because they love me. Loving someone means that you want to please them, right? I know that my children love me, of course, but when they deliberately disobey me I don't sense their love so much. Of course, everyone disobeys sometimes (even adults), but it shouldn't be a pattern.

As I consider my children's behavior, I must also think about how I relate to God, whom I love. Do I disobey Him sometimes? Do I ever get a rebellious attitude and disobey Him deliberately? I must admit that yes, I do.

So as I explain the importance of obedience to my children I am also speaking to myself. Love and obedience go hand in hand. Love spurs us to obedience. I want my children to understand that I'm working on learning this, just as they are. We can work on it together.

Dear Father, I do love You — even if I don't always act like it. Please forgive my disobedience and my stubbornness, even as I forgive my children. Help us all to love more purely and let that love move us to obedience. Amen.

Happiness Shines Through

A happy heart makes the face cheerful, but
heartache crushes the spirit. Proverbs 15:13

It's hard to fake happiness, at least with people you know well ... or live with. Don't you find that the "true you" comes out most at home? Our families have to deal with our happiness, anger, depression, sadness, uncertainty and whatever else we feel. The public masks come off when we walk in the door. It's good that home is a "safe place" to work through your emotions, but it's sad that the people you love the most have to deal with your darkest side.

Often you hear that the mother in a home sets the atmosphere of the home, which means that the rest of the family reflects your emotions. That's frustrating because it is a big responsibility, but it can also be a big motivator to deal with your negative emotions and get to a more positive place. Sometimes that happens easily; sometimes it is a long journey.

Teach your children not to sink into negative emotions, but to deal with the causes and move forward. Then you show them how to deal with their emotions in a healthy way.

Dear Father, because I set the mood in my house I need to deal with whatever tries to wreck it. Help me to do so in a healthy way and show my children how to deal with the ups and downs of life. Amen.

OCTOBER 20

Benefits of Hard Work

Even when we were with you, we gave you this rule:
"If a man will not work, he shall not eat." 2 Thessalonians 3:10

I work hard to take care of my family and so does my husband. We both have jobs outside the home, but our work isn't done when we get home. Caring for our children, our home and our yard is another full-time job. The benefit of our hard work is that we can provide a home for our family as well as food, clothing and fun things.

I want my children to begin to grasp that the things we have, even our home, were not just given to us. I want them to understand that hard work brings results. Granted, for some, those results are more generous than for others. Still, the thing I want my kids to understand is that working hard at something brings benefits. Some of the benefits are financial; another benefit is the pride of a job well done. Working hard at something also gives an opportunity to learn more about that job.

Families, ministries, churches, towns and societies are built on hard work. Becoming a contributing member of society means learning to work.

Dear Father, sometimes work is fun, and sometimes it isn't. Regardless, I want my children to learn to work and not just expect things to be handed to them. Help them work hard and take pride in the job they do. Amen.

Close to the Source

Flee from all this, and pursue righteousness, godliness, faith, love, endurance and gentleness. 1 Timothy 6:11

Grrr! I just totally lost it with my children. I was shouting and crying and even threw a pillow across the room. Why did I get so crazy over something that wasn't really that major? Because I'm running on empty. Imagine a tube of toothpaste that has been squeezed dry and, try as you might to eek out one more drop; there is nothing left inside it.

I'm exhausted from dealing with my three energetic children and the rest of life. I've got no resources of peace or strength to draw on. So when my children started fighting today, my response was to blow up at them. I don't like behaving that way. Losing my temper shows no love to my kids, no self-control and does not honor God on any level. What am I going to do about it? I've got to get back to the source of peace, strength and love ... God.

No matter how busy my days are I must make time to spend with God and let His Word fill me with the resources I need to be me.

Dear Father, I'm so tired and feel so empty. I know this is because I haven't made time for You in my life. Please forgive me. Help me to carve out time each day to spend with You. Fill me with Your Spirit, love and strength so I can be the best mom to my children. Amen.

Tough Love

Do not withhold discipline from a child; if you punish him with the rod,
he will not die. Punish him with the rod and save his soul from death.
Proverbs 23:13-14

Can you identify with this scenario? A crowded grocery store with canned music playing over the speaker system ... However, the temper tantrum your two-year-old is pitching drowns out all other sounds in the store. Everyone is looking at you.

How about this one? A play date for your child and a few other children is going well when your child suddenly decides that all the toys belong to her and no one else can touch them. End of play date.

All parents have these moments at one time or another. Discipline is necessary though, isn't it? Some parents don't like to discipline their children because they don't want to deal with the anger that discipline brings. However, discipline is biblical. It's a good thing that, in the long run, doesn't hurt your children, but actually helps them.

Discipline teaches children the need to obey and to play nicely with others. If they learn that now it will make their lives a lot more pleasant.

Dear Father, discipline isn't easy, but I know it's necessary so help me to discipline when needed and to be fair about it. Help me to always discipline in love and not out of anger. Amen.

OCTOBER 23

Frightening Nights

There is no fear in love. But perfect love drives out fear.
The one who fears is not made perfect in love. 1 John 4:18

Crashing thunder wakes me in the middle of the night. I start counting slowly, "One ... two ... three" ... the door flings open and my five-year-old son comes flying in, pillow in hand. He doesn't say a word but comes to my side of the bed, pulls his sleeping bag out from underneath, climbs into it and reaches up for my hand. We hold hands as the thunder crashes and the lightning flashes until he finally falls asleep.

Storms really scare my son. We have talked about his fear often; we've talked about trusting God and how God takes care of him. But the bottom line is that for a five-year-old, storms are really loud and scary. It's OK for him to be afraid; I'm afraid, too, sometimes. I'll use these thunderstorm nights to continue teaching my son that God loves him and will take care of him. We'll continue praying for fewer thunderstorms (his prayer) and for our trust in God to take care of us to grow (my prayer).

Dear Father, I know You love me and my son. You understand our fears and why certain things scare us more than others. Help my son to learn to trust You and find comfort in that trust during times of fear. In the meantime, thanks that I get to hold hands with him during thunderstorms! Amen.

Praise God for His Word

Your word, O LORD, is eternal; it stands firm in the heavens.
Your faithfulness continues through all generations.
Psalm 119:89-90

I don't have all the answers; I don't even know what the questions are sometimes. As my children have grown from babies into teenagers, the questions have gotten more complicated. If it weren't for the advice of other moms, I don't know what I would have done sometimes; not the right thing that's for sure!

But my real strength and wisdom has always come from one source ... God's Word. When I had days where I was so frustrated with my children that I could have walked away, I found peace and guidance in His Word. When I had days where I didn't know how to handle them, I found examples in Jesus' life. When I had days where I just had no joy, I found it in the words of God.

I'm so thankful that God gave us His Word to teach, guide, inspire and help us through each circumstance and relationship that life throws at us. He knew exactly what I would need for each day of my life. If I spend time reading the Bible, I know I will find what I need to help me to be the best wife, mom, daughter and friend I can be.

Dear Father, thank You for the Bible. I am learning to love more and more and finding from it what I need each day. Amen.

OCTOBER 25

Living in Contentment

I have learned to be content whatever the circumstances.
I know what it is to be in need, and I know what it is to have plenty.
I have learned the secret of being content in any and every situation.
Philippians 4:11-12

My children have a serious case of the "gimmes." OK, I'm going to be honest; sometimes I have the "gimmes" too. What are the "gimmes"? The major characteristic of this disease is a yearning to have more stuff. It always wants more and is never satisfied with what it has.

My major struggle with this is clothing. I like clothes; I like to look stylish and current. But my closet is so jammed that I know I don't actually need more clothes. My children struggle with wanting the newest toys, video games and even vacations. "Why can't we go to Disney World? Mark's family goes every year." My children don't want to be satisfied with what we can afford.

We all need to learn to be content with what we have. After all, we already have all we need, the things we want (the "gimmes") are luxuries and we can do without them.

Dear Father, I'm sorry that I have such a gluttonous attitude toward life. How can I expect my children to have anything less? Forgive me, Father, and help me begin to model contentment and appreciation for all we have. Amen.

Great Delight

The LORD your God is with you, He is mighty to save.
He will take great delight in you, He will quiet you with His love,
He will rejoice over you with singing. Zephaniah 3:17

Delight is such a great word. It's fun to think about what brings me delight. My children, my husband and my friends all bring me delight in various ways. What is totally incomprehensible, however, is to think that I bring delight to God.

Scripture tells me that even when I'm grumpy, selfish, angry, disobedient ... God still delights in me. That changes my whole attitude about myself! Reading Zephaniah 3:17 opens my eyes to His love for me. I'm never alone; His strength is always with me. He will calm me down when life makes me crazy. He sings over me and He rejoices in me. That's amazing – the Creator God rejoices over me with singing!

This reminds me of when I used to rock my precious newborn baby and sing to him with peace and joy in my heart. Realizing that God delights in me enough to sing over me makes me more peaceful and delighted. That will make me a better wife, mom and friend. Praise God for His love!

Dear Father, I'm amazed that You delight in me. Thank You so much. Help that knowledge grow a love in me that I can share with those around me. Amen.

Gratitude Lessons

Praise the LORD, O my soul, and forget not all His benefits — who forgives all your sins and heals all your diseases, who redeems your life from the pit and crowns you with love and compassion. Psalm 103:2-4

How often do any of us feel real, sincere gratitude? I'm convicted that I cannot truly praise God for all His benefits if I do not know true gratitude. Even more, I'm convicted that I cannot teach my children to be grateful if I am not grateful. Often I come to God in prayer with, "Do this. Help that. Fix this. Guide him. Show me." Do you see a theme here?

The challenge for my children and me is to spend one full prayer time each week just praising God for all He does. "Thanks for this. I appreciate that You did that. What a cool thing You made."

It is actually a blessing to remember all that God does for us each and every day and not take for granted one single moment of sunshine, one flower, one smile, one relationship or even one breath that we take. Life and all that it involves is a blessing and gift from God. Replacing requests with praise renews my energy and zest for life. I pray that it does the same for my children.

Dear Father, thank You so much for everything You do for me and my family. Help me as I strive to praise You more and teach my children to be filled with gratitude. Amen.

Hope for the Future

Jesus said to her, "I am the resurrection and the life. He who believes in Me will live, even though he dies; and whoever lives and believes in Me will never die. Do you believe this?" John 11:25-26

Death is a tough thing for kids to understand. My teenager just had a really difficult experience – one that I hoped she would never have to go through. One of her really close friends died in a car accident this weekend. Oh my, the questions she has now – and I don't really have answers. Her heart is aching and I just want to help her but all I can do really is hold her, comfort her, let her talk about her friend and share memories that I have of the beautiful young girl too.

As her pain settles a bit I will remind her that her friend knew Jesus so she is now with Him. That's a good thing, no, a wonderful thing for her friend. I can remind my daughter of the promise of resurrection for believers and that she will see her friend again one day – forever.

But for now, I will let her cry; in fact, I'll cry with her, as we struggle to understand how such a young life could be cut so short.

Dear Father, death is hard. We miss our loved ones so much when they leave. Thank You for the promise of resurrection and eternal life. Help my daughter through this grief and may that eternal promise give her peace. Amen.

OCTOBER 29

Choosing Good Friends

The godly give good advice to their friends; the wicked lead them astray.
Proverbs 12:26

Reality check ... the more my children grow up, the less influence I have on who they choose to be friends with. When they were young I could more or less determine who they spent time with. Now, because they are in school, they decide who they will eat lunch with and who they will play with at recess. Those friends and their values can have such an influence on my kids, and that kind of scares me.

I pray they understand the need to be careful about their choice of friends. Good friends can stretch their minds and interests but they shouldn't pull them away from their faith or the values of their family. I will pray diligently for my children as they choose their friends. I pray they will find friends who will help them to be the wonderful people God desires. I pray they will find friends who help them grow and develop and learn. I pray for friends who are so precious that they become lifelong friends.

Dear Father, it's kind of scary for me to realize that friends have become so important to my children. I pray that they make good choices in friendships. Father, guide them to friends who will encourage and enhance their lives. Guide them to friends who will be their friends for life! Amen.

Striving for Consistency

Jesus Christ is the same yesterday and today and forever.
Hebrews 13:8

Parenting experts say that the key to being a good parent is to be consistent. Once you make house rules, be consistent in enforcing them. Make the punishment fit the disobedience. Don't overreact. In other words, be steady.

Yeah, sometimes I wonder if the parenting experts have ever parented. Being consistent and, therefore, not being controlled by moods or circumstances is not easy! But I do want my children to know what to expect and to not have to be concerned that one day Mom is patient and kind but the next day she is short-tempered and unreasonable.

My example for this is Jesus. Scripture tells us that He is the same today as He was yesterday and as He will be tomorrow. He never changes. The example for me is that I know that Jesus is always forgiving, loving, and willing to teach. I am not perfect like Jesus was, but I can strive to be more consistent and steady, regardless of bad circumstances, so that my children know what to expect from me.

Dear Father, I want to model the consistency of Jesus in my life. I know I can never be as consistent as He is, but help me to grow closer and closer to His model. Amen.

OCTOBER 31

November

Counting My Blessings

Every good and perfect gift is from above. James 1:17

It's been a difficult day ... and it's only two o'clock in the afternoon. I have a two-year-old and a one-month-old and they have both been switched on to continuous cry all day. My nerves are shot, my ears are ringing and my head hurts. Just now, though, they both finally went to sleep – at the same time!

I've gotten them each into their beds, kissed their little heads and can't wait to sit down and put my feet up. However, as I leave each room, I glance back at the sleeping child. How angelic they each look! How precious they are! Yes, that's what I need to remember. That angelic-looking little person is precious. Neither of them intends to give me a headache (they don't even know what a headache IS). I must remember that they are just being children; that's all they know how to be.

Standing here watching them sleep, I am overwhelmed with love for them. Someday I will look back on these days with fondness, forgetting the headaches and crying, and I will long to have these tiring, wonderful days back. So I'm going to take a moment to enjoy them right now.

Dear Father, thank You for my children. While I don't enjoy tough days like today, I know that soon they'll be all grown up. Help me to relax so that I can focus on enjoying my babies. Amen.

NOVEMBER 1

Just like Dad

And so you became a model to all the believers in
Macedonia and Achaia. 1 Thessalonians 1:7

It's so funny when my son copies his dad. My eighteen-month-old son absolutely adores his father. The little guy studies his dad's movements and mimics them carefully. He pretends to put gel in his hair just like Dad. He holds the TV remote just like Dad. He works in the yard just like Dad. Some of his imitations are so exact that it's scary.

As we've become aware of how much our little guy notices, we have all become much more careful about what we do and say ... and none so much as my husband!

What a great tool this adoration can be if it's channeled in the right direction. When our son sees his dad reading the Bible and praying, will he copy that also? When my husband goes out of his way to help a neighbor, will my son mimic that? When my son sees his big, strong dad going to church, will he follow suit? I pray that he does.

Dear Father, it is really fun to see what my son is picking up on these days. I pray that he will quickly see his father's love for You and that because his dad loves You, he will soon be curious about knowing You too. Amen.

A Special Thanksgiving

*The man with two tunics should share with him who has none,
and the one who has food should do the same. Luke 3:11*

My children are so excited about our Thanksgiving plans. No, we're not traveling to some exotic, warm destination, we're not having a big family reunion with relatives traveling from far-off places; actually I'm not even cooking a big dinner. Instead, we have decided that this holiday celebration is going to be spent together working for the poor. We're volunteering together as a family to serve dinners to the homeless in a nearby city.

I'm so thankful that my children immediately grasped the joy of giving their time and energy to others. Each year of my children's lives we have driven to grandmom's house to celebrate this holiday with family so there is a little feeling of sacrifice for us to not go there. But my children aren't bemoaning this; they are celebrating the chance to do something nice for others. It is going to be a special day!

Dear Father, for Christians life should be about others. I'm so grateful and joyful that my children are excited about this opportunity. Use this time to open their eyes a little to the great needs of those around them. Begin to teach them how to give of their time and energy to help others. Amen.

What to Do …

Fear God and obey His commands, for this is everyone's duty.
Ecclesiastes 12:13 NLT

I once heard a mom with two small children at home say, "I'm so busy that I don't even have time to sin." Ha. Obviously she was joking, but you get the idea. Life gets really busy, especially when you have young children at home. Those little people take up so much time and energy! It's easy to get to the point where you feel like you're just checking tasks off a list and never really engaging in them, even if those tasks have spiritual implications.

When you get that busy, it's hard to find meaning in anything you do. Then you cheat the people you're doing the tasks for, whether it's your children, your husband … even yourself.

The Bible says that the whole duty of man is to fear God and obey His commandments. Use those two points as filters for all the tasks that fill up your days. If a task doesn't fit under one of those things, it may not be worth your time and energy!

Dear Father, I want to respect You and I desire to obey Your commandments. Help me to de-junk my life so that I can give You the attention I need to focus on You and give my children the attention they deserve. Help me get my priorities straight! Amen.

Difficult Choices

"You shall have no other gods before Me." Exodus 20:3

God is a jealous God. He wants to be Number One in each of our lives. That means He wants to matter the most. He wants to be the impetus behind our decisions and actions. He wants to be Lord. He will accept no less.

This truth is something I really want to explain to my young adult son. It's not an easy concept to convey but it is so important. My son has made some other things his "gods." His pursuit of money is the number one thing in his life; he has put it above God, above relationships, even above family. Nothing is more important to him than making lots and lots of money.

I just wish he would understand that there are more important things in life than money. It's true that money can't buy happiness. Relationships with family and friends should be important, yes, but nothing, absolutely nothing, should take the place of his relationship with God, who loves him and wants to guide and direct his life.

Dear Father, I don't know how to tell my son this without him getting angry and walking away. Father, grab his heart. Remind him of Your love and care for him. Remind him that You want to be Number One in his heart. Amen.

Birthday Gifts

*Be completely humble and gentle; be patient, bearing
with one another in love. Ephesians 4:2*

A friend of mine threw a party for her three-year-old at an indoor playground and my son was invited. All the kids were having fun, but then came the gift-opening time … and my son's display of strong will.

Oh, he gave his friend his gift quite willingly, as did the other party guests, but as soon as the birthday boy opened it, my little guy snatched it back. I guess he thought the boy was providing a gift-opening service. My son threw a royal fit because he wanted to keep the gift for himself. I pried his fingers off the gift and returned it to the birthday boy, but my son continued crying for it. He cried for the rest of the party, as I put his coat on, and as we left the building.

It's a challenge to teach my son that he can't always get his way. He hasn't yet understood that life is not all about him. Hmmm, I guess I have times where I struggle with the same thing; times when I throw little temper tantrums because God doesn't do what I want. I guess we'll both have to work on learning that we can't always get our way.

Dear Father, I need Your wisdom to teach my son that he can't always get his way. And, as I teach him, help me remember this truth too. Amen.

Middle-School Muddle

By Him all things were created: things in heaven and on earth,
all things were created by Him and for Him. Colossians 1:16

A teacher at my daughter's middle school openly teaches evolution as truth. He dismisses Creationism with a wave of his hand and a sarcastic comment. His class has my daughter asking a lot of questions and even wondering if all the truths of the Bible are just fairy tales.

I think it's good that she is asking questions, because as she works through the questions and understands the answers her faith will become her own. I am scrambling to find some of the answers and I'm praying a lot for God's wisdom, but my daughter must understand that some aspects of the truths of the Bible simply have to be accepted by faith. God has certainly made Himself known in our family; she has seen His work first-hand in answered prayers and incredible blessings.

I see this as an opportunity to show my faith and Christian love in my responses. I will not say negative things about her teacher. I will affirm my own faith and beliefs. I will pray non-stop.

Dear Father, help my daughter as she thinks through the evolution vs. Bible truths issue. Father, remind her of Your love and work in her life. Help her to think clearly, without the pressure of her teacher's beliefs influencing her. Amen.

NOVEMBER 7

Circle of Friends

Love does not delight in evil but rejoices with the truth.
It always protects, always trusts, always hopes, always perseveres.
1 Corinthians 13:6-7

Friends are so important to teenagers. They almost seem to travel in herds ... everywhere. I seldom see my daughter alone any more except when she's getting ready to go to bed. I'm pleased with her choice of friends and I'm glad to know that a few of them are believers. I've watched the dynamics of this group of friends and I'm impressed with the way they support each other, encourage each other and even protect each other. It's really a nice thing.

Actually, by watching my daughter's friends I've come to appreciate my own friends even more. I appreciate the same things about them – their encouragement, support and protection. Friends are truly a gift from God and they provide a chance to show His love to others as well as receive His love from His people.

Dear Father, thank You that my daughter has such a nice group of friends and that some of them are believers who can encourage her walk with You. Thank You, too, for my friends and all they do for me. I pray that both my daughter and I will give to our friends as freely as we receive from them. Amen.

Take Him Back

*Those who know Your name will trust in You, for You, Lord,
have never forsaken those who seek You.* Psalm 9:10

A week ago we brought our second baby home from the hospital. Our schedule quickly shifted to revolve around the baby's schedule. Our three-year-old daughter is not very pleased with the shift. For the past three years our lives have revolved around her. She quickly observed that our attentions are now diverted and just yesterday loudly ordered, "Take him back." Yeah, she's finished with sharing our attention and energy.

We've tried to include her in his care by asking her to do things for him and to help us, and I invite her to snuggle with us while he nurses. Those things work well, but when she wants my attention or wants me to do something, she is not at all patient with the fact that I'm busy with the baby. My husband and I know that we need to make opportunities for each of us to do things alone with our daughter so she can see that she is still special to us and we love her very much. We'll make daddy/daughter dates and mommy/daughter dates. She'll grow to love her brother, of course, but in the meantime we want her to know she's still very loved!

Dear Father, help us to show our daughter that we love her. Help us to remember that she's adjusting to this change in her world. Amen.

NOVEMBER 9

Consuming Fear

*So we say with confidence, "The Lord is my helper;
I will not be afraid. What can man do to me?" Hebrews 13:6*

I'm scared. Everything seems out of control. My husband and I bought practically my dream home last year – but now we have very high mortgage payments. We also have two young children and I'm a stay-at-home mom, happily caring for my kids.

Why am I scared? My husband lost his job. He was let go – just like that. The job market is awful and the economic situation in our country is worse than it has ever been. Stories abound on the news of middle-class families who are suddenly homeless and have lost everything. The stress of this situation is putting a strain on our marriage. Our children are reflecting all this emotion too. I fear that we're going to lose everything – not just our lifestyle and home ... but our family.

I'm clinging to God these days and calling on Him for help. My trust is shaky as each day brings more dark news, but I believe God loves us and will help us survive this.

Dear Father, I'm scared. I don't want to lose my family. The stuff we have means nothing to me without my family. Save our family, God. Amen.

Adopted Grandmas and Grandpas

"If anyone gives even a cup of cold water to one of these little ones because he is My disciple, I tell you the truth, he will certainly not lose his reward." Matthew 10:42

A group from our church visits a local senior citizens facility each month. We bring them cupcakes and sometimes do a small craft with them. Once in a while a group of children sing a song and do a short program for the residents.

This week I brought my son along. He's only four and I've never brought him because I thought he would be disruptive rather than helpful. I was wrong; his outgoing personality and friendly spirit played right into the setting. My son wandered from resident to resident, chatting, talking and asking questions. It was amazing.

The residents fell in love with him right away and took turns waving him over to chat some more. He really brought a lot of joy to them and by the time we left my son had several adopted grandmas and grandpas who asked if he would come back and visit them. We will.

Dear Father, thank You for my son's outgoing personality. He really is a joy to be around and I loved seeing him interact with the seniors today. Thank You for a wonderful experience for him and for them. Amen.

NOVEMBER 11

Hugs and Kisses

Whatever is true, whatever is noble, whatever is right, whatever is pure,
whatever is lovely, whatever is admirable — if anything is excellent
or praiseworthy — think about such things. Philippians 4:8-9

My friends often told me how fun grandparenthood is, but I must admit that I had my doubts. However, the way my daughter and her husband's finances have gone has necessitated me helping them by caring for my grandson a couple of days a week while they both work. I'm glad I can help them but at first I wasn't super excited about babysitting.

My grandson is now about eighteen months old and I can't wait to see him on my babysitting days. What changed my attitude?

Ha. The first time he leaned over to give me a sloppy, wet kiss, he had my heart. Then the first time he put his arm around my neck in a baby bear hug sealed my heart. He is a delight and, yes, grandparenthood is a lot of fun. I appreciate that I'm getting to know my grandson and am building a relationship that will always be special for us.

Dear Father, my grandson is amazing, gorgeous, intelligent and so much fun! Thank You that I can share in his life. Bless him as he grows and learns. Thank You for his hugs and kisses! Amen.

"Just a Mom"

Continue in what you have learned because you know those from whom you learned it, and how from infancy you have known the holy Scriptures, which are able to make you wise for salvation through faith in Christ Jesus.
2 Timothy 3:14-15

When I attend an office event with my husband, inevitably someone asks me what I do. I used to be intimidated by this question, especially when it came from a professional woman. I often hung my head and mumbled something like, "I'm just a mom." It was almost like I was apologizing.

However, one night after I had mumbled my response, an older woman pulled me aside. "Don't apologize for having the most important job in the world!" she told me. "Investing your time, energy, creativity, values and love into your children is the best thing you will ever do. Remember that companies come and go, careers come and go, but the opportunity to change a child's life is an investment in God's kingdom and in the world itself!"

Well, she convinced me. Now when someone asks what I do, I hold my head high and announce that I have the privilege of being home with my children ... and I love every minute of it!

Dear Father, being a mom is a high calling. Please keep reminding me of that. Don't let me take it lightly! Amen.

NOVEMBER 13

The Journey of Prayer

*The eyes of the Lord are on the righteous and
His ears are attentive to their prayer.* 1 Peter 3:12

From the moment I learned I was going to have a baby, I began praying for my child. I prayed for her as God was forming her little body inside me; I prayed that she would be healthy and strong; I prayed for her safe arrival. Then I prayed for my daughter to come to know God early in life and to live for Him. I prayed for good choices in friendships and for the strength to stand strong against temptations.

One of my most dedicated prayers was about her future spouse. I prayed for a man of God who would love God first and my daughter second ... a man with whom she could serve the Lord. God has honored those prayers and my daughter is now married to a wonderful Christian man. It has been a privilege to pray for her through the years ... but I'm not finished yet. I continue to pray for her, her marriage, and the children she will one day mother. I'm investing in her future through my prayers.

Dear Father, it is a privilege to pray for my daughter. Thank You for honoring so many of my prayers. Although there have been difficult times; You've always seen us through them. Continue to bless and guide her life and her family. Amen.

Is This Right?

It is God who arms me with strength and makes my way perfect.
2 Samuel 22:33

I've read every book I can find and searched websites about being a mom and taking care of a newborn baby. I am armed out the wazoo with information. But my baby is still crying 24/7. Is this right? Am I doing something wrong? Have I missed a step somewhere? I'm frustrated, I have a headache, I feel like a failure, and I'm so tired I can barely form words. Why does my baby cry all the time? Why can't I make him stop?

OK, deep breath. Apparently some babies do this; the doctor says I'm not doing anything wrong. More importantly, the experts (my mom and mom-in-law) say I'm doing just fine. I'm just going to have to endure the crying until it stops. It could be a week or it could be months. Another deep breath. If we're going the "months" route I will need a lot of patience and strength from God. Good thing He has some to share!

Dear Father, You know what I'm going through and You know how tired and frustrated I am. I want my baby to be OK — that's the big thing, so if You wouldn't mind … make him stop crying so much. If that isn't going to happen, then please bless me with extra patience and strength to get through this. Amen.

Amazing Brains

Your hands made me and formed me; give me
understanding to learn Your commands. Psalm 119:73

I think my son is the most intelligent, amazing toddler that ever walked this planet. Of course I may be a bit prejudiced ... Each time my son learns something new I am struck by how amazing the human brain is. I don't have any scientific knowledge or anything like that but, as a mom, may I just say the brain is amazing!

My son got a new toy – the kind with graduated sized rings that stack on a little pole. We hadn't played with it yet, but it was on the floor. He dumped the rings, and then proceeded to put them back on. One at a time he picked up a ring and placed it on the pole. Amazing!

OK, I know he isn't doing anything that other toddlers haven't done, I'm just saying that God has placed so much potential and information in the human brain that is just waiting to be tapped into! It makes me stop and praise God each time I see my little son learn something new or do something new without being taught it. What amazing minds God gave us!

Dear Father, I don't know how anyone could watch a baby grow and not believe in You. The human body is a work of art. Thank You for giving us life and for making our complex bodies and brains so amazing! Amen.

Comfort Time

Even though I walk through the valley of the shadow of death, I will fear no evil, for You are with me; Your rod and Your staff, they comfort me.
Psalm 23:4

When a small child gets a "boo-boo," what does she do? Generally she comes running to mom, who picks her up, kisses her "boo-boo," cuddles her on her lap and makes her feel all better.

Wow, I'm an adult, but I wish comfort came that easily to me. I wish there was someone with a lap big enough for me to climb up in and sit for a while. Oh wait, there is Someone ... my Father, God.

Admittedly it's not the same as finding comfort from a real person, but in many ways it's better. I don't have to tell God my problem because He already knows. I don't have to worry that He will accidentally tell someone else and make me a topic of gossip, because He won't tell anyone. Best of all, He knows exactly what I need and if I will sit still and listen, He will give me the comfort I need. I guess we never outgrow the need for a lap to snuggle in or a hug of comfort.

Dear Father, thank You for caring about my problems. Thank You for always being there to comfort and care. Help me, Father, to choose You first over other things that wouldn't really give me comfort anyway. Amen.

NOVEMBER 17

Family Nights

"I will bless them and the places surrounding My hill. I will send down showers in season; there will be showers of blessing." Ezekiel 34:26

I love spending time with my friends, going to dinner or a movie. I yearn for date nights with my husband when we can get away to talk and laugh. I enjoy activities at church, especially the ones that are targeted at women. But my absolute favorite night is Family Night. When our children were quite young, my husband and I established Family Night. We take no phone calls (except emergencies). No friends come over. Everyone is home.

Each Family Night is different, sometimes we watch a movie – usually all piled on our king-sized bed. We munch popcorn and laugh so much that we hardly see the movie. Other times we get pizza and play board games all evening. Sometimes the kids put on a play for us. Once in a while my husband reads a book out loud and uses hilarious voices that have the kids (and me) rolling on the floor in laughter. Whatever we end up doing is always fun because we're together. It's so easy to let the craziness of life crowd out the important things. Family Nights protect an important thing – us.

Dear Father, thank You that we enjoy being together. Thank You that we find such fun things to do and to laugh about and talk about. Thank You for my wonderful family. What a blessing they are. Amen.

Always "On"

Being confident of this, that He who began a good work in you will carry it on to completion until the day of Christ Jesus.

Philippians 1:6

I pray often that my children come to know Christ early. I pray that from a young age they will begin developing a relationship with Him. Even as I pray those prayers though, God reminds me ... of me. He reminds me that the most influential example they have of the importance of Christ in their lives is my own life.

They are with me every day, so they see how I act and react. They hear what I say about others. They notice whether I'm worried to the point of not trusting God with my problems. They sense how much I truly care about other people and see how generous I am with my time and energy to help others. In short, they see if my faith really has impacted my life enough to change me. If it doesn't work for me, why should they think it will work for them?

I'm aware that I'm always "on," my children are always watching. I don't want to fake my faith to try to fool them; I want to live it to the point that they know how important it is to me.

Dear Father, my faith matters a lot to me but sometimes I get lazy. When I'm tempted to take a short cut, remind me that my children are watching. The reality of You in my life can influence them. Amen.

NOVEMBER 19

What Do You Need?

You are my portion, O Lord, I have promised to obey Your words.
Psalm 119:57

Parents often accuse their children of always wanting more and more stuff and seldom being satisfied with what they have. I've even used the ever popular phrase, "Money doesn't grow on trees" with my children.

I wonder, though, if we don't sometimes feed that desire for more stuff in our kids by giving them so much. They see our comfortable lifestyles and how we like to have the latest gadgets and conveniences. They see how we give them as much as possible so they follow the natural course to want to accumulate more and more. Perhaps we as parents are guilty, too, of focusing on accumulating more and more material things. When in reality we don't need more stuff – stuff will never make us happy – we just need more God in our lives.

Think about it ... if we had a deeper understanding of His love for us; if we grasped the possibilities of His power in our lives and had a truer belief that He wants a close relationship with us, then our striving wouldn't be for stuff; it would be only for Him.

Dear Father, oh my, what an eye-opener this is. My kids want stuff because I want stuff. Father, help me break that cycle. Help me to focus on You; on wanting more of You in my life! Amen.

All or Nothing

"You will seek Me and find Me when you seek Me with all your heart."
Jeremiah 29:13

It must be difficult to be a teenager these days. My daughter is seventeen and is trying to decide who she is. She has been raised in a Christian home where we strive to honor Christ in our lives. We attend church as a family and she goes to youth group – she's even been on some church mission trips. But the pressures of peers who don't know Christ are beginning to wear on her. I see the confusion in her eyes. I know she is struggling to make her faith her own … not Mom and Dad's faith.

She's searching, but she's not committing to what she's finding – when God shows her something of Himself, she either ignores it or explains it away. Faith must be trusted; that's the nature of faith; and she isn't doing that. If she would just give her whole heart to searching for God and not try to ride the fence between two worlds, I know she would find Him. I know it's not my place to bombard her with a lot of "You should's …" but I can pray and trust that God will draw her to Himself.

Dear Father, meet my daughter in a way where her faith can become her own. That's so important. Draw her heart to You and help her to know without a doubt that she has found You. Amen.

Honoring My Parents

Honor your father and your mother, so that you may live long in the land the LORD your God is giving you. Exodus 20:12

My husband and I joke with our children that someday one of them will support us. We tease that we're nice to them so they will choose a nice seniors home to put us in. It's all in good fun, except when it's not. Maybe one day we will actually be dependent on our children to make decisions for us and perhaps even help us financially.

Since I'm caring for my ageing mother in much that way right now, I take our teasing more seriously. I'm also aware that my children pay attention to how I treat my mother. Am I obeying God's commands to honor her? Do I respect her and speak kindly to her and about her ... even when I'm frustrated with her? Do I grasp the confusion and frustration she feels about growing older and not being able to do what she used to do or remember what she knows she once knew? Do I view the responsibility of caring for her as a privilege or a burden?

My mother gave me life, I am happy to help with hers. I'm aware that I'm laying groundwork for the future – for my children to someday honor me in my golden years.

Dear Father, thank You for the privilege of caring for my mother. Help me to always treat her with respect and love, to be an example for my children of what it means to honor your mother. Amen.

Loose Lips Sink Ships

Too much talk leads to sin. Be sensible and keep your mouth shut.
Proverbs 10:19 NLT

If you've ever been hurt because someone blabbed one of your confidences to the world then you understand the meaning of Proverbs 10:19. What an important truth to impress on our young children. Teach your child that when someone tells her a secret ... keep it secret. Don't break her trust. Just remind your child that if a friend is in danger, then it's OK to tell the secret to an adult, but still not make the situation a point for gossip.

It is difficult to restore trust when someone breaks a confidence. Breaking someone's trust is a sin. So, yes, when words flow freely there is probably sin present – it may show in bragging, criticism, gossip or sharing a friend's secrets. These not only damage friendships but they set terrible examples of what Christ intended for relationships based on love. Children pick up on these things. Not to say that gossip begets gossip ... but it sure sets an example! How can you condemn your children for doing what they have observed you doing?

Dear Father, help my children grasp the importance of thinking before they speak. I pray they will choose to keep confidences and thus become known as trustworthy friends. Amen.

Praying All the Time

Are any of you suffering hardships? You should pray.
Are any of you happy? You should sing praises. James 5:13 NLT

What do my children see me do when problems come into our lives? Do they see me turn first to Christ for wisdom, guidance, comfort and help? If I'm not modeling a lifestyle that shows that, then why should I expect them to turn to Christ in times of need? When I'm in a good place because God has smoothed the path before me and everything is happy, do I praise God? Do I give Him the credit? If I don't praise and thank Him for the blessings in my life, then why should my children do so?

Scripture tells us to go to God with our problems and to praise Him for the answers. If my first request isn't of God, then I'm sinning. If my first praise isn't to Him, I'm also sinning. In order to teach my children to go to God all the time, whether with painful problems or joyous praises, I must show them that I do it. If it's not real for me, why should it be real for them?

Dear Father, I need some help here. I do pray, but often only when I'm alone or when the kids are asleep. Give me the courage to let them see me praying throughout the day. Give me the courage to let them see my pain and my celebrations. Let them see that I go to God with everything. Amen.

NOVEMBER 24

Walking on Eggshells

*A hot-tempered person starts fights; a cool-tempered
person stops them.* Proverbs 15:18 NLT

Isn't that a funny expression ... "walking on eggshells" around someone? What does it even mean? Well, eggshells break easily and when they are broken they have sharp edges, so in order not to break them, a person would have to tread lightly and carefully. If the shells were broken she would have to walk even more carefully to avoid getting hurt.

Wow, if there is a person who is so temperamental that you have to walk on eggshells around her you know it's not fun. People with explosive tempers are like that. You're always wondering if you are going to say the wrong thing at the wrong time and cause an explosion.

This makes me wonder how my children perceive me – am I an "eggshell" kind of mom who explodes when they argue and just makes things worse? Or do they see me as a patient mom who can calm their quarrels and settle their battles? That's the kind of mom I want to be. If I'm not there yet, then perhaps I have some work to do.

Dear Father, I don't want to be hot-tempered but I know I am sometimes. Forgive me for that, Father, and help me to be more patient and calm. Help me to show love to my children, not anger. Help them to learn to do the same. Amen.

Just Let It Go

*Starting a quarrel is like breaching a dam; so drop
the matter before a dispute breaks out.* Proverbs 17:14

My son loves to torment his older sister. I think he wakes up in the morning with a plan for the day of ways to make her miserable. She is a "reactor" (like me). So when he begins teasing her, she seldom lets his comments roll off her back. She usually responds with a critical comment, which just eggs him on to tease her more because he is getting what he wants. Almost every time they are together this exchange escalates into a war.

I keep telling my daughter to just let it go and not react to his comments. If he doesn't get a reaction, he will eventually stop teasing her. But she doesn't seem to be able to do that. She thinks the best way to handle it is to punish him ... and I do ... but it is such a game to him that he doesn't stop. It is important for her to learn to stop the quarrel before it becomes a war, and that she can diffuse the situation by her response.

Dear Father, I want my daughter to understand that she is the one in control – she just has to discipline herself to stop reacting to her brother's teasing. Help her see that and put it into practice. Amen.

Gentle, Not Weak

Let your gentleness be evident to all.
Philippians 4:5

My son can be incredibly gentle. I've seen him tenderly pick up an injured animal and carry it to safety. When he plays with small children he is careful with them. I know he is capable of being gentle. But, with his siblings, there is no gentleness evident. He acts like such a tough guy.

Sometimes I think that in his ten-year-old brain he equates gentleness with weakness. How do I get him to understand that being gentle with his six-year-old sister does not mean he is weak but that he is sensitive to a younger, weaker person? He doesn't need to knock her against the wall to get past her. He also doesn't need to speak so loudly or harshly to other members of the family either – that won't get him what he wants anyway.

I want to help him understand that gentleness is a reflection of how Jesus related to people, especially people who had great needs. He was gentle in His words and in His actions but He was never weak. Gentle words and actions are the bridge that God's love crosses over from us to others.

Dear Father, my son has so much energy and so much strength. Help him to channel that into living for You and loving others. I pray that a part of that process will be his gentleness toward others. Amen.

Living Together

How good and pleasant it is when brothers live together in unity!
Psalm 133:1

One of my greatest accomplishments in life is really not my accomplishment at all ... it's God's. I think, though, that I did play a role as His tool once in a while. This is the accomplishment that gives me such pleasure: my children like each other. Does that sound like a little thing? It isn't.

I have friends whose children are grown up and do not even talk to each other. How sad is that? I love that when my children all come home, there is non-stop chatter and laughter. They have so much fun together. A complete stranger even stopped us in public to comment on how pleasant it was to see a family getting along so well. It's true ... we do. I believe it is a gift from God.

There were certainly times when one of us could have walked away from the others, but none of us ever did because we have a foundation of love and care for one another. Now, even their stories of disagreements from the past sparkle with humor and laughter. No hard feelings have been carried over. Praise God ... they like each other!

Dear Father, I'm so happy that my adult children like each other. Each of them is so different, I'm just thrilled that they love each other and would really do anything for one another. What a gift. Thank You. Amen.

Teamwork

The body is a unit, though it is made up of many parts; and though all its parts are many, they form one body. 1 Corinthians 12:12

My children know what a team is; they understand the concept of working together with your teammates, helping and encouraging each other.

I'd like them to carry over that team concept to their understanding of family too. It's true that the five of us are different from one another in many ways: We have different hobbies, different likes and dislikes, and we look different. But we have one important thing in common; we belong to the same family. So the five of us make up one family. Five parts, one whole.

When kids get to the teenage years they act as though they want nothing to do with their family. They are often "too cool" to be seen with their parents and siblings. I don't believe that, though, because the awareness that they are an important part of a body means that they know they have a role to play. I pray that deep down inside my kids have affirmed that they would each be there for the other should the need ever arise. I pray that their commitment to the family is strong.

Dear Father, thank You for my family. I pray that my children will stay connected and understand the joy of belonging to a family. Amen.

Say It ... Mean It

*Dear children, let us not love with words or tongue
but with actions and in truth. 1 John 3:18*

Sometimes people say that if you repeat something often enough you will believe it. That's great but I'm not sure whoever said that was thinking about siblings.

My two boys are only a year apart and they fight constantly. Often my intervention is to suggest that they say something nice to each other – sometimes I even make them say that they love each other. Yeah, that goes over well.

Beyond that, I encourage them to actually do things that show they love each other. Sometimes, when they've had a particularly rough day together, we sit down and they make lists of the nice things they could do for each other. Then they each have to secretly choose one thing and quietly do it for his brother before the day is over. It's awesome! It's nearly impossible to stay angry with someone when you're doing a nice thing for that person.

I'm seeing my boys put feet on their faith – and this means loving each other even when it's hard.

Dear Father, thank You for my boys. Continue to channel their energy and enthusiasm into good things. Help them learn that good actions mean so much more than just good words by themselves. Amen.

December

Hanging On

*The LORD upholds all those who fall and lifts up
all who are bowed down. Psalm 145:14*

I'm sick – very sick. I just left the doctor's office where I got the worst possible news. I'm numb. The major thought stuck in my mind; the thought I can't see around; is this ... what will happen to my children? I mean, if I don't make it. I can't believe that God would give me these wonderful children, then not let me live to see them grow up ... but I know it happens all the time.

I know I need to trust God to do what's best for me and to take care of my children no matter what. I want to trust Him. I need to trust Him. I know that God's ways are not my ways so I guess this is when my faith is going to have to take hold and be my strength.

There have been plenty of times in my life when I've needed God's strength, but I've never had an experience like this. I have nothing to compare it to and therefore nothing to draw on ... except my history with God, which proves He loves my children and me. I know He will take care of us – no matter what.

Dear Father, I'm scared. I don't want to leave my children but I know You won't leave me or my kids, because You love us. I know that. I'll keep trusting You and keep believing You will do what's best. Amen.

Fretting Queen

Refrain from anger and turn from wrath; do not fret —
it only leads to evil. Psalm 37:8

The Bible says that God has given everyone some special talent or ability. I know what mine is — I'm really good at fretting. What is fretting? It's worry that doesn't let go.

When I fret about something I think about it constantly and try everything to fix the problem or stop it from happening. I fret about my children being safe in this crazy world where children are randomly attacked. I fret about whether they are living up to their potential in school. I fret about whether I'm doing a good job as a mom.

Why is fretting so bad? Fret and trust can't co-exist. If I'm fretting about these things, then I'm not trusting God to guide and protect me. That means my proclamations of faith have little meaning when life gets difficult. Do I really trust God or do I just give Him lip service while I go right on fretting? Yeah, that's pretty convicting, isn't it? I need to dethrone myself as the fretting queen and get on my knees before God.

Dear Father, fretting takes a lot of energy and it doesn't really get me anywhere. I know fretting isn't what You want for me. Forgive me for not trusting You more and help me to give up fretting and trust You instead. Amen.

How to Live with Others

The commandments are summed up in this one rule:
"Love your neighbor as yourself." Romans 13:9

One of the most important things I can teach my children is how to get along with others. The "play nice with others" characteristic will carry them through all of life. Romans 13:9 verifies that all of God's commandments about how to get along with others can be summed up in one singular command, "Love your neighbor as yourself."

Teaching my children to think about others' feelings and desires with the same intensity that they look out for their own is a big thing for them to understand. It's sometimes hard for a child to get past the "Life is all about me" thought process (it's hard for adults sometimes too). Modeling an open and caring attitude for others is one subtle way to teach this.

Loving others as I love myself means putting others first. It means I don't always need to be the star or in the spotlight. It means I don't always get my way. It means encouraging and helping others instead of promoting myself.

Dear Father, loving others is key to living the Christian life. I want my children to understand that living a life of love is Your goal for all of us. Help them to learn to put others first. Amen.

Purifying Life

"You are the salt of the earth. But if the salt loses its saltiness, how can it be made salty again? It is no longer good for anything, except to be thrown out and trampled by men." Matthew 5:13

Living for Christ in a public high school is not easy. My daughter is trying, but other kids make fun of her and call her unkind names. Part of the reason for their antagonism may be that those kids are making choices they know are not right. A girl who is trying to live a pure life and who openly lives for God can be seen as salt in a wound.

My daughter understands it's a good thing (although it's not always easy for her). She knows that one of the descriptions of a believer's life is that of being salt, so she leans into this challenge. My support is to encourage her, give her chances to talk about her feelings, and pray, pray, pray.

I know it's hard – it's hard for me as an adult to live my faith in front of skeptics – so I have no doubt it is more difficult for a teenager. I'm proud of her but I'm aware of her need for constant prayer support. She's got it!

Dear Father, strengthen and encourage my daughter as she lives her love for You openly. Give her wisdom and power to withstand attacks on her choices and on her faith. Amen.

United through Love

If you have any encouragement from being united with Christ, if any comfort from His love, if any fellowship with the Spirit, if any tenderness and compassion, then make my joy complete by being like-minded, having the same love, being one in spirit and purpose. Philippians 2:1-2

Have you heard the old expression, "Blood is thicker than water"? It refers to the fact that family loyalties should be stronger than friendship loyalties. Family members should stick together, support each other, defend each other and love each other – no matter what!

This gets a little sticky once in a while because, even though we love each other as family, it doesn't mean we always like each other or what each family member chooses to do. Your family should be a safe place. So, even if I don't like my teenager sometimes, I love her to the depths of my soul; I'll stand up for her, support her, encourage her, challenge her and pray for her.

As family we share more than just a name: we share DNA, we share memories; we share our lives. We are to be like-minded and have the united purpose of loving one another, loving Christ and living for Him. It's not always easy, but it's always worthwhile.

Dear Father, my family is very important to me. Sometimes it takes a little work (or a lot of work) to be united and supportive of one another. Let us never give up on that, though. Amen.

Feeling Slighted

Trust in the LORD forever, for the LORD, the LORD, is the Rock eternal.
He humbles those who dwell on high. Isaiah 26:4-5

Oh my, my heart is aching for my child. She's hurting so badly because, once again, she didn't make the team. This child has literally tried out for everything her school offers: cheerleading, sports teams, plays, talent nights, variety shows ... and she has made nothing!

The school says it encourages school spirit and participation by all students, but it seems like the same kids make everything. To make matters worse, there is one girl (who is on every team and in every play) who really enjoys rubbing her success in my daughter's face and putting her down.

My daughter is wondering where God is in all this. She is a believer and does try to obey Him and live for Him. She's kind of wondering why He doesn't help her with one victory ... just one. I don't have an answer for her except to keep trusting God. Eventually, life will even out and she will get her chance. True, it may not be in this school, but the school years don't last forever.

Dear Father, one thing ... just give her one thing. OK, encourage her to keep believing in herself. Help her to see her worth and to recognize the abilities You gave her. Don't let her give up. Amen.

DECEMBER 6

Fooling Yourself

Do not merely listen to the word, and so deceive yourselves.
Do what it says. James 1:22

I wonder how many times in a child's life a parent asks, "Do you hear me?" Kids seem to have selective hearing, don't they? Parents give instructions or correction and the words seem to float right over their child's head. It can be so frustrating. So, we follow up our words with, "Do you hear me?" Of course our children always answer affirmatively, but the key to the hearing is in the actions. Do they put our words into action? Do we see a difference in their behavior? If not, then the "hearing" didn't translate into action.

In much the same way, I wonder how often God wants to ask me, "Do you hear Me?" I may read His Word each day in my daily quiet time, but how often am I reading the words while thinking about my agenda for the day? The key to reading His Word and it changing my life will be seen in changes in my behavior. Just as the proof of my children listening to me is shown in their behavior, the proof of God's Word changing me is seen in my behavior.

Dear Father, just as I want my children to not just hear me but actually put my instructions and corrections into action, I also long to have my behavior changed by Your Word. Help me to pay attention and put Your Word into practice. Amen.

God Knows

"When you pray, do not keep on babbling like pagans, for they think they will be heard because of their many words. Do not be like them, for your Father knows what you need before you ask Him." Matthew 6:7-8

It always makes me laugh when my husband and I pray together for our children because as he prays, he names each child like God doesn't know who they are. Oh, I'm not being critical, just smiling. I know that as my husband says each name his heart is uttering a prayer that he can't even verbalize for each individual child. My husband is an awesome pray-er! I pray so simply and struggle to find the right words at times.

I find great comfort, especially in praying for my children, that God knows what they need before I can even verbalize my requests. I don't need to keep babbling and telling God what to do, because spewing more words out doesn't make Him listen any more carefully. God loves me. He loves my children. He knows what we all need before we ever utter a prayer. Yes, He wants me to pray – I need to pray – but I can trust Him to take care of us when I don't even know what to pray.

Dear Father, thank You for loving us so much. Thank You for taking such good care of us. Thank You for hearing my fumbling efforts at prayer and seeing the passion of my heart. Amen.

God Has a Plan

Continue to work out your salvation with fear and trembling, for it is God who works in you to will and to act according to His good purpose.
Philippians 2:12-13

Sometimes I wonder if cultures where parents plan their children's lives by choosing their careers and spouses have life figured out. My children don't want me to tell them who to marry or even who to date. They don't want me to choose their career or even what to study at college. I raised them to be independent people who can actually think ... but then I don't want them to. Go figure.

The comfort I take in their thinking is that each of them is seeking God's guidance in their lives and I know He has a plan for each of them that He will continue to work out. Of course there will be ups and downs in their lives (from which I'd like to protect them), and there will be times when they do not obey God (intentionally or accidentally), but God sees their hearts. He will continue to teach them through the hard times and guide them through the mess that life sometimes becomes. I can trust God with them a whole lot more than I trust myself with them.

Dear Father, I pray for my children to keep seeking Your guidance. I pray for strength not to try to fix everything, because You will teach them important lessons through hard times. Amen.

DECEMBER 9

A New Believer

*You were taught, with regard to your former way of life,
to put off your old self, and to put on the new self, created to
be like God in true righteousness and holiness. Ephesians 4:22-24*

I'm a new Christian – the first believer in my family. I'm pretty enthusiastic about my faith so I talk about it a lot. I want my husband and children to know the joy of recognizing what Christ did for them and to grasp how much God loves them. But I'm learning that my enthusiasm for my new faith needs to be shown by actual changes in my life.

Because this is all so new to me, sometimes I slip back into my selfish attitudes and critical judgments. I'm learning that, in order for my family to take my new faith seriously, they need to see that every day I consciously allow the Holy Spirit to take control of my life and make me more like God.

Yes, I'm still a sinner and some days will be better than others, but I want my family to come to know Christ so I will consciously make this effort – every day – with the help of God who loves us all.

Dear Father, I'm so excited about all You have done for me. Take control of my heart, my mind, my words and make me more and more like Christ. Let my family see the difference You make in my life. Amen.

"I Didn't Do It!"

*If we claim to be without sin, we deceive ourselves and the truth is not in us.
If we confess our sins, He is faithful and just and will forgive
us our sins and purify us from all unrighteousness.* 1 John 1:8-9

Someone spilled grape juice on my beige sofa. Dark grape juice ... a big stain. When I questioned my nine-year-old son, his response, of course, was, "I didn't do it." Our household consists of me, my husband, my son and our dog. I didn't do it, my hubby didn't do it ... that leaves the dog. It's funny how my son is always guilt-free. He seldom voluntarily accepts responsibility for his actions. How did he learn to be so deceptive?

I confess to him that I'm certainly not guilt-free; I make mistakes and commit sins for which I must take responsibility. The best thing is to accept responsibility by admitting and confessing my wrongs. Just as I will forgive my son for his mistakes, God will also forgive. He will cleanse me from the stain of that sin.

If I don't confess and ask for forgiveness, that stain will be a constant reminder of my deceit. I love my son, which means I want to forgive him. God loves him even more and encourages confession so that forgiveness can be given.

Dear Father, it's hard to admit our sins, but help my son to see how important it is. Experiencing forgiveness, both from others and from You, is such a blessing. Help him to learn to be honest. Amen.

Who Does It Hurt?

Remember, it is sin to know what you ought to do and then not do it.
James 4:17 NLT

My teenage son has gotten into pornography. It makes me sad and angry at the same time. My husband and I challenged our son about his exploration of this dirt and his response was, "So what? It's not a big deal." Oh my, that made me even sadder. I could shout at him regarding how this stuff affects his view of women and how unrealistic his expectations of women and even of sex will be because of what he is watching. Of course, he will have a flip answer for that.

We're dealing with the practicalities, like monitoring his computer time, but I'm more concerned with the condition of his heart. My son has accepted Christ as his Savior. But the fact that this addiction has been allowed to creep into his heart is sin, plain and simple. That's what I want him to understand. It's not just a harmless hobby.

Even if no other human was directly or indirectly hurt by his actions, his relationship with God is hurt because it placed sin between them. He knows the right thing to do and he's not doing it – that's sin.

Dear Father, grab my son's heart. Pull him back to You. Pull him away from this desire. Open his eyes to the sin of what he's allowing into his mind and heart. Please, help him. Amen.

DECEMBER 12

Breaking the
"Quitter" Attitude

Do not be afraid or discouraged, for the LORD God, my God,
is with you. He will not fail you or forsake you until all the work
for the service of the temple of the LORD is finished. 1 Chronicles 28:20

My son's first grade teacher called me in for a meeting – never a good sign. Actually, she was just concerned about something that I'd noticed too: My son does not like to fail. He is so afraid of failing that unless he is absolutely certain he can accomplish a task, he won't even try it. He'd rather not try than fail. I so appreciate his teacher picking up on this and we will work together to help my son understand that failure is not necessarily a bad thing.

Good lessons can be learned from failing, like how to approach a task the next time. Today's verse is the words of a parent to his child. David is encouraging Solomon to keep working at his task and not be afraid of failure. David reminds his son that God helps him and will not fail him until the work is done.

I can similarly encourage my son that God will help him with his work and that, even if he fails sometimes, God will help him get back up and try again.

Dear Father, please encourage my son to be willing to try new things. He will never know the joy of learning new things or being successful at them if he isn't willing to try. Remind him of Your help. Amen.

More and More Stuff

Godliness with contentment is great gain. For we brought nothing into the world, and we can take nothing out of it. 1 Timothy 6:6-7

Contentment is not a word that is used in today's society very often. We're generally not content with much, but are constantly striving for more. More cars, more clothes, more money, more stuff, more friends ... more, more, more. We seem to feel that what we have is not enough and we always deserve more.

We chastise our children for feeling this way. We tell them to appreciate the toys they have but then they watch us get better cars, bigger TVs, faster computers, the newest cell phones ... and our chastisement falls on deaf ears. Can you blame them?

Encouraging a simpler lifestyle begins by living one, not just preaching about one. It may not be easy, but living contentedly will eventually bring more peace in our lives and the means to be more generous in our giving to those who have so much less.

Dear Father, help me incorporate simplicity into my lifestyle. If I model it perhaps my children will see that it's a good thing. As we accept this lifestyle of being content with what we have, show us where we can give to those who don't have enough to even live, let alone have abundance. Amen.

DECEMBER 14

Dark Times

These have come so that your faith — of greater worth than gold, which perishes even though refined by fire — may be proved genuine and may result in praise, glory and honor when Jesus Christ is revealed. 1 Peter 1:7

My husband left us. I don't understand why God let this happen. We were a Christian family. We were super-involved at our church. I thought we were happy. This has shaken my faith because I'm not sure where God is in this situation. I can't seem to find Him and yet, in my heart, I know that it is in these darkest times of life when faith in God matters the most. If I can see Him through my pain, then I will always know that He is with me, regardless of what happens.

This is one of those "going through the fire" times of life that hurt so very much, but once I get to the other side, I will look back and see the evidence of God's presence and how it has made my faith so much stronger.

I have to get myself together and be strong for my children. I have to let them know that we will be just fine. God is our strength and we will come out on the other side stronger than ever!

Dear Father, I'm saying the words but I don't fully believe them right now – the hurt is too fresh. Strengthen me, show me how to get through this. Be my security and my hope. Help me pass that along to my children. Amen.

Beautiful People

"What do you benefit if you gain the whole world but lose your own soul? Is anything worth more than your soul?" Matthew 16:26

From the time my daughter was a little girl she has cared about having lots of friends and being the leader of her group of friends. Now that she's in high school ... well, let's just say that I worry a bit about where this yearning to be popular might take her. Her faith doesn't seem to be strong enough to face-off against what the "crowd" says so it's quite possible that she might compromise her values and beliefs in order to fit in and be popular.

I feel like I've talked until I'm blue in the face about standing up for what she believes, and being a light in a dark place, and how friends that make you do things you disagree with are not really friends. But I don't know if she's heard a word. She could gain tons of momentary popularity, but forfeit her soul in the process. I'm an adult and I understand that; but it is a tougher concept for a teenager. I will keep on talking, of course, but more than anything I'll pray for her and I'll enlist my friends to pray for her too.

Dear Father, I pray that my daughter will get her priorities straight and realize that living for You is more important than the fleeting popularity of a high school group. Protect her, Father. Amen.

Beauty from Within

*Charm is deceptive, and beauty is fleeting; but a woman
who fears the LORD is to be praised.* Proverbs 31:30

Women put a lot of time and money into their appearance and comfort – we spend money on hair, manicures, pedicures, massages, skin lotions, make-up, jewelry, clothing, shoes and a myriad of other things I can't think of right now. All of the things on this list contribute to our outer beauty.

Proverbs 31 doesn't mention much about a woman's outer appearance; it focuses importance on a woman's heart. I wonder how equal the time spent between outward preparations for our appearance and preparations in our heart's appearance would be. What are we teaching our young daughters regarding what is important if we focus most of our energy, money and time on outward stuff, while inward care gets a fraction of the time?

Inward care? That's reading our Bibles … really reading it so that God can speak to us. It's also praying, spending quiet time before God while waiting to hear His voice. This inner beauty treatment can't be rushed; it takes time and is well worth the effort.

Dear Father, help me to see the greater need to spend time on myself, hearing from You, learning from Your Word. I want to be known for being a woman of God, not just for my appearance. Amen.

Heartwarmers

A cheerful look brings joy to the heart, and good
news gives health to the bones. Proverbs 15:30

You know the feeling of a long hard day. The kids got up way too early after you stayed up way too late the night before. Your two-year-old throws his bowl of cereal across the kitchen. The dog eats it, and then promptly throws up ... on the carpet. Your husband calls to say that he forgot his lunch and wonders if you could bring it to him. Your four-year-old blocks the toilet trying to flush a washcloth. Then the kids start fighting and well ... things go downhill from there. By the end of the day you are exhausted. Your patience is completely gone and you are secretly considering locking the door and running away.

Every mom has had a day like this. There is one thing that happens almost every bad day, though, that completely changes my attitude. Do you know what it is? A simple smile from one of my little ones. Yes, so simple, but that little heartfelt smile warms my heart more than anything I can imagine. I'm refreshed and ready to give another 200% to my little ones. I love them so much.

Dear Father, thank You for the honest smiles and hugs from my children. They make the struggles, work and effort worthwhile. I love them so much. Thank You for them. Amen.

DECEMBER 18

Family Life

All of you, clothe yourselves with humility toward one another, because,
"God opposes the proud but gives grace to the humble." 1 Peter 5:5

Why is it that my kids can be so nice when they are out in public, but when they get home they behave with such arrogance and pride? The way my children treat each other, and even me sometimes, is just not acceptable. I guess I'm glad they behave politely to outsiders, but seriously, it would be nice to have a little peace in our home. There is such a "life is all about me" attitude in the way they interact. Everyone is looking out for Number One.

Emulating Christ's humility seldom crosses their minds, I guess. The lesson of humility involves emptying self of ... self. It means thinking about others first and even desiring to push others to the forefront for a little glory, a chance to succeed and recognition. Humility is glad to take a back seat. Being humble is a chance to be a conduit of Christ's love to those around us. It's a goal for all of us ... even at home.

Dear Father, thank You that my children do show humility when they are out in public, but I pray that a little of it would come home with them. Bless our family with love and concern for each other. Show us each how to share Christ's love with one another. Amen.

No Soap Operas Here!

*She watches over the affairs of her household and
does not eat the bread of idleness. Proverbs 31:27*

The Proverbs 31 woman has always been a pain in the neck. There was nothing that woman could not do! I always cringe when a speaker says, "Turn to Proverbs 31." Who could live up to the standard that woman set? In reality ... most moms can cover most of the bases; and do it without the servants that "31 woman" had. A woman who has a husband, children, a house to manage, a part-time job and who is engaged in the lives of her family does not have time to sit around and watch soap operas and eat bon bons all day (OK, an occasional TV show and a candy bar, maybe).

The point is that the Proverbs 31 woman didn't eat the bread of idleness and, while I love bread, I don't have time to be idle either. If a mom gets sick and has to miss even one day of doing her jobs around the house ... it's a disaster! So, no more intimidation by the Proverbs 31 woman. We can do a lot of what she did ... but I'm thinking having those servant girls sounds pretty appealing!

Dear Father, Proverbs 31 gives me a standard to attempt to live up to. At the very least it's a reminder to stay true to my jobs, keep busy and not eat the bread of idleness. Thanks for the reminder. Amen.

DECEMBER 20

For the Love of Money

For the love of money is a root of all kinds of evil. Some people, eager for money, have wandered from the faith and pierced themselves with many griefs. 1 Timothy 6:10

It's so easy to get caught up in the "Keeping up with the Joneses" syndrome. Living in a nice neighborhood in a nice town and going to a nice church almost makes it worse. I find myself wanting the same things my friends and neighbors have, and even feeling like a bit of a failure if I don't have them. This attitude places all kinds of stress on my relationship with my husband.

Loving money and other things gets in the way of loving people. Of course, there's nothing wrong with having money or having stuff, but those should never be more important than the people in my life or my relationship with God – it should not pull me away from my walk with Him. No good can come of that.

I must beware of the temptation to care about money and stuff too much. If that begins creeping into my life, turning to God's Word is the best antidote to help me get my priorities straight again.

Dear Father, I'm sorry that sometimes stuff becomes so important to me. Help me to keep my priorities straight and focus on You and the people I love. Amen.

Careless Words

*Reckless words pierce like a sword, but the tongue
of the wise brings healing. Proverbs 12:18*

I can't believe I did that. The look I just saw on my young son's face is one I never, ever want to see again. Granted, he has been a stinker today; into one thing after another, disobedient and difficult to handle. I just lost my temper and shouted at him. I said words to him that no loving, Christian mother should ever say to her child. I saw by the look in his eyes that my words pierced his heart.

I want to grab him in a giant hug, apologize profusely and promise him that I will never do that again. I love him so much and I really enjoy being his mother. He's a good boy who had a tough day and I'm a good mother who had a tougher day.

I'm the adult, so I will apologize, ask his forgiveness and assure him of my total and complete love. I really hate it when I lose control like that, especially if my words hurt my son.

Dear Father, why do I do that? Why can't I control myself better? It breaks my heart when I hurt my son by losing control. Please forgive me and please let him forgive … and forget. Please don't allow my loose, cruel words to damage his tender, loving heart. Help me, Father, to not allow that to happen again. Amen.

DECEMBER 22

Staying Focused

Look to the LORD and His strength; seek His face always.
Psalm 105:4

My daughter's gymnastic training is teaching me a couple of important spiritual lessons. She trains so hard, working out for five hours six days a week. But she has had to skip over some activities that she might have enjoyed because gymnastics takes so much of her time. She made the choice to work at being the best gymnast she can be.

That's one lesson my daughter has taught me – living for Christ means daily choosing to follow Him. It means forgoing some things that you might enjoy because living for Christ is more important.

Another thing I've learned from her is focus. Her specialty is the balance beam. I'm blown away by her ability to jump, spin on one foot, or tumble and land upright on the beam. I ask her how she does those tricks without falling off and her response is ... focus. She chooses one spot to look at and keeps her eyes on it, so when she spins or tumbles she is looking for that one spot to focus on so she knows where to land. I must keep my eyes focused on Jesus so that when life experiences make me tumble or spin, I know where to land by when I see Him.

Dear Father, thank You again for powerful lessons from a practical experience. Help me to stay focused on You. Amen.

Never Give Up

"Nothing is impossible with God." Luke 1:37

My son is all grown up. It's weird being the parent of an adult sometimes. I still have all the "momma" feelings and desires ... but he doesn't want to be mothered. So I can either fret about the things I want him to do or I can trust God with them. Hmmm, choices.

The biggest thing I struggle with is that my son is not walking with the Lord. That breaks my heart. I've prayed and prayed that he will return to the faith of his childhood, but he isn't interested at all. He says he's doing just fine without God, thank you very much. The truth is ... he is, at least as far as his career and money goes. But I wouldn't care if he didn't have two coins to rub together if he was living for Christ.

I've talked and prayed until I've run out of ways to tell my son about Christ. He kindly tells me that there is no way he is going to become a Christian, but I haven't given up because I have a secret weapon. I know, from a myriad of examples in God's Word, that nothing, absolutely nothing, is impossible where God is concerned. So I'm going to keep right on praying!

Dear Father, bring my son to You. Break down the barriers he has built around his heart. Show him his need for You! Nothing is impossible with You, God. Nothing! Amen.

An Amazing Gift

The angel said to them, "Do not be afraid. I bring you good news
of great joy that will be for all the people. Today in the town of David
a Savior has been born to you; He is Christ the Lord." Luke 2:10-12

Since becoming a mother I have a much greater understanding of the magnitude of God's gift of Jesus. I would
do anything for my son ... anything ... die for him, if necessary. So, to understand that God's love for me is so
powerful that He would send His Son to earth to live
and die for me is completely humbling and completely
amazing. I can't even find words to describe how I feel
about this.

Before I became a mother I understood that Jesus is
God's Son and that He came to earth as part of the plan that
would allow me to have a place in God's family for eternity.
I understood it with my head, but since my son was born,
now I understand it with my heart.

Sending Jesus was such an unselfish act of love that I
cannot comprehend it. I'm saddened by what God must
have felt; I'm grateful for such a gift; I'm humbled by His
love; I'm motivated to love Him back ... more and more.

Dear Father, I can't find the words to express my gratitude.
Thank You seems way too simple. But ... thank You. Amen.

Powerful Belief

"I tell you the truth, if you have faith as small as a mustard seed, you can say to this mountain, 'Move from here to there' and it will move. Nothing will be impossible for you." Matthew 17:20

Faith as powerful as Jesus described in Matthew 17:20 seems to escape me, even though I long for it. I want to be able to trust Jesus that much. I've never really wanted a physical mountain to move, but there are things in my life that look as big as mountains and I'd love to face into them with powerful faith.

My marriage is teetering on destruction; I'd like to believe that it can be mended. My children are angry and distant; I want to believe that we can reconnect. Our finances are in turmoil; I pray that we can recover.

Jesus said that even a tiny bit of real faith means nothing is impossible. God is more powerful than any damaged relationship. He is the great Healer of broken hearts. He is the best Accountant ever.

God can do anything if I just believe it. I'm working on it ... for me and for my family. It's going to take the power of God to heal our problems and put us back together.

Dear Father, heal us. Help us. Show me how to find that tiny, deep faith that can move mountains. We have a few mountains in our lives right now. I give them to You. I trust them to You. Amen.

Precious Protection

He will cover you with His feathers, and under His wings you will find refuge; His faithfulness will be your shield and rampart.
Psalm 91:4

We have to move. My husband got a new job, but it's across the country. It's a promotion and will be really great for him and for us financially, but moving isn't going to be easy for our teenage children. They are not willing to even discuss it. We've heard the usual, "My life will be over." "How can you ask me to leave my friends and my school?"

I understand their fears. The truth is I'm a little nervous too. We'll be starting over in a brand-new place. That's pretty scary. However, I trust God's promise to be our refuge. I know we won't be moving across the country by ourselves; God will protect us. He will cover us and His faithfulness will see us through this time.

It may be that the hardest part of this move is walking our kids through it. I want them to understand, too, that God will be their refuge and strength through this difficult time. It's hard but sometimes good things come out of difficult situations.

Dear Father, I'm scared and excited at the same time. I'm most concerned, though, for my children. Father, I know this is going to be hard for them. Help them through it. Help them make new friends quickly and easily settle in to their new schools. Amen.

Praising, Praising Always

Great is the LORD and most worthy of praise;
His greatness no one can fathom. Psalm 145:3

My children and I have a fun activity we enjoy doing together: We settle in the backyard with glasses of lemonade and look up at the clouds in the sky, describing what we see. As the clouds move and change formation we see different things. Sometimes we get a bit silly and see the most incredible things; sometimes the cloud pictures are quite complex.

From this simple activity I often guide our conversation to how amazing and awesome our God is. We each start listing our favorite things that God makes. My children are so observant! I love hearing them praise God for the simplest of His creations, from a tiny ant to rainbows to kangaroos to mountains. The longer we talk, the more detailed our lists get.

I love that my kids are learning to praise God. They are appreciating how amazing God's creation is. The longer our list gets, the more aware my kids become of the greatness of God. I just pray that this praise exercise lasts their whole lifetime!

Dear Father, praise You God for Your amazing creation. Praise You for Your love and care. Praise You for Your creativity. You are awesome and powerful. You are love! Amen.

DECEMBER 28

Forgiving Others

"Forgive us our sins, for we also forgive everyone who sins against us."
Luke 11:4

Forgiveness is not my strong suit. I'm not too apologetic about it, either, because life has dealt me some pretty hard blows. My husband deciding to bail out on the kids and me was the final blow. He said it was too much stress for him to have to worry about earning a living for a whole family. He couldn't take it so he left. Now I get to worry about earning a living, being both mom and dad, and answering my kids' questions about where daddy is. It stinks. I'm really mad at him and feel completely betrayed.

My kids have picked up on that anger and now they are angry at their dad too. I know I need to forgive him; it isn't right to pass my anger along to my kids, after all, he is their father.

To forgive when I've been so deeply hurt and feel so completely abandoned is difficult. I can only do it through God's power. I know I need forgiveness sometimes, too – maybe even from my husband. I probably didn't always make life easy for him. Forgiveness is sometimes a two-way street.

Dear Father, I need Your help to forgive my husband. His abandonment has made my life so difficult. But I don't want to poison my children. So, help me to forgive him. Help me, please. Amen.

Held Together

He is the image of the invisible God, the firstborn over all creation.
For by Him all things were created: things in heaven and on earth,
visible and invisible, whether thrones or powers or rulers or authorities;
all things were created by Him and for Him. He is before all things,
and in Him all things hold together. Colossians 1:15-17

It feels like our lives are spinning out of control. Perhaps you've been in one of those places in life where it feels like everything that could possibly go wrong does. It's those times when all of your kids have some kind of uproar in their lives, your personal finances are in a mess, your family isn't getting along … Nothing seems to be going well; there's no place where you can see peace.

So where do you turn? What will hold your family together in these kinds of crises? Scripture says that only Christ has the power to hold things together when it feels like they are in danger of exploding in a million directions.

So when things look the darkest, turn to Him. Ask Him for help. After all, He has the power and knowledge to hold you steady and make your family unit strong.

Dear Father, there is no greater thing to hold on to than You. Keep my family together, Father, keep us strong. Hold us together during these difficult times. Amen.

Staying Strong

Dear children, continue in Him, so that when He appears we may be confident and unashamed before Him at His coming. 1 John 2:28

Parenting is a full-time job. It's a lifelong job. Regardless of how old my children get, I will always be their mom. As long as we all walk on this earth, my children will be my children. From the time they were toddlers I have sought to help them learn to be productive adults who enjoy life and contribute to society. The key to that is to live in Christ, read God's Word, pray and grow in relationship with Christ.

I pray that my children have learned that lesson by the way I've raised them and the model my life has been for them. Each of my children has accepted Christ as Savior; now my prayer for them is that they will continue to grow in their faith and that each of them finds God's purpose in their lives.

We know that someday in the future each of us will stand before Christ and we don't want to be found disobedient. Or, perhaps we'll still be here on earth when Christ returns to take believers to heaven. Regardless of how it happens, I pray for my children and myself to be unashamed before Him at His return.

Dear Father, thank You that my children know You. I pray, Father, that each of my children will serve You with all their hearts. Amen.